2021 AP EXAM FORMAT INFORMATION

The COVID-19 pandemic affected the administration of AP exams in both 2020 and 2021. Although things remain subject to change at any time, it appears we are now on our way back to the traditional AP track. College Board continues to make decisions based on the health and safety of students and educators across the country, so it's a good idea to stay informed of the latest changes to your AP course and exam as the school year progresses.

The big news for the 2021 tests was the introduction of varied testing date and format options. Rather than offering the traditional single test approach, AP exams were administered three times—in early May, late May, and early June—with some subjects having been administered in a digital format in addition to the traditional paper format. Several exams offered different formats for paper- and digital-based exams, and the differences varied by subject. **All exams, however, were full length and covered the full scope of content for each AP course.**

AP Microeconomics exam used the following format:

- Exams were offered on paper in early May, and as a digital exam in late May and early June

- Both the paper and digital versions contained the typical multiple-choice and free-response sections

- Per the AP Exam Calculator Policy, calculators were not permitted on the paper exam. On the digital exam, calculators were permitted

- On the digital exam, students answered free-response questions with a keyboard, rather than by hand. Students taking digital exams were not asked to draw graphs as part of their response—rather, these skills were assessed with questions about given diagrams. No handwritten or photographed work was required or accepted

Is this *5 Steps* guide relevant and up-to-date?

Yes! Everything in this book is reflective of the current course and exam as it was originally designed. The *5 Steps* team strives to keep all information relevant and as up-to-date as possible, both in print and online.

What will happen in May 2022?

Your guess is as good as ours. Whether the AP exams return fully to their original paper format, continue in the 2021 hybrid (paper and online) models, or morph into something entirely new – remains uncertain. However, no matter what College Board will decide for next year - we have you covered! We'll be updating our materials whenever any new information becomes available, and will make every effort to revise our digital resources as quickly as possible.

So, whatever this AP school year may bring, please continue to check in to your *5 Steps* Cross-Platform course at **mheducation.com/5stepsmicro**. We will make every effort to keep the practice tests on the platform reflective of what you'll see on test day.

Most importantly, look for regular updates on the College Board website for the latest information on your course at **apcentral.collegeboard.org**. This will be your best resource for the most up-to-date information on all AP courses.

5 STEPS TO A 5™

AP Microeconomics
2022

Eric R. Dodge, PhD

McGraw Hill

New York   Chicago   San Francisco   Athens   London   Madrid   Mexico City
Milan   New Delhi   Singapore   Sydney   Toronto

1 2 3 4 5 6 7 8 9   LHS   26 25 24 23 22 21 (Cross-Platform Prep Course only)
1 2 3 4 5 6 7 8 9   LHS   26 25 24 23 22 21 (Elite Student Edition)

ISBN   978-1-264-26748-4 (Cross-Platform Prep Course only)
MHID   1-264-26748-7

e-ISBN   978-1-264-26749-1 (e-book Cross-Platform Prep Course only)
e-MHID   1-264-26749-5

ISBN   978-1-264-26750-7 (Elite Student Edition)
MHID   1-264-26750-9

e-ISBN   978-1-264-26751-4 (e-book Elite Student Edition)
e-MHID   1-264-26751-7

The series editor was Grace Freedson, and the project editor was Del Franz. Series design by Jane Tenenbaum.

McGraw Hill products are available at special quantity discounts to use as premiums and sales or for use in corporate training programs. To contact a representative, please visit the Contact Us pages at www.mhprofessional.com.

CONTENTS

So, you've decided to bite the bullet and invest in a book designed to help you earn a 5 on your AP Microeconomics exam. Congratulations! You have taken the first of many small steps toward this goal. An important question remains: Why this book?

Priority number one, both for your AP course and for this book, is to prepare you to do well enough on the AP Microeconomics exam to earn college credit. I firmly believe that this book has a comparative advantage over your other options. First, I have written this text with a certain conversational approach, rather than a flurry of formulas and diagrams that you must remember. Sure, some memorization is required for any standardized test, but a memorizer of formulas is in deep trouble when asked to analyze the relative success of several possible economic policies or to draw fine distinctions between competing economic theories. Using this book to supplement and reinforce your understanding of the theories and relationships in economics allows you to apply your analytical skills to the exam, and this gives you a significant advantage over the formula-memorizing exam taker. If you spend less time memorizing formulas and take the extra time to understand the basics, you will get along just fine with this book, and you will do extremely well on the AP Economics exams.

Second, as a college professor who has taught economics to thousands of students, I have a strong understanding of where the learning happens and where the mistakes are made.

Third, as a reader and writer of AP exams, I can tell you where points are lost and where a 5 is made on the free-response questions. Most important, I am a realist. You want to know what it takes to earn a 5 and not necessarily the finer points of the Federal Reserve System, the Sherman Antitrust Act, or the NAFTA.

Take the time to read the first four chapters of this book, which are designed to help you understand the challenge that lies ahead and to provide you with tips for success on the exam.

Take the diagnostic exam to see where you stand before beginning your review. The bulk of this book is a comprehensive review of microeconomics with practice questions at the end of each chapter. These questions are designed to quickly test your understanding of the material presented in each chapter, not necessarily to mirror the AP exam. For exam questions that are more typical of what you will experience in May, I have provided you with two practice exams in microeconomics. These are practice exams, complete with essay questions, sample responses, and scoring guidelines.

There have been several important updates since the first edition. The second edition included expanded coverage of game theory, reflecting the growing use of game theory in the AP Microeconomics curriculum. In that edition, I included a free-response question involving game theory because the people who develop the AP exam had been urging high school AP teachers to devote more time to game theory. Such urgings are usually a strong hint of a future free-response question, and indeed in 2007, the Microeconomics exam included, for the first time, a free-response game-theory question.

In the 2018 edition of this book, I included details of the impact that trade barriers, such as tariffs and quotas, have on competitive markets. While the topic of trade barriers has been present in the AP Microeconomics course outline for several years, it was not tested extensively in the free-response section until 2012. That edition also added coverage of the market for capital in the factor markets chapter to reflect a growing emphasis in both teaching and testing more than simply labor markets. I also brought some of the coverage of externalities more in line with recent AP exams and the rubrics that were used to grade them.

To reflect more recent points of emphasis in the AP exam, the 2019 edition expanded the explanation of how certain costs can be identified and computed in a graph. I also provided additional graphing tips and modified some questions in the practice exams.

This new edition reflects some changes that the College Board has made to the AP Microeconomics curriculum. For the most part, the content is quite similar to what has been taught, and tested, for the last decade or more. While the changes are not fundamentally changing the Microeconomics course, it is important that this book keeps pace with those changes. More specific details about the changes to the Microeconomics course are given in Chapter 1. As with every edition, I adjust free-response questions and rubrics to better reflect how those questions are being scored at the annual Reading.

I do not see any reason to continue talking about the book when we could just dive in. I hope that you enjoy this book and that you find it a useful resource. Good luck!

ACKNOWLEDGMENTS

This book is dedicated to my wife, Dr. Melanie Fox, and our three sons, Eli, Max, and Theo. My utility for you is increasing at an increasing rate. Thank you.

ABOUT THE AUTHOR

Eric R. Dodge was born in Portland, Oregon, and attended high school in Tigard, Oregon. He received a bachelor's degree in business administration from the University of Puget Sound in Tacoma, Washington, before attending the University of Oregon for his master's and doctoral degrees in economics. While at the University of Oregon, he received two graduate student awards for teaching and became a die-hard fan of the Ducks. Since 1995, he has been teaching economics at Hanover College in Hanover, Indiana, the oldest private college in the state. The author teaches principles of microeconomics and macroeconomics, intermediate microeconomic theory, labor economics, environmental economics, industrial organization, statistics, econometrics, and the economics of dams.

Since 2000, Eric Dodge has served as a faculty consultant for the AP economics program, and has been a reader and writer of free-response questions, table leader, and question leader at the annual AP Economics Reading. With coauthor Melanie Fox, he has also written three recently published books: *Economics Demystified, 500 Microeconomics Questions: Ace Your College Exams,* and *500 Macroeconomics Questions: Ace Your College Exams.* He lives in historic Madison, Indiana, with his wife, Melanie; sons Eli, Max, and Theo; and a neurotic, rain-fearing dog.

INTRODUCTION: THE FIVE-STEP PROGRAM

The Basics

Not too long ago, you agreed to enroll in AP Microeconomics. Maybe you saw a flyer and the allure of economic knowledge was just too much to resist, or maybe a respected teacher encouraged you to challenge yourself and you took the bait. Either way, you find yourself here, flipping through a book that promises to help you culminate this life-changing experience with the highest of honors, a 5 in AP Microeconomics. Can it be done without this book? Sure, there are many excellent teachers of AP Microeconomics out there who teach, coax, and cajole their students into a 5 every year. But for the majority of students in your shoes, the marginal benefits of buying this book far outweigh the marginal costs.

Introducing the Five-Step Preparation Program

This book is organized as a five-step program to prepare you for success on the exam. These steps are designed to provide you with the skills and strategies vital to the exam and the practice that can lead you to that perfect 5. Each of the five steps will provide you with the opportunity to get closer and closer to that prize trophy 5.

Following are the five steps:

Step 1: Set Up Your Study Program

In this step, you'll read a brief overview of the AP Microeconomics exam, including an outline of topics and the approximate percentage of the exam that will test knowledge of each topic. You will also follow a process to help determine which of the following preparation programs is right for you:

- Full school year: September through May
- One semester: January through May
- Six weeks: Basic training for the exam

Step 2: Determine Your Test Readiness

In this step, you'll take a diagnostic exam in microeconomics. This pretest should give you an idea of how prepared you are to take the real exam before beginning to study for it.

- Go through the diagnostic exam step by step and question by question to build your confidence level.
- Review the correct answers and explanations so that you see what you do and do not yet fully understand.

Step 3: Develop Strategies for Success

In this step, you'll learn strategies to help you do your best on the exam. These strategies cover both the multiple-choice and free-response sections of the exam. Some of these tips are based upon my understanding of how the questions are designed, and others have been gleaned from my years of experience reading (grading) the AP Economics exams.

- Learn to read multiple-choice questions.
- Learn how to answer multiple-choice questions, including whether or not to guess.
- Learn how to plan and write the free-response questions.

Step 4: Review the Knowledge You Need to Score High

In this step, you'll review the material you need to know for the test. This review section takes up the bulk of this book. It contains a comprehensive review of microeconomics.

There is a lot of material here, enough to summarize a yearlong experience in AP Microeconomics and highlight the, well, highlights. Some AP courses will have covered more material than yours; some will have covered less. The bottom line is that if you thoroughly review this material, you will have studied all that is tested on the exam, and you will significantly increase your chances of scoring well. This edition gives new emphasis to some areas of microeconomics to bring your review more in line with recent exams. For example, recent editions included more discussion of tariffs and game theory, whereas this edition includes more graphing tips in the microeconomics review.

Step 5: Build Your Test-Taking Confidence

In this step, you'll complete your preparation by testing yourself on practice exams. This section contains two complete exams in microeconomics, solutions, and, sometimes more important, advice on how to avoid the common mistakes. Once again, the 2020 edition of this book has updated the free-response exams to more accurately reflect the content tested on recent AP exams. Be aware that these practice exams are *not* reproduced questions from actual AP Microeconomics exams, but they mirror both the material tested by AP and the way in which it is tested.

Lastly, at the back of this book you'll find additional resources to aid your preparation. These include the following:

- A brief bibliography
- A list of websites related to AP Microeconomics
- A glossary of terms related to the AP Microeconomics exam
- A summary of formulas related to the AP Microeconomics exam

Introduction to the Graphics Used in This Book

To emphasize particular skills and strategies, several icons appear in the margins, alerting you to pay particular attention to the accompanying text. We use these three icons:

This icon indicates a very important concept or fact that you should not pass over.

This icon calls your attention to a strategy that you might want to try.

This icon alerts you to a tip that you might find useful.

Boldfaced words indicate terms that are included in the glossary. Throughout the book you will also find marginal notes, boxes, and starred areas. Pay close attention to these areas because they can provide tips, hints, strategies, and further explanations to help you reach your full potential.

STEP

1

Set Up Your Study Program

CHAPTER 1

What You Need to Know About the AP Microeconomics Exam

IN THIS CHAPTER

Summary: Learn what topics are tested, how the test is scored, and basic test-taking information.

Key Ideas
- ✪ Most colleges will award credit for a score of 4 or 5; some will award credit for a score of 3.
- ✪ Multiple-choice questions account for two-thirds of your final score.
- ✪ Free-response questions account for one-third of your final score.
- ✪ Your composite score on the two test sections is converted to a score on the 1-to-5 scale.

Background Information

The AP Economics exams that you are taking were first offered by the College Board in 1989. Since then, the number of students taking the tests has grown rapidly. In 1989, 3,198 students took the Microeconomics exam, and by 2012 that number had increased to 62,351.

Some Frequently Asked Questions About the AP Economics Exams

Why Take the AP Economics Exams?

Although there might be some altruistic motivators, let's face it: most of you take the AP Economics exams because you are seeking college credit. The majority of colleges and universities will accept a 4 or 5 as acceptable credit for their Principles of Microeconomics or Macroeconomics courses. A number of schools will even accept a 3 on an exam. This means you are one or two courses closer to graduation before you even begin working on the "freshman 15." Even if you do not score high enough to earn college credit, the fact that you elected to enroll in AP courses tells admission committees that you are a high achiever and serious about your education. In recent years, close to two-thirds of students have scored a 3 or higher on their AP Microeconomics exam.

What Is the Format of the Exams?

Table 1.1 Summarizes the format of the AP Micro and Macro exams

AP MACROECONOMICS		
Section	*Number of Questions*	*Time Limit*
I. Multiple-Choice Questions	60	1 hour and 10 minutes
II. Free-Response Questions	3	Planning time: 10 minutes Writing time: 50 minutes

AP MICROECONOMICS		
Section	*Number of Questions*	*Time Limit*
I. Multiple-Choice Questions	60	1 hour and 10 minutes
II. Free-Response Questions	3	Planning time: 10 minutes Writing time: 50 minutes

Who Writes the AP Economics Exams?

Development of each AP exam is a multiyear effort that involves many education and testing professionals and students. At the heart of the effort is the AP Economics Development Committee, a group of college and high school economics teachers who are typically asked to serve for three years. The committee and other college professors create a large pool of multiple-choice questions. With the help of the testing experts at Educational Testing Service (ETS), these questions are then pretested with college students enrolled in Principles of Microeconomics and Macroeconomics for accuracy, appropriateness, clarity, and assurance that there is only one possible answer. The results of this pretesting allow each question to be categorized by degree of difficulty. Several more months of development and refinement later, Section I of the exam is ready to be administered.

The free-response essay questions that make up Section II go through a similar process of creation, modification, pretesting, and final refinement so that the questions cover the necessary areas of material and are at an appropriate level of difficulty and clarity.

The committee also makes a great effort to construct a free-response exam that allows for clear and equitable grading by the AP readers.

At the conclusion of each AP reading and scoring of exams, the exam itself and the results are thoroughly evaluated by the committee and by ETS. In this way, the College Board can use the results to make suggestions for course development in high schools and to plan future exams.

What Topics Appear on the Exams?

The College Board, after consulting with teachers of economics, develops a curriculum that covers material that college professors expect to cover in their first-year classes. This curriculum has just undergone a revision and the new outline for the Microeconomics course is provided below. Based upon this outline of topics, the multiple-choice exams are written such that those topics are covered in proportion to their importance to the expected economics understanding of the student. If you find this confusing, think of it this way: Suppose that faculty consultants agree that market failure and the role of government topics are important to the microeconomics curriculum, maybe to the tune of 8 to 13 percent. So if about 10 percent of the curriculum in your AP Microeconomics course is devoted to these topics, you can expect roughly 10 percent of the multiple-choice exam to address these topics. This curriculum has just undergone a revision and the outline is provided below. Remember, this is just a guide and each year the exam differs slightly in the percentages.

Microeconomics

Unit 1: Basic Economic Concepts
This unit covers the foundations of microeconomic thinking, decision-making under constraints, and rational choice.

Topics:
  Scarcity
  Resource allocation and economic systems
  Production possibilities curve
  Comparative advantage and gains from trade
  Cost-benefit analysis
  Marginal analysis and consumer choice

Exam Coverage
  12%–15%

Unit 2: Supply and Demand
This unit provides the basics for understanding how markets work, with an introduction to the supply and demand model.

Topics:
  Demand
  Supply
  Elasticity
  Market equilibrium, disequilibrium, and changes in equilibrium
  The effects of government intervention in markets
  International trade and public policy

Exam Coverage
  20%–25%

Unit 3: Production, Cost, and the Perfect Competition Model

This unit describes the factors that drive the behavior of companies and the model of perfect competition.

Topics:
  The production function
  Short- and long-run production costs
  Types of profit
  Profit maximization
  Perfect competition

Exam Coverage
22%–25%

Unit 4: Imperfect Competition

This unit explores how imperfectly competitive markets work and how game theory is used to predict behavior in oligopolies.

Topics:
  Monopoly
  Price discrimination
  Monopolistic competition
  Oligopoly and game theory

Exam Coverage
15%–22%

Unit 5: Factor Markets

This unit demonstrates how markets and marginal decision-making are used to describe the workings of factor markets.

Topics:
  Introduction to factor markets
  Changes in factor demand and factor supply
  Profit-maximizing behavior in perfectly competitive factor markets
  Monopsonistic markets

Exam Coverage
10%–13%

Unit 6: Market Failure and the Role of Government

This unit looks at the conditions under which markets may fail and the effects of government intervention in markets.

Topics:
  Socially efficient and inefficient market outcomes
  Externalities
  Public and private goods
  The effects of government intervention in different market structures
  Income and wealth inequality

Exam Coverage
8%–13%

My Teacher (and the Syllabus) Keeps Talking About "Big Ideas" and "Skill Categories." What Are These?

Most of the new curricular revision was a big-picture way of describing, and teaching, the key concepts in the AP Microeconomics course. While these are critical to your teacher's preparation, and fundamentally guide the way in which she structures the course, as a student preparing for the exam you probably don't need to have a deep understanding of what is happening behind the scenes. In other words, your course will be new and improved because of these revisions, but your fantastic teacher is doing the heavy lifting on making sure these are woven throughout the course.

But in case you're still curious, there are four skill categories that identify important skills that an AP Micro student should master throughout the course. The table below provides a brief summary.

	Title	An example
Category 1	Principles of Models: define economic principles and models	Can you describe the similarities and differences between the model of perfect competition and monopolistic competition in the long run?
Category 2	Interpretation: explain given economic outcomes	If production of a good is creating external costs on third parties, can you prescribe a policy for addressing these external costs?
Category 3	Manipulation: determine outcomes of specific economic situations	If the price elasticity of demand for a good is 2.5, and the price falls by 10%, can you calculate the estimated change in total spending on this good?
Category 4	Graphing and Visuals: model economic situations using graphs or visual representations	Can you draw an accurately labeled graph that shows a profit-maximizing monopolist earning positive economic profit?

There also four Big Ideas that will appear throughout your course. These are intended to reinforce common concepts that are key to a deep understanding of microeconomics. The four Big Ideas are:

1. Scarcity and Markets
2. Costs, Benefits, and Marginal Analysis
3. Production Choices and Behavior
4. Market Inefficiency and Public Policy

Much more detail on these Big Ideas and the Skill Categories can be found in the "AP Microeconomics Course and Exam Description" that is found at https://apcentral .collegeboard.org/pdf/ap-microeconomics-course-and-exam-description.pdf?course= ap-microeconomics.

Who Grades My AP Economics Exam?

From confidential sources, I can tell you that nearly 100,000 free-response essay booklets are dropped from a three-story building, and those that fall into a small cardboard box are given a 5, those that fall into a slightly larger box are given a 4, and so on until those that fall into a dumpster receive a 1. It's really quite scientific!

Okay, that's not really how it's done. Instead, every June a group of economics teachers gather for a week to assign grades to your hard work. Each of these "Faculty Consultants," or "Readers," spends a day or so getting trained on one question and one question only. Because each reader becomes an expert on that question, and because each exam book is anonymous, this process provides a very consistent and unbiased scoring of that question. During a typical day of grading, a random sample of each reader's scores is selected and cross-checked by other experienced "Table Leaders" to ensure that the consistency is maintained throughout the day and the week. Each reader's scores on a given question are also statistically analyzed to make sure that he or she is not giving scores that are significantly higher or lower than the mean scores given by other readers of that question. All measures are taken to maintain consistency and fairness for your benefit.

Will My Exam Remain Anonymous?

Absolutely. Even if your high school teacher happens to randomly read your booklet, there is virtually no way he or she will know it is you. To the reader, each student is a number and to the computer, each student is a bar code.

What About That Permission Box on the Back?

The College Board uses some exams to help train high school teachers so that they can help the next generation of economics students to avoid common mistakes. If you check this box, you simply give permission to use your exam in this way. Even if you give permission, your anonymity is still maintained.

How Is My Multiple-Choice Exam Scored?

The multiple-choice section of each Economics exam is 60 questions and is worth two-thirds of your final score. Your answer sheet is run through the computer, which adds up your correct responses. The total scores on the multiple-choice sections are based on the number of questions answered correctly. The "guessing penalty" has been eliminated, and points are no longer deducted for incorrect answers. As always, no points are awarded for unanswered questions. The formula looks something like this:

$$\text{Section I Raw Score} = N_{\text{right}}$$

How Is My Free-Response Exam Scored?

Your performance on the free-response section is worth one-third of your final score and consists of three questions. Another change to the exam is that the first question will always be scored out of 10 points, and the second and third questions will each be scored out of 5 points. Because the first question is longer than the other two, and therefore scored on a higher scale, it is given a different weight in the raw score. If you use the following sample formula as a rough guide, you'll be able to gauge your approximate score on the practice questions.

$$\text{Section II Raw Score} = (1.50 \times \text{Score 1}) + (1.50 \times \text{Score 2}) + (1.50 \times \text{Score 3})$$

So How Is My Final Grade Determined and What Does It Mean?

With a total composite score of 90 points, and 60 being determined on Section I, the remaining 30 must be divided among the three essay questions in Section II. The total composite score is then a weighted sum of the multiple-choice and the free-response sections. In the end, when all of the numbers have been crunched, the Chief Faculty Consultant converts the range of composite scores to the 5-point scale of the AP grades.

Table 1.2 gives you a very rough example of a conversion, and as you complete the practice exam, you may use this to give yourself a hypothetical grade, keeping in mind that every year the conversion changes slightly to adjust for the difficulty of the questions from year to year. You should receive your grade in early July.

Table 1.2 Sample Score Conversion

MICROECONOMICS		
Composite Score Range	*AP Grade*	*Interpretation*
73–90	5	Extremely well qualified for college credit
58–72	4	Well qualified
45–57	3	Qualified
33–44	2	Possibly qualified
0–32	1	No recommendation

Example:

In Section I, you receive 50 correct and 10 incorrect responses on the microeconomics practice exam. In Section II, your scores are 7/10, 5/5, and 5/5.

$$\text{Weighted Section I} = 50$$

$$\text{Weighted Section II} = (1.50 \times 7) = (1.50 \times 5) + (1.50 \times 5)$$
$$= 10.50 + 7.5 + 7.5 = 25.5$$

Composite Score = 50 + 25.5 = 75.5, which would be assigned a 5.

How Do I Register and How Much Does It Cost?

If you are enrolled in AP Microeconomics in your high school, your teacher is going to provide all of these details, but a quick summary wouldn't hurt. After all, you do not have to enroll in the AP course to register for and complete the AP exam. When in doubt, the best source of information is the College Board's website: www.college-board.com.

In 2019–2020 the fee for taking an exam was $94 for each exam. Students who demonstrate financial need may receive a partial refund to help offset the cost of testing. There are also several *optional* fees that *can* be paid if you want your scores rushed to you or if you wish to receive multiple grade reports.

The coordinator of the AP program at your school will inform you where and when you will take the exam. If you live in a small community, your exam might not be administered at your school, so be sure to get this information.

What If My School Only Offered AP Macroeconomics and Not AP Microeconomics, or Vice Versa?

Because of budget and personnel constraints, some high schools cannot offer both Microeconomics and Macroeconomics. The majority of these schools choose the macro side of the AP program, but some choose the micro side. This puts students at a significant disadvantage when they sit down for the Microeconomics exam without having taken the course. Likewise, Macroeconomics test takers have a rough time when they have not taken the Macroeconomics course. If you are in this situation, and you put in the necessary effort, I assure you that buying this book will give you more than a fighting chance on either exam even if your school did not offer that course.

What Should I Bring to the Exam?

On exam day, I suggest bringing the following items:

- Two sharpened number 2 pencils and an eraser that doesn't leave smudges.
- Two black or blue-colored pens for the free-response section. Some students like to use two colors to make their graphs stand out for the reader.
- A watch so that you can monitor your time. You never know whether the exam room will have a clock on the wall. You cannot have a watch that accesses the Internet, and make sure you turn off any beep that goes off on the hour.
- Your school code.
- Your photo identification and social security number.
- Tissues.
- Your quiet confidence that you are prepared!

What Should I *Not* Bring to the Exam?

It's probably a good idea to leave the following items at home:

- A calculator. It is not allowed for the Microeconomics or Macroeconomics exam. However, this does not mean that math will not be required. Questions involving simple computations have recently appeared on the exams, and later in the book I point out a few places where knowing a little math can earn you some points.
- A cell phone, smart watch, camera, tablet, laptop computer, or walkie-talkie.
- Books, a dictionary, study notes, flash cards, highlighting pens, correction fluid, a ruler, or any other office supplies.
- Portable music of any kind.
- Clothing with any economics on it.
- Panic or fear. It's natural to be nervous, but you can comfort yourself that you have used this book well and that there is no room for fear on your exam.

CHAPTER 2

How to Plan Your Time

IN THIS CHAPTER

Summary: The right preparation plan for you depends on your study habits and the amount of time you have before the test.

Key Idea

✪ Choose the study plan that's right for you.

Three Approaches to Preparing for AP Exams

What kind of preparation program for the AP exam should you use? Should you carefully follow every step, or are there perhaps some steps you can bypass? That depends not only on how much time you have but also on what kind of student you are. No one knows your study habits, likes, and dislikes better than you do. So you are the only one who can decide which approach to use. This chapter presents three possible study plans, labeled A, B, and C. Look at the brief profiles that follow. These will help you determine which plan is right for you. Table 2.1 summarizes each study plan, with a suggested timetable for each.

You're a **full-school-year prep student** if:

1. You are the kind of person who likes to plan for everything very far in advance.
2. You buy your best friend a gift two months before his or her birthday because you know exactly what to choose, where you will buy it, and how much you will pay for it.
3. You like detailed planning and everything in its place.
4. You feel that you must be thoroughly prepared.
5. You hate surprises.

If you fit this profile, consider **Plan A**.

You're a **one-semester prep student** if:

1. You buy your best friend a gift one week before his or her birthday because it sort of snuck up on you, yet you have a clear idea of exactly what you will be purchasing.
2. You are willing to plan ahead to feel comfortable in stressful situations but are okay with skipping some details.
3. You feel more comfortable when you know what to expect, but a surprise or two is cool.
4. You're always on time for appointments.

If you fit this profile, consider **Plan B**.

You're a **six-week prep student** if:

1. You buy your best friend a gift for his or her birthday, but you need to include a belated card because you missed it by a couple of days.
2. You work best under pressure and tight deadlines.
3. You feel very confident with the skills and background you've learned in your AP Economics classes.
4. You decided late in the year to take the exam.
5. You like surprises.
6. You feel okay if you arrive 10 to 15 minutes late for an appointment.

If you fit this profile, consider **Plan C**.

Table 2.1 Three Different Study Schedules

MONTH	PLAN A: FULL SCHOOL YEAR	PLAN B: ONE SEMESTER	PLAN C: SIX WEEKS
September to October	Introduction; Chapters 1 to 4	—	—
November	Chapters 5 to 6	—	—
December	Chapter 7	—	—
January	Chapter 8	Chapters 1 to 4	—
February	Chapter 9; Micro Practice Exam 1	Chapters 5 to 7; Micro Practice Exam 1	—
March	Chapter 10	Chapters 8 to 9	—
April	Chapter 11	Chapters 10 to 11	Skim Chapters 1 to 9; all rapid reviews; Micro Practice Exam 1
May	Review everything; Micro Practice Exam 2	Review everything; Micro Practice Exam 2	Skim Chapters 10 to 11; Micro Practice Exam 2

Calendar for Each Plan

Plan A: You Have a Full School Year to Prepare

Use this plan to organize your study during the coming school year.

SEPTEMBER–OCTOBER (Check off the activities as you complete them.)

_____ Determine the student mode (A, B, or C) that applies to you.

_____ Carefully read Chapters 1 to 4 of this book.

_____ Take the diagnostic exam.

_____ Pay close attention to your walk-through of the diagnostic exam.

_____ Get on the web and take a look at the AP website(s).

_____ Skim the review chapters in Step 4 of this book. (Reviewing the topics covered in this section will be part of your yearlong preparation.)

_____ Buy a few color highlighters.

_____ Flip through the entire book. Break the book in. Write in it. Toss it around a little bit . . . highlight it.

_____ Get a clear picture of your own school's AP Economics curriculum.

_____ Begin to use this book as a resource to supplement the classroom learning.

NOVEMBER (the first 10 weeks have elapsed)

_____ Read and study Chapter 5, "Fundamentals of Economic Analysis."

_____ Read and study Chapter 6, "Demand, Supply, Market Equilibrium, and Welfare Analysis."

DECEMBER

_____ Read and study Chapter 7, "Elasticity, Microeconomic Policy, and Consumer Theory."

_____ Review Chapters 5 to 6.

JANUARY (20 weeks have elapsed)

_____ Read and study Chapter 8, "The Firm, Profit, and the Costs of Production."

_____ Review Chapters 5 to 7.

FEBRUARY

_____ Take Microeconomics Practice Exam 1 in the first week of February.

_____ Evaluate your Micro strengths and weaknesses.

_____ Study appropriate chapters to correct your Micro weaknesses.

_____ Read and study Chapter 9, "Market Structures, Perfect Competition, Monopoly, and Things Between."

_____ Review Chapters 5 to 8.

MARCH (30 weeks have now elapsed)

_____ Read and study Chapter 10, "Factor Markets."

_____ Review Chapters 5 to 9.

APRIL

_____ Read and study Chapter 11, "Public Goods, Externalities, and the Role of Government."

_____ Review Chapters 5 to 10.

MAY (first two weeks) (THIS IS IT!)

_____ Review Chapters 5 to 11—all the material!

_____ Take Practice Exam 2.

_____ Score yourself.

_____ Get a good night's sleep before the exam. Fall asleep knowing that you are well prepared.

GOOD LUCK ON THE TEST!

Plan B: You Have One Semester to Prepare

If you have already completed one semester of economic studies, the following plan will help you use those skills you've been practicing to prepare for the May exam.

JANUARY–FEBRUARY

_____ Carefully read Chapters 1 to 4 of this book.

_____ Take the diagnostic exam.

_____ Pay close attention to your walk-through of the diagnostic exam.

_____ Read and study Chapter 5, "Fundamentals of Economic Analysis."

_____ Read and study Chapter 6, "Demand, Supply, Market Equilibrium, and Welfare Analysis."

_____ Read and study Chapter 7, "Elasticity, Microeconomic Policy, and Consumer Theory."

_____ Take Microeconomics Practice Exam 1 in the last week of February.

_____ Evaluate your Micro strengths and weaknesses.

_____ Study appropriate chapters to correct your Micro weaknesses.

MARCH (10 weeks to go)

_____ Read and study Chapter 8, "The Firm, Profit, and the Costs of Production."

_____ Read and study Chapter 9, "Market Structures, Perfect Competition, Monopoly, and Things Between."

_____ Review Chapters 5 to 7.

APRIL

_____ Read and study Chapter 10, "Factor Markets."

_____ Read and study Chapter 11, "Public Goods, Externalities, and the Role of Government."

_____ Review Chapters 5 to 9.

MAY (first two weeks) (THIS IS IT!)

_____ Review Chapters 5 to 11—all the material!

_____ Take Microeconomics Practice Exam 2.

_____ Score yourself.

_____ Get a good night's sleep before the exam. Fall asleep knowing that you are well prepared.

GOOD LUCK ON THE TEST!

Plan C: You Have Six Weeks to Prepare

Use this plan if you have been studying economics for six months or more and intend to use this book primarily as a specific guide to the AP Microeconomics exam. If you have only six weeks to prepare, now is not the time to try to learn everything. Focus instead on the essential points you need to know for the test.

APRIL 1–15

_____ Skim Chapters 1 to 4 of this book.

_____ Skim Chapters 5 to 6.

_____ Carefully go over the Rapid Review sections of Chapters 5 to 8.

_____ Complete the Microeconomics Practice Exam 1.

_____ Score yourself and analyze your errors.

_____ Skim and highlight the Glossary at the end of the book.

APRIL 15–MAY 1

_____ Skim Chapters 9 to 11.

_____ Carefully go over the Rapid Review sections of Chapters 9 to 11.

_____ Continue to skim and highlight the Glossary at the end of the book.

MAY (first two weeks) (THIS IS IT!)

_____ Carefully go over the Rapid Review sections of Chapters 5 to 11.

_____ Take Microeconomics Practice Exam 2.

_____ Score yourself and analyze your errors.

_____ Get a good night's sleep before the exam. Fall asleep knowing that you are well prepared.

GOOD LUCK ON THE TEST!

STEP 2

Determine Your
Test Readiness

CHAPTER 3   Take the Diagnostic Exam

CHAPTER 3

Take the Diagnostic Exam

IN THIS CHAPTER

Summary: This chapter includes a diagnostic exam for microeconomics. It is intended to give you an idea of where you stand with your preparation. The questions have been written to approximate the coverage of material that you will see on the AP exam and are similar to the review questions at the end of each chapter in this book. Once you are done with the exam, check your work against the given answers, which also indicate where you can find the corresponding material in this book. Also provided is a way to convert your score to a rough AP score.

Key Ideas

✪ Practice the kind of multiple-choice and free-response questions you will be asked on the real exam.

✪ Answer questions that approximate the coverage of topics on the real exam.

✪ Check your work against the given answers.

✪ Determine your areas of strength and weakness.

✪ Earmark the pages that you must give special attention.

Diagnostic Exam

MICROECONOMICS—SECTION I

ANSWER SHEET

Record your responses to the exam questions in the spaces below.

1 (A) (B) (C) (D) (E)	21 (A) (B) (C) (D) (E)	41 (A) (B) (C) (D) (E)
2 (A) (B) (C) (D) (E)	22 (A) (B) (C) (D) (E)	42 (A) (B) (C) (D) (E)
3 (A) (B) (C) (D) (E)	23 (A) (B) (C) (D) (E)	43 (A) (B) (C) (D) (E)
4 (A) (B) (C) (D) (E)	24 (A) (B) (C) (D) (E)	44 (A) (B) (C) (D) (E)
5 (A) (B) (C) (D) (E)	25 (A) (B) (C) (D) (E)	45 (A) (B) (C) (D) (E)
6 (A) (B) (C) (D) (E)	26 (A) (B) (C) (D) (E)	46 (A) (B) (C) (D) (E)
7 (A) (B) (C) (D) (E)	27 (A) (B) (C) (D) (E)	47 (A) (B) (C) (D) (E)
8 (A) (B) (C) (D) (E)	28 (A) (B) (C) (D) (E)	48 (A) (B) (C) (D) (E)
9 (A) (B) (C) (D) (E)	29 (A) (B) (C) (D) (E)	49 (A) (B) (C) (D) (E)
10 (A) (B) (C) (D) (E)	30 (A) (B) (C) (D) (E)	50 (A) (B) (C) (D) (E)
11 (A) (B) (C) (D) (E)	31 (A) (B) (C) (D) (E)	51 (A) (B) (C) (D) (E)
12 (A) (B) (C) (D) (E)	32 (A) (B) (C) (D) (E)	52 (A) (B) (C) (D) (E)
13 (A) (B) (C) (D) (E)	33 (A) (B) (C) (D) (E)	53 (A) (B) (C) (D) (E)
14 (A) (B) (C) (D) (E)	34 (A) (B) (C) (D) (E)	54 (A) (B) (C) (D) (E)
15 (A) (B) (C) (D) (E)	35 (A) (B) (C) (D) (E)	55 (A) (B) (C) (D) (E)
16 (A) (B) (C) (D) (E)	36 (A) (B) (C) (D) (E)	56 (A) (B) (C) (D) (E)
17 (A) (B) (C) (D) (E)	37 (A) (B) (C) (D) (E)	57 (A) (B) (C) (D) (E)
18 (A) (B) (C) (D) (E)	38 (A) (B) (C) (D) (E)	58 (A) (B) (C) (D) (E)
19 (A) (B) (C) (D) (E)	39 (A) (B) (C) (D) (E)	59 (A) (B) (C) (D) (E)
20 (A) (B) (C) (D) (E)	40 (A) (B) (C) (D) (E)	60 (A) (B) (C) (D) (E)

Diagnostic Exam: AP Microeconomics

SECTION I
Time—70 Minutes
60 Questions

For the following multiple-choice questions, select the best answer choice and record your choice on the answer sheet provided.

1. Scarcity is best defined as

   (A) the difference between limited wants and limited economic resources.
   (B) the difference between the total benefit of an action and the total cost of that action.
   (C) the difference between unlimited wants and limited economic resources.
   (D) the opportunity cost of pursuing a given course of action.
   (E) the difference between the marginal benefit and marginal cost of an action.

2. Which of the following statements is most consistent with a capitalist market economy?

   (A) Economic resources are allocated according to the decisions of the central bank.
   (B) Private property is fundamental to innovation, growth, and trade.
   (C) A central government plans the production and distribution of goods.
   (D) Most wages and prices are legally controlled.
   (E) Most economic resources are owned by the government and leased to the citizens in exchange for lower taxes.

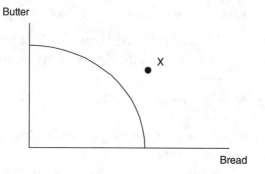

Figure D.1

3. The graph in Figure D.1 shows a nation's production possibilities curve (PPC) for the production of bread and butter. Which of the following is true?

   (A) The opportunity cost of producing more butter is a decreasing amount of bread.
   (B) Point X represents unemployed economic resources.
   (C) The opportunity cost of producing more butter is a constant amount of bread.
   (D) Point X represents a labor force that has become less productive.
   (E) The opportunity cost of producing more butter is an increasing amount of bread.

4. The graph in Figure D.1 shows a nation's production possibilities curve (PPC) to produce bread and butter. Suppose that production technology in butter production improves. All else being equal, how will this affect the PPC and the opportunity cost of producing bread?

   (A) The vertical intercept of the PPC increases; the opportunity cost of bread decreases.
   (B) The vertical intercept of the PPC decreases; the opportunity cost of bread decreases.
   (C) The horizontal intercept of the PPC increases; the opportunity cost of bread increases.
   (D) The vertical intercept of the PPC increases; the opportunity cost of bread increases.
   (E) The horizontal intercept of the PPC decreases; the opportunity cost of bread decreases.

5. Jess likes to purchase $1 tacos from the taco truck near her school. If Jess uses marginal analysis, how many tacos will she consume on a given day?

   (A) Jess will stop consuming tacos when the marginal benefit of the next taco is equal to zero.
   (B) Jess will stop consuming tacos when the marginal benefit of the next taco is less than zero.
   (C) Jess will stop consuming tacos when the marginal benefit of the next taco is equal to $1.
   (D) Jess will stop consuming tacos when the marginal cost of the next taco is equal to $1.
   (E) Jess will stop consuming tacos when the marginal cost of the next taco is equal to zero.

6. A small bakery has been so busy that they have hired two part-time employees. This is an example of a business changing its _____ resource.

   (A) capital
   (B) profit
   (C) land
   (D) entrepreneurial
   (E) labor

7. Felipe wants to go see a concert next month. He knows that the concert, including his drive to and from the arena, will take five hours. Which of the following is the best example of an implicit cost that Felipe should consider before deciding whether to attend the concert?

   (A) The price of the concert ticket
   (B) The highest wage he could earn if he worked five hours
   (C) The cost of gasoline needed to drive to the concert
   (D) The price of snacks and drinks he would buy at the arena
   (E) His estimate of how much he will enjoy the concert

8. Theo and Eliza can both paint the fence and wax the car after school. For every hour of waxing the car, Theo can paint eight sections of fence and Eliza can paint two sections of fence. Based on this information, the most efficient division of labor would be

   (A) Theo should paint the fence because he has a comparative advantage in painting.
   (B) Eliza should wax the car because she has an absolute advantage in waxing.
   (C) Theo should wax the car because he has a comparative advantage in painting.
   (D) Eliza should paint the fence because she has an absolute advantage in painting.
   (E) Theo should paint the fence because he has an absolute advantage in waxing.

9. Which of the following is true of equilibrium in a purely (or perfectly) competitive market for good X?

   (A) A shortage of good X exists.
   (B) The quantity demanded equals the quantity supplied of good X.
   (C) A surplus of good X exists.
   (D) The government regulates the quantity of good X produced at the market price.
   (E) Deadweight loss exists.

10. The competitive market for gasoline, a normal good, is currently in a state of equilibrium. Which of the following would most likely increase the price of gasoline?

    (A) Household income falls.
    (B) Technology used to produce gasoline improves.
    (C) The price of subway tickets and other public transportation falls.
    (D) The price of crude oil, a raw material for gasoline, rises.
    (E) The price of car insurance rises.

11. If the demand for grapes increases simultaneously with an increase in the supply of grapes, we can say that

    (A) equilibrium quantity rises, but the price change is ambiguous.
    (B) equilibrium quantity falls, but the price change is ambiguous.
    (C) equilibrium quantity rises, and the price rises.
    (D) equilibrium quantity falls, and the price falls.
    (E) the quantity change is ambiguous, but the equilibrium price rises.

12. In the competitive market for cherry pie, we observe the equilibrium price has risen and the equilibrium quantity has fallen. Which of the following could explain this?

    (A) Income has increased, and cherry pie is a normal good.
    (B) The price of raw cherries has increased.
    (C) The technology used to produce cherry pies has increased.
    (D) The price of apple pies has decreased.
    (E) The number of cherry pie producers has increased.

13. In Figure D.2, identify the area that corresponds to total dollars spent on this product.

    (A) 0ACB
    (B) 0FCB
    (C) AFC
    (D) ACE
    (E) FCE

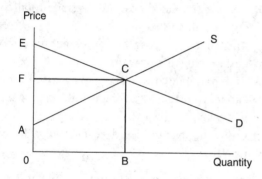

Price

Figure D.2

14. In Figure D.2, identify the area of consumer surplus.

    (A) 0ACB
    (B) 0FCB
    (C) AFC
    (D) ACE
    (E) FCE

15. Suppose the price of beef rises by 10 percent and the quantity of beef demanded falls by 20 percent. We can conclude that

    (A) demand for beef is price elastic and consumer spending on beef is falling.
    (B) demand for beef is price elastic and consumer spending on beef is rising.
    (C) demand for beef is price inelastic and consumer spending on beef is falling.
    (D) demand for beef is price inelastic and consumer spending on beef is rising.
    (E) demand for beef is unit elastic and consumer spending on beef is constant.

16. If the price of firm A's cell phone service rises by 5 percent and the quantity demanded for firm B's cell phone service increases by 10 percent, we can say that

    (A) demand for firm B is price elastic.
    (B) supply for firm B is price elastic.
    (C) firms A and B are substitutes because the cross-price elasticity is greater than zero.
    (D) firms A and B are complements because the cross-price elasticity is less than zero.
    (E) firms A and B are complements because the cross-price elasticity is greater than zero.

17. A binding price floor is imposed in a competitive market. How will this change consumer surplus and producer surplus, and will there be a shortage or surplus of the product exchanged?

	CONSUMER SURPLUS	PRODUCER SURPLUS	SHORTAGE OR SURPLUS?
(A)	Decreases	Increases	Surplus
(B)	Decreases	Increases	Shortage
(C)	Increases	Decreases	Shortage
(D)	Increases	Decreases	Surplus
(E)	Decreases	Decreases	Surplus

18. An excise tax of $T is imposed on the sellers of a product exchanged in a competitive market. Which of the following statements accurately describes the outcome?

    (A) If the supply curve is less elastic than the demand curve, consumers pay a higher share of the tax and there is deadweight loss.

    (B) If the supply curve is more elastic than the demand curve, consumers pay a lower share of the tax and there is deadweight loss.

    (C) If the demand curve is perfectly elastic, producers pay the entire burden of the tax and there is zero deadweight loss.

    (D) If the supply curve is perfectly elastic, consumers pay the entire burden of the tax and there is zero deadweight loss.

    (E) If the demand curve is perfectly inelastic, consumers pay the entire burden of the tax and there is zero deadweight loss.

19. Professor Peach spends her entire budget on tea and biscuits to maximize her utility. The price of tea is $2 per cup and the price of each biscuit is $3. At her current consumption levels, the marginal utility of tea is 22 utils and the marginal utility of biscuits is 33 utils, and she has used her entire budget. What should Professor Peach do to maximize her utility?

    (A) She should increase tea consumption and decrease biscuit consumption.

    (B) She should decrease both tea consumption and biscuit consumption.

    (C) She should decrease tea consumption and increase biscuit consumption.

    (D) She should increase both tea consumption and biscuit consumption.

    (E) She should change nothing.

20. Which of the following describes the theory behind the demand curve?

    (A) Decreasing marginal utility as consumption rises

    (B) Increasing marginal cost as consumption rises

    (C) Decreasing marginal cost as consumption rises

    (D) Increasing total utility at an increasing rate as consumption rises

    (E) The substitution effect is larger than the income effect.

21. If a consumer is not required to pay a monetary price for each cookie she consumes, the consumer will stop eating cookies when

    (A) the total utility from eating cookies is equal to zero.

    (B) the substitution effect outweighs the income effect from eating cookies.

    (C) the ratio of marginal utility divided by total utility is equal to one.

    (D) the marginal utility from eating the last cookie is zero.

    (E) the marginal utility from eating the next cookie is increasing at a decreasing rate.

22. In the short run, a firm employs labor and capital to produce gadgets. If the annual price of capital increases, what will happen to the short-run cost curves?

    (A) The marginal cost and average variable cost curves will shift upward.

    (B) The average fixed cost and average total cost curves will shift upward.

    (C) The marginal cost and average fixed cost curves will shift upward.

    (D) The marginal cost, average fixed cost, average variable cost, and average total cost curves will all shift upward.

    (E) Only the average fixed cost curve will shift upward.

23. A pizza restaurant is operating in the short run and looking at expenses for next month. Which of the following is a variable cost for the owners of the restaurant?

    (A) Rent on the building

    (B) Cost of Wi-Fi in the building

    (C) Cost of deliveries of cheese and pepperoni

    (D) Insurance payments on pizza delivery cars

    (E) Payments to keep the website updated

Questions 24 and 25 are based on the production data in the following table.

QUANTITY OF LABOR EMPLOYED (L)	TOTAL PRODUCT OF LABOR (Q)
0	0
1	10
2	18
3	24
4	28
5	30
6	31
7	30

24. What is the marginal product of labor for the third unit of labor?

(A) 24
(B) 6
(C) 8
(D) 3
(E) 12

25. What is the average product of labor for the fifth unit of labor?

(A) 5
(B) 30
(C) 6
(D) 2
(E) 25

Questions 26 to 28 are based on the table of costs below for a perfectly competitive firm.

OUTPUT	AVERAGE FIXED COST	AVERAGE VARIABLE COST	MARGINAL COST
0			
1	$10	$5	$5
2	$5	$3.50	$2
3	$3.33	$4.33	$6
4	$2.50	$5	$7
5	$2	$5.60	$8

26. The total fixed cost of producing a quantity of 4 is

(A) $5.
(B) $7.50.
(C) $7.
(D) $2.50.
(E) $10.

27. The first unit of output to exhibit diminishing marginal productivity is the _____ unit.

(A) 1st
(B) 2nd
(C) 3rd
(D) 4th
(E) 5th

28. At a quantity of 4, what is the total cost of production?

(A) $7.50
(B) $2.50
(C) $15
(D) $30
(E) $14.50

Questions 29 to 30 are based on Figure D.3, which illustrates the short-run cost curves of a perfectly competitive firm.

Figure D.3

29. The shutdown point is seen at:

(A) $P0$, $q0$
(B) $P1$, $q1$
(C) $P2$, $q2$
(D) $P3$, $q3$
(E) $P3$, $q4$

30. If the market price of the output increases from $P1$ to $P3$, the profit-maximizing firm will

    (A) increase output from $q1$ to $q4$ and earn positive economic profits.
    (B) increase output from $q1$ to $q4$ and earn a normal profit.
    (C) increase output from $q1$ to $q3$ and earn positive economic profits.
    (D) increase output from $q1$ to $q3$ and earn a normal profit.
    (E) increase output from $q1$ to $q2$ and earn economic losses.

31. If the perfectly competitive price is currently below minimum average total cost, we can expect which of the following events in the long run?

    (A) The price will rise and each firm's output will fall as firms exit the industry.
    (B) Market equilibrium quantity will increase as firms exit the industry.
    (C) Nothing. The industry is currently in long-run equilibrium.
    (D) Profits will fall as the market price increases.
    (E) The price will rise to the breakeven point as firms exit the industry.

32. If a perfectly competitive firm is maximizing profit and short-run profits are positive, which of the following must be true?

    (A) $P = MR = MC = ATC$
    (B) $P > MR = MC = ATC$
    (C) $P = MR = MC > ATC$
    (D) $P = MR = MC < ATC$
    (E) $P = MR > MC = ATC$

33. Which of the following is a characteristic of perfectly competitive markets?

    (A) Product differentiation
    (B) Barriers to entry
    (C) Strategic behavior
    (D) Very few producers
    (E) Price-taking behavior

34. When a perfectly competitive market has come to long-run equilibrium, we know that

    (A) economic profit is zero and accounting profit is greater than zero.
    (B) economic profit and accounting profit are both zero.
    (C) price is greater than average total cost.
    (D) price is equal to average variable cost.
    (E) accounting profit is zero and economic profit is greater than zero.

35. Perfectly competitive markets are said to be allocatively efficient because output is where

    (A) P = ATC.
    (B) P = MC.
    (C) P = AVC.
    (D) economic profit is zero.
    (E) P = MR.

36. When a monopolist has maximized profit,

    (A) price is set equal to marginal cost, creating zero economic profit.
    (B) output is set where price is equal to average total cost.
    (C) price is set above marginal cost, creating allocative inefficiency.
    (D) any short-run profit will be eliminated through the long-run entry of new firms.
    (E) output is set where price is equal to marginal cost, eliminating any deadweight loss.

37. Assuming positive profits are possible, when a monopolist sets output to maximize profit, we know that

    (A) $P = MR = MC = ATC$.
    (B) $P = MR = MC > ATC$.
    (C) $P > MR > MC = ATC$.
    (D) $P > MR > MC > ATC$.
    (E) $P > ATC > MR = MC$.

Questions 38–40 are based on Figure D.4, which illustrates a profit-maximizing monopolist.

Figure D.4

38. When the monopolist maximizes profit, output will be set at _____ and price will be set at _____.

    (A) Q2; P1
    (B) Q1; P1
    (C) Q1; P2
    (D) Q3; P3
    (E) Q2; P2

39. At the monopoly outcome, consumer surplus is equal to the following area:

    (A) (P2 − P1) × Q1
    (B) 1/2 × (P3 − P1) × Q2
    (C) 1/2 × (P2 − P1) × (Q2 − Q1)
    (D) 1/2 × P3 × Q3
    (E) 1/2 × (P3 − P2) × Q1

40. If this monopolist were regulated to produce a break-even level of output, output will be set at _____ and price will be set at _____.

    (A) Q2; P1
    (B) Q1; P1
    (C) Q1; P2
    (D) Q3; P3
    (E) Q2; P2

41. Which of the following is necessarily a characteristic of oligopoly?

    (A) Free entry into and exit from the market
    (B) A few large producers
    (C) One producer of a good with no close substitutes
    (D) A homogenous product
    (E) No opportunities for collusion between firms

42. The market structures of perfect competition and monopolistic competition share which of the following characteristics?

    (A) Ease of entry and exit in the long run
    (B) Homogenous products
    (C) Perfectly elastic demand for the firm's product
    (D) Long-run positive profits
    (E) Rigid or "sticky" prices

43. Monopolistic competition is often characterized by

    (A) strong barriers to entry.
    (B) a long-run price that exceeds average total cost.
    (C) a price that exceeds average variable cost, causing excess capacity.
    (D) a homogenous product.
    (E) many resources devoted to advertising.

44. If the government wishes to regulate a natural monopoly so that it produces an allocatively efficient level of output, it would be at an output

    (A) where price is equal to average total cost.
    (B) where marginal revenue equals marginal cost.
    (C) where normal profits are made.
    (D) where price is equal to average variable cost.
    (E) where price is equal to marginal cost.

Use the following payoff matrix to answer Questions 45 and 46.

		FIRM Z	
		Ph	Pl
FIRM Y	Ph	Y: $15,000 Z: $13,000	Y: $20,000 Z: $12,000
	Pl	Y: $14,000 Z: $22,000	Y: $16,000 Z: $15,000

45. Two oligopolists must simultaneously decide upon a pricing strategy, either set a high price (Ph) or a low price (Pl). Once the price is set, it cannot be changed. If the firms do not collude, the outcome of the game will be

    (A) both firms set a low price.
    (B) Firm Y sets a high price and Firm Z alternates between the high price and low price.
    (C) both firms set a high price.
    (D) Firm Y sets the high price and Firm Z sets the low price.
    (E) Firm Y sets the low price and Firm Z sets the high price.

46. Two oligopolists must simultaneously decide upon a pricing strategy, either set a high price (Ph) or a low price (Pl). Once the price is set, it cannot be changed. If the firms can successfully collude, the outcome of the game will be:

    (A) both firms set a low price.
    (B) both Firm Y and Firm Z alternate between the high price and low price.
    (C) both firms set a high price.
    (D) Firm Y sets the high price and Firm Z sets the low price.
    (E) Firm Y sets the low price and Firm Z sets the high price.

47. Which of the following is most likely to decrease the demand for kindergarten teachers?

    (A) An increase in funding for education
    (B) Increased immigration of foreign citizens and their families
    (C) A decrease in the average number of children per household
    (D) Subsidies given to college students who major in elementary education
    (E) A decrease in the number of classes the state requires for a teaching certificate

48. Which of the following statements is true about the demand for labor?

    (A) It rises if the price of a substitute resource falls and the output effect is greater than the substitution effect.
    (B) It falls if the price of the output produced rises.
    (C) It falls if the price of a complementary resource falls.
    (D) It falls if the demand for the output produced by labor increases.
    (E) It falls if the labor becomes more productive.

Questions 49 and 50 are based on the table of employment data below.

WAGE (W)	QUANTITY OF LABOR SUPPLIED	MARGINAL REVENUE PRODUCT OF LABOR (MRP$_L$)
$4	0	
$5	10	$7
$6	20	$6
$7	30	$5
$8	40	$4

49. If a firm is hiring labor in the perfectly competitive labor market, the wage and employment will be

    (A) $4 and 0.
    (B) $5 and 10.
    (C) $6 and 20.
    (D) $7 and 30.
    (E) $8 and 40.

50. If the above firm were a monopsonist, the wage would be _____ and employment would be _____ the competitive outcome.

    (A) greater than; less than
    (B) less than; greater than
    (C) greater than; greater than
    (D) less than; less than
    (E) less than; the same as

51. Interstate trucking companies hire three factors of production in shipping goods from point A to point B: labor (drivers), capital (trucks and trailers), and diesel fuel. Which of the following would cause the demand for capital to increase?

    (A) A recession decreases the demand for goods.
    (B) Wages paid to drivers are increasing in the labor market.
    (C) Diesel fuel prices are decreasing in the fuel market.
    (D) Interest rates on borrowing are increasing in credit markets.
    (E) The price of capital is decreasing.

Questions 52 and 53 are based on Figure D.5, which illustrates a profit-maximizing employer.

Figure D.5

52. If this firm is the sole employer in the labor market, how much labor would be employed and what is the wage that would be paid?

    (A) Q1; W3
    (B) Q1; W1
    (C) Q2; W2
    (D) Q1; W2
    (E) Q2; W1

53. If this firm hires the efficient quantity of labor in this market, employment would be _____ and the wage would be _____.

    (A) Q1; W3
    (B) Q1; W1
    (C) Q2; W2
    (D) Q1; W2
    (E) Q2; W1

54. A firm hires labor and capital in competitive-factor markets. The price of labor is $6, and the price of capital is $12. Currently the marginal product of labor is 24 units, and the marginal product of capital is 36 units. Can the firm adjust the hiring of labor and capital to produce the same output at a lower cost?

    (A) No, the firm is hiring the least-cost combination of labor and capital.
    (B) Yes, the firm should hire more of both labor and capital.
    (C) Yes, the firm should hire less of both labor and capital.
    (D) Yes, the firm should hire more labor and less capital.
    (E) Yes, the firm should hire less labor and more capital.

55. Which of the following is the best example of a public good?

    (A) A visit to the orthodontist
    (B) A session at the tanning salon
    (C) A large pizza
    (D) A cup of coffee
    (E) The International Space Station

56. A negative externality in the market for a good exists when

    (A) the market overallocates resources to the production of this good.
    (B) spillover benefits are received by society.

(C) the marginal social benefit equals the marginal social cost.
(D) total welfare is maximized.
(E) the marginal private cost exceeds the marginal social cost.

57. Which of the following tax systems is designed to redistribute income from the wealthy to the poor?

    (A) A progressive tax system
    (B) A regressive tax system
    (C) A proportional tax system
    (D) An excise tax system
    (E) A tariff system

58. The two characteristics of a private good are

    (A) excludable and rival.
    (B) open-access and rival.
    (C) nonexcludable and nonrival.
    (D) excludable and nonrival.
    (E) nonexcludable and rival.

59. Suppose we observe a nation's Gini ratio has fallen from .75 to .45 over 20 years. What might explain this change?

    (A) The nation's level of human capital has fallen.
    (B) The nation has used more regressive taxes.
    (C) The nation's markets have become less competitive.
    (D) The nation has used more progressive taxes.
    (E) The nation's degree of social and economic discrimination has worsened.

60. Consumers of gadgets generate spillover benefits to their communities, and the gadget market does not account for these social benefits. Which of the following would be an appropriate government response to improve efficiency in the gadget market?

    (A) Impose a tax on each gadget produced.
    (B) Ban the consumption of gadgets.
    (C) Impose a tax on each gadget consumed.
    (D) Set a price ceiling in the gadget market.
    (E) Provide a subsidy for each gadget consumed.

❯ Answers and Explanations

This diagnostic exam was designed to test you on topics that you will see on the AP Microeconomics exam in the approximate proportions that you will see them. Chronologically they appear in the approximate order of their review in Step 4 of this book, but this is not the case on the AP exam. Topics on the practice exams are shuffled.

Questions from Chapter 5

1. **C**—This is the definition of scarcity.

2. **B**—In a capitalistic market economy, the central government has minimal roles in the production and distribution of goods. Resources are allocated based on relative, not absolute, prices, and prices are determined in markets. The role of private property is central to capitalism.

3. **E**—A concave, or bowed out, PPC illustrates the principle of increasing opportunity costs. It is more and more difficult (costly) to produce increasing amounts of a good.

4. **D**—When technology improves for butter production, it means that the same number of resources can produce more butter; this shifts the vertical intercept upward. The opportunity cost of bread rises because every additional unit of bread now comes at a larger sacrifice of butter production.

5. **C**—The marginal cost of the next taco is always $1, so a rational consumer will stop when the marginal benefit falls to equal marginal cost.

6. **E**—Employees are the labor resource for a firm.

7. **B**—If Felipe could work for five hours instead of attending the concert, those forgone wages are an implicit cost of the concert. An explicit cost is something he directly pays out of his pocket.

8. **A**—If Theo waxes the car, he gives up eight sections of painted fence, while Eliza would only give up two sections of fence. Because the opportunity cost of waxing is higher for Theo, he has a comparative advantage in painting and Eliza has a comparative advantage in waxing. Theo should paint the fence and Eliza should wax the car.

Questions from Chapter 6

9. **B**—In a market free of price controls or other distortions, equilibrium occurs at a price where $Q_d = Q_s$. Graphically this is where the demand curve intersects the supply curve. Here, social welfare is maximized, allocative efficiency is attained, and there exists no deadweight loss.

10. **D**—If the price of a production input (or resource) increases, the supply curve shifts leftward and the price of gasoline rises. Hint: Having a strong grasp of what shifts supply and demand curves will really pay off. Draw these shifting curves in the margin of the exam book!

11. **A**—Increased demand, by itself, increases equilibrium quantity and increases the price of grapes. Increased supply, by itself, increases equilibrium quantity and decreases the price of grapes. So quantity definitely increases, but the price change is unknown because it depends on how far the curves shift in relation to each other. Quickly draw these in the exam book.

12. **B**—If the price has risen and quantity has fallen, look for something that would cause the supply curve to decrease, or shift leftward. The higher price of raw cherries, a key input in the production of cherry pie, would decrease the supply of cherry pies.

13. **B**—Total spending is the price multiplied by the quantity demanded, or the area of the rectangle with height to point F and width of point B.

14. **E**—Consumer surplus is the area above the price and below the demand curve. It is the difference between the price consumers would have paid and the price they did pay.

Questions from Chapter 7

15. **A**—If the percentage change in Q_d is greater than the percentage change in price, the good is elastic. In this situation of rising prices, total spending on beef will fall because the upward effect of prices is outweighed by the downward effect of quantity.

16. **C**—The cross-price elasticity measures how sensitive the Q_d of good X is to a change in the price of good Y. If this elasticity is greater than zero, the two goods are substitutes; if it is negative, the two goods are complements.

17. **A**—A binding price floor is designed to help producers, so it is set above the equilibrium price. At this price floor, $Q_s > Q_d$, so a surplus of the product exists. The higher price and decreased quantity cause consumer surplus to fall and producer surplus to rise.

18. **E**—A vertical demand curve will put the entire burden of the tax on consumers because the price will rise by exactly $T. There is no deadweight loss because the equilibrium quantity doesn't change. It's important to remember that the group, buyers or sellers, that pays the higher burden of the tax is the group that has the lowest price elasticity. And any time a tax decreases the market equilibrium quantity, deadweight loss will emerge.

19. **E**—A consumer has maximized her utility when the marginal utility per dollar is equal for both products. When we divide marginal utility by the price, we see that $MU_{tea}/P_{tea} = MU_{biscuits}/P_{biscuits} = 11$ utils per dollar.

20. **A**—One of the foundations of the law of demand is falling marginal utility as more of a good is consumed. You can eliminate any choices that refer to marginal cost, and a downward-sloping demand curve would not be the result of total utility that increases at an increasing rate.

21. **D**—A consumer stops eating cookies when total utility is maximized, which corresponds to when $MU = 0$. Because marginal utility falls with consumption, the very next cookie will give the consumer disutility ($MU < 0$), so she stops.

Questions from Chapter 8

22. **B**—An increase in the price of capital is an increase in total fixed costs. This increases AFC. Since ATC = AFC + AVC, it also increases ATC. Because fixed costs do not change with output, marginal cost and variable cost remain the same.

23. **C**—A variable cost is something that increases and decreases with output. If the restaurant is busy, they will need more cheese and pepperoni next month. All other options would remain constant, or fixed, no matter if the restaurant was busy or slow next month.

24. **B**—Marginal product of labor is the change in output when the next unit of labor is employed. When the third unit of labor is hired, output rises from 18 to 24 units, so marginal product is 6 additional units of output.

25. **C**—Average product of labor is the total output divided by the units of labor hired to produce that output. In other words, it is output per unit of labor. At the fifth unit of labor, total output is 30, so average product is equal to 30 divided by 5, or 6 units per worker.

26. **E**—TFC are constant, so if AFC = $10 at $q = 1$ and AFC = TFC/q, then TFC must be $10 at *any* quantity. Know the way in which all total and average costs are related.

27. **C**—This question tests whether you know the relationships between production and cost. Marginal cost and marginal product are inverses of each other. Because the MC of producing the third unit is rising, the MP must be falling.

28. **D**—At a quantity of 4, TFC = $10 and TVC = AVC × q = $5 × 4 = $20. Since TC = TFC + TVC, TC = $30.

Questions from Chapter 9

29. **B**—The shutdown point is at minimum AVC. If the price falls below this point, the firm finds it rational to produce nothing in the short run and incur losses equal to TFC.

30. **C**—When the price rises, the perfectly competitive firm finds a higher level of output where $P = MR = MC$. Since this price lies above the ATC curve, positive economic profits are possible.

31. **E**—The question describes a situation where short-run losses are being incurred. In the long run, firms exit, shifting market supply leftward, increasing market price until the firms earn normal, or breakeven, profits.

32. **C**—In perfect competition, price and marginal revenue are identical, and the firm maximizes profit by producing where price and marginal revenue are equal to marginal cost. If positive

profits are being made, it must be the case that price is greater than average total cost.

33. **E**—Perfect competition is described by many firms producing identical products in a market with no barriers to entry. These characteristics imply that firms cannot affect the price; they're price takers. Strategic behavior, like advertising, is impossible under these conditions.

34. **A**—In the long run, perfectly competitive firms earn zero economic profit. Unlike economic profit, accounting profit does not include the implicit costs of operating the business, so accounting profit will always be greater than economic profit.

35. **B**—Allocative efficiency is achieved when the marginal benefit to society is equal to the marginal cost to society. In perfectly competitive markets, this occurs because price equals marginal cost for the last unit produced and consumed. This is true even if profits are positive, zero, or negative.

36. **C**—One of the important results of monopoly is that while output is set where MR = MC, price is set from the demand curve, so $P >$ MC. This creates inefficient resource allocation and deadweight loss that is not eliminated in the long run.

37. **E**—For a monopolist, price is always greater than marginal revenue, and profit is maximized when marginal revenue equals marginal cost, so you can eliminate any choices where these conditions are not met. If profit is positive, price must also be greater than average total cost.

38. **C**—A monopolist sets output where MR = MC, and this happens at Q1. But price comes from the demand curve, so from Q1 go up to demand, and the price is set at P2.

39. **E**—Consumer surplus is the area above the price and below the demand curve at the monopoly output. This area forms a triangle with a width of Q1 units and a height of (P3 – P2) units. The area of a triangle is 1/2 × (width) × (height).

40. **A**—The breakeven point would occur at the output where price equals average total cost.

41. **B**—Oligopolies are industries dominated by a few large firms but can have either homogenous or differentiated products. All other choices describe other market structures in the chapter.

42. **A**—These two market structures are fairly similar, and free entry and exit is one of the characteristics that they share. They also share the characteristic of normal profits in the long run but do not share homogenous products or efficiency.

43. **E**—Monopolistic competition is characterized by product differentiation. One way that firms differentiate their products and protect market share is through extensive advertising.

44. **E**—In perfect competition, $P =$ MR = MC and resources are allocated efficiently. Since a monopoly will not have the situation where $P =$ MR, regulators might try to force the firm to produce where $P =$ MC. This point may or may not ensure a long-run profit for the firm.

45. **C**—Both firms have dominant strategies to always choose the high price. This means that no matter what the other firm does, each firm sees that Ph is always more profitable than Pl.

46. **A**—When firms cannot collude, they will pursue their individual dominant strategies and price high. However, if they can successfully collude, they can both increase profits by agreeing to set the low price.

Questions from Chapter 10

47. **C**—Demand for any type of labor is derived from the demand for the good or service that the labor produces. With fewer children in the household, there will be less demand for kindergarten classes and teachers.

48. **A**—When the price of a substitute resource (like capital) falls, two effects move the demand for labor in opposite directions. The firm wants to substitute for more capital and less labor, but lower costs prompt more output to be produced, and this can require more labor. If the output effect outweighs the substitution effect, demand for labor may increase even if capital is less expensive. Labor demand will increase if the labor becomes more productive or if the price of the output produced rises.

49. C—Competitive labor markets are characterized by hiring where $W = $ MRPL. This is another example of decision making where marginal costs (wage paid) equal marginal benefits (MR $\times$ MPL).

50. D—A monopsonist is like a monopolist on the hiring side of the firm. Monopsonists hire where MFC $=$ MRPL, and because MFC lies above the labor supply curve, this means that they will hire fewer workers and pay lower wages than the competitive outcome.

51. D—Diesel fuel is a complementary input for the capital trucks and trailers, so a lower price of this input would increase demand for capital. The lower price of capital would increase the quantity of capital hired, but wouldn't shift the entire demand curve.

52. B—The monopsonist hires to the point where marginal factor cost is equal to the marginal revenue product of labor, and this happens at Q1 units of labor. The wage comes from the labor supply curve, so the wage paid is W1.

53. D—The efficient quantity of employment is where the demand curve intersects the supply curve. This would correspond to the outcome for a perfectly competitive labor market.

54. D—The least-cost combination of labor and capital is employed when the marginal product per dollar is equal for both inputs. Currently the marginal product per dollar is 4 units per dollar for labor (24/\$6) compared to 3 units per dollar (36/\$12) for capital. Since each dollar paid to labor produces more output, the firm should increase labor hiring and decrease capital hiring until $MP_L/w = MP_K/r$.

Questions from Chapter 11

55. E—Public goods cannot be divided among consumers. If one consumes a public good, the next person is not denied consumption of it. All other choices are goods and services that are both rival and excludable.

56. A—When individuals and firms exchange a good that imposes costs on third parties, they have created a negative externality. The market produces "too much" because these spillover costs are not reflected in the private (or market) supply curve.

Resources are overallocated to the production of this good.

57. A—A progressive tax system means that higher levels of income pay higher proportions of their income to the tax collector. This system is designed to redistribute income from higher tax brackets to lower tax brackets.

58. A—A private good, like a hamburger, is excludable because sellers can exclude nonpayers from consuming the good. Private goods are also rival because one person's consumption of a unit means another person cannot also consume that same unit of the good.

59. D—When a Gini ratio has fallen, it means that the income distribution has become more equal in a nation. Progressive taxes are those that tax a higher percentage of income as income rises. This is one way that government can redistribute income from the wealthiest to the poorest segments of society.

60. E—Positive externalities should be encouraged, but markets ignore the spillover benefits to the rest of society. Subsidies would promote more transactions and move the market outcome closer to the socially efficient outcome.

AP Microeconomics Diagnostic Exam

SECTION II

Free-Response Questions
Planning Time—10 minutes
Writing Time—50 minutes

At the conclusion of the planning time, you have 50 minutes to respond to the following three questions. Approximately half of your time should be given to the first question, and the second half should be divided evenly between the remaining two questions. Be careful to clearly explain your reasoning and to provide clear labels to all graph axes and curves.

1. The following graph shows a typical seller of burritos in a monopolistically competitive market for burritos.

(A) Using the labels in the graph, identify the following:

   i. The profit-maximizing quantity
   ii. The price of a burrito when the monopolist has maximized profit
   iii. The allocatively efficient output

(B) Using the labels in the graph, identify the following:

   i. The area of short-run economic profit or loss
   ii. The area of consumer surplus

(C) In the long run, do you expect there to be the same number of firms, more firms, or fewer firms in this market? Explain.

(D) Given your response in (C), will the long-run price of burritos be higher, lower, or the same as the short-run price of burritos?

(E) In the long-run equilibrium, will deadweight loss exist? Explain.

2. The market for apples is perfectly competitive and in long-run equilibrium. Due to consumer unrest about the price of apples, the government is considering a price ceiling.

(A) In a correctly labeled graph, draw the market for apples. In the graph, identify

   i. The equilibrium price and quantity in the market, labeled P_M and Q_M respectively.
   ii. An effective price ceiling, labeled P_C.
   iii. The quantity of apples exchanged at the price floor, labeled Q^*.

(B) If the price ceiling is effective, is there a shortage of apples, a surplus of apples, or neither? Explain.

(C) In your graph from (A), shade the area of deadweight loss due to the effective price ceiling.

3. Sissy is an employer of labor in a competitive labor market at a wage of $12. Sissy's firm produces cat toys in a competitive output market at a price of $2. The table below shows how output changes in the short run with different levels of employment. Labor is Sissy's only variable input, and the firm has fixed costs equal to $8.

UNITS OF LABOR (L)	CAT TOYS PRODUCED (Q)
0	0
1	8
2	15
3	21
4	26
5	30
6	33
7	35
8	31

(A) Using marginal analysis, how units of labor should Sissy employ to maximize her short-run profits? Explain.

(B) Based on your answer to (A),

  i. Identify the number of cat toys that will be produced.
  ii. Calculate Sissy's short-run economic profit. Show your work.

(C) Based on your answer to (B) (ii), should Sissy shut down in the short run? Explain.

Free-Response Grading Rubric

Question 1 (10 points)

Part (A): 3 points
i. One point is earned for identifying Q2 as the profit-maximizing output.
ii. One point is earned for identifying P4 as the price.
iii. One point is earned for identifying Q3 as the allocatively efficient output (where $P = MC$).

Part (B): 2 points
i. One point is earned for identifying the area $(P5 - P4) \times Q2$ as the area of economic losses. Alternatively, the point could be earned by stating the area of $(P4 - P5) \times Q2$ is the economic profit (a negative value).
ii. One point is earned by identifying the area $1/2 \times (P6 - P4) \times Q2$ as the area of consumer surplus.

Part (C): 2 points
• One point is earned for stating there will be fewer firms in the long run.
• One point is earned for explaining that the short-run losses will prompt exit of some firms in the long run.

Part (D): 1 point
One point is earned for stating that the price of burritos will be higher in the long run.

Part E: (2 points)
• One point is earned for stating that deadweight loss will exist in the long run.
• One point is earned for explaining that in the long run the price will still be greater than marginal cost.

Question 2 (5 points)
Part A: 3 points
These are graphing points.
i. One point is earned for drawing a correctly labeled graph of the apple market with P_M and Q_M. The market demand curve must be downward sloping, and the market supply curve must be upward sloping.
ii. One point is earned for drawing a horizontal P_c that lies below P_M.
iii. One point is earned by identifying Q^* from the intersection of P_c and the supply curve.

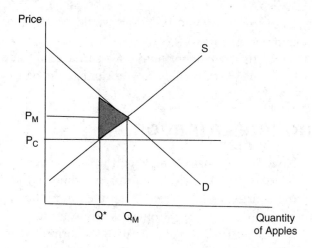

Part B: 2 points
- One point is earned for stating that there is a shortage of apples.
- One point is earned by explaining that at P_c the quantity demanded exceeds the quantity supplied.

Part C: 1 point
One point is earned for correctly shading the area of deadweight loss in the graph.

Question 3 (5 points)
Part A: 1 point
- One point is earned for stating that the firm should employ 3 units of labor and for explaining that at 3 units of labor, the marginal revenue product of labor (MRPL) is equal to the wage (W), but at the fourth unit of labor, $MRP_L < W$.

Part B: 2 points
i. One point is earned for stating that Sissy will produce 21 cat toys.
ii. One point is earned for calculating profit and showing the work.
    Profit = $\$2 \times 21 - \$12 \times 3 - \$8 = -\$2$

Part C: 2 points
- One point is earned for stating that Sissy should not shut down in the short run.
- One point is earned for explaining that her total revenue exceeds total variable cost. If she shut down, she would lose $8 rather than $2.

Are there ever any opportunities for extra credit in FRQs?
Yes, these are often called "consistency points," and these allow you to earn points on subsequent sections of an FRQ, so long as your responses are consistent with earlier incorrect responses.

For example, let's look at Problem 1. In part (B)(i) you should have found an area of economic losses, but suppose you state that you have found positive economic profits. You are not going to earn the point in (B)(i). However, in part (C) you state that there will be more firms because the profit attracts entry. You would most likely earn the two points in (C) because you were consistently correct. You could even earn the point in (D) for stating that the price of burritos would fall.

In Problem 3, maybe you stated in (A) that Sissy will hire 4 units of labor. Wrong, no point there. However in part (B)(i) you state that her output is 26 cat toys (consistent with

4 units of labor) and her losses would be $4 (consistent with 26 cat toys), so you could earn both points.

So there are opportunities for partial credit in the FRQs, but you really want to shoot for earning perfect credit so you can bag the perfect 5.

Scoring and Interpretation

Now that you have completed the diagnostic exam and checked your answers, it is time to assess your knowledge and preparation. If you saw some questions that caused you to roll your eyes and mutter "What the . . . ?" then you can focus your study on those areas. If you breezed through some questions, great!

Calculate your raw score with the formula that follows. If you left any multiple-choice questions blank, there is no penalty. Take this raw score on the diagnostic exam and compare it to the table that follows to estimate where you might score at this point.

Calculate Your Score:

Multiple-Choice Questions:

$$\frac{\qquad\qquad}{\text{(# right)}} = \frac{\qquad\qquad}{\text{MC raw score}}$$

Free-Response Questions:

Free-Response Raw Score $= (1.50 \times \text{Score 1}) + (1.50 \times \text{Score 2}) + (1.50 \times \text{Score 3})$

$= \underline{\qquad}$

Add the raw scores from the multiple-choice and free-response sections to obtain your total raw score for the diagnostic exam. Use the following table to determine your grade, remembering these are rough estimates using questions that are not actually from AP exams, so do not read too much into this conversion from raw score to AP score.

MICROECONOMICS	
Raw Diagnostic Score	AP Grade
73–90	5
58–72	4
45–57	3
33–44	2
0–32	1

No matter how you scored on the diagnostic exam, it is time to begin to review for your AP Microeconomics exam.

STEP 3

Develop Strategies for Success

CHAPTER **4**   How to Approach Each Question Type

CHAPTER 4

How to Approach Each Question Type

IN THIS CHAPTER

Summary: Use these question-answering strategies to raise your AP score.

Key Ideas

Multiple-Choice Questions
- ✪ Read the question carefully.
- ✪ Try to answer the question yourself before reading the answer choices.
- ✪ Guess if you can eliminate one or more answer choices.
- ✪ Remember that drawing a picture can help.
- ✪ Don't spend too much time on any one question.

Free-Response Questions
- ✪ Write clearly and legibly.
- ✪ Be consistent from one part of your answer to another.
- ✪ Draw a graph if one is required.
- ✪ If the question can be answered with one word or number, don't write more.
- ✪ Pay attention to the prompts.

Section I: Multiple-Choice Questions

Because you are a seasoned student accustomed to the educational testing machine, you have surely participated in more standardized tests than you care to count. You probably know some students who always seem to ace the multiple-choice questions and some students who would rather set themselves on fire than sit for another round of "bubble trouble." I hope that with a little background and a few tips, you might improve your scores in this important component of the AP Microeconomics exam.

First, the background. Every multiple-choice question has three important parts:

1. The **stem** is the basis for the actual question. Sometimes this comes in the form of a fill-in-the-blank statement, rather than a question.

   Example
   Average fixed cost is computed by dividing total fixed cost by to the end

   Example
   If a negative externality exists in the production of a good, what must be true of the market for this product?

2. The **correct answer option.** Obviously, this is the one selection that best completes the statement, or responds to the question in the stem. Because you have purchased this book, you will select this option many, many times.

3. **Distractor options.** Just as it sounds, these are the incorrect answers intended to distract the person who decided not to purchase this book. You can locate this person in the exam room by searching for the individual who is repeatedly smacking his or her forehead on the desktop.

Students who do well on multiple-choice exams are so well prepared that they can easily find the correct answer, but other students do well because they are savvy enough to identify and avoid the distractors. Much research has been done on how to best study for, and complete, multiple-choice questions. You can find some of this research by using your favorite Internet search engine, but here are a few tips that many economics students find useful.

1. *Let's be careful out there.* You must carefully read the question. This sounds pretty obvious, but you would be surprised how tricky those test developers can be. For example, rushing past and failing to see the use of a negative can throw a student.

   Example
   Which of the following is *not* true of firms in perfect competition?

   A. Firms produce a homogenous good.
   B. Firms engage in price discrimination.
   C. Firms earn a normal profit in the long run.
   D. Firms have no ability to influence the market price.
   E. Firms produce the output where price is equal to marginal cost.

   A student who is going too fast and ignores the negative *not* might select option (A) because it is true of perfectly competitive firms, and it was the first option that the student saw.

2. *See the answer, be the answer.* Many people find success when they carefully read the question and, before looking at the alternatives, visualize the correct answer. This allows the person to narrow the search for the correct option and identify the distractors. Of course this visualization tip is most useful for students who have used this book to thoroughly review the economic content.

Example

The profit-maximizing monopolist sets output where:

> Before you even look at the options, you should know that the answer is "MR = MC". Find that option, and then quickly confirm to yourself that the others are indeed wrong.

3. *Never say never.* Words like "never" and "always" are called absolute qualifiers. If these words are used in one of the choices, it is rarely the correct choice.

Example

Which of the following is true about production in the short run?

A. MP is always greater than AP.
B. MP is never increasing.

If you can think of any situation where the statements in (A) and (B) are untrue, then you have discovered distractors and can eliminate these as valid choices.

4. *Easy is as easy does.* It's exam day and you're all geared up to set this very difficult test on its ear. The first question looks like a no-brainer. Of course! The answer is 7, choice C. But rather than smiling at the satisfaction that you knew the answer, you doubt yourself. Could it be that easy? Sometimes they are just that easy.

5. *Sometimes a blind squirrel finds an acorn.* Should you guess? If you have no clue which choice is correct, guessing is a no-lose strategy. Even with a wild guess, you have a 20 percent chance of getting it right. If you leave it blank, you have no chance. I am sure that you can do the math.

6. *Draw it, nail it.* Many questions can be easily answered if you do a quick sketch in the margins of your test book. Hey, you paid for that test book; you might as well use it.

Example

In the market for new automobiles, a normal good, a decrease in consumer income will cause output and the price to change in which of the following ways?

	OUTPUT	PRICE
(A)	No change	Increase
(B)	Decrease	Decrease
(C)	Increase	No change
(D)	No change	No change
(E)	No change	Decrease

These types of questions are particularly difficult because the answer requires two ingredients. It also requires a very thorough understanding of the demand and supply model, and here is where your graph comes in. The first thing you should do is quickly draw the situation given to you in the question: the market for automobiles. Show a downward-sloping demand curve shifting to the left and you can see that option (B) is correct. The graph speaks for itself.

7. *Come back, come back!* There are 60 questions and none of these is worth more than the other. If you are struggling with a particular question, circle it in your exam book and move on. Another question deeper into the exam might jog a memory of a theory you studied or something you learned from a practice exam in this book. You can then go back and quickly slay the beast. But if you spend a ridiculous amount of time on one question, you will feel your confidence and your time slipping away. This leads to my last tip.

8. *Timing is everything, kid.* You have about 70 seconds of time for each of the 60 questions. Keep an eye on your watch as you pass the halfway point. If you are running out of time and you have a few questions left, skim them for the easy (and quick) ones so that the rest of your scarce time can be devoted to those that need a little extra reading or thought.

Other things to keep in mind:

- Take the extra half of a second required to clearly fill in the bubbles.
- Don't smudge anything with sloppy erasures. If your eraser is smudgy, ask the proctor for another.
- Absolutely, positively check that you are bubbling the same line on the answer sheet as the question you are answering. I suggest that every time you turn the page you double-check that you are still lined up correctly.

Section II: Free-Response Questions

Your score on the FRQs amounts to one-third of your grade, and as a longtime reader of essays, I assure you there is no other way to score highly than to know your stuff. While you can guess on a multiple-choice question and have a one-in-five chance of getting the correct answer, there is no room for guessing in this section. There are, however, some tips that you can use to enhance your FRQ scores.

1. *Easy to read = easy to grade.* Organize your responses around the separate parts of the question and clearly label each part of your response. In other words, do not hide your answer; make it easy to find and easy to read. It helps you, and it helps the reader see where you're going. *Trust me, helping the reader can never hurt.* This leads to a related tip: Write in English, not Sanskrit. Even the most levelheaded and unbiased reader has trouble keeping their patience while struggling to read sloppy handwriting. I have seen three readers waste almost 10 minutes using the Rosetta stone to decipher a paragraph of text that was obviously written by a time-traveling student from the Byzantine Empire.

2. *Consistently wrong can be good.* The free-response questions are written in several parts, each building upon the first. If you are looking at an eight-part question, it can be scary. However, these questions are graded so that you can salvage several points even if you do not correctly answer the first part. The key thing for you to know is that you must be consistent, even if it is consistently wrong. For example, you might be asked to draw a graph showing a monopolist who has chosen the profit-maximizing level of output. Following sections might ask you to label the price, economic profit, consumer surplus, and deadweight loss—each being determined by the choice of output. So let's say you draw your diagram, but you label an incorrect level of output. Obviously you

are not going to receive that point. But if you proceed by labeling price, economic profit, consumer surplus, and deadweight loss correctly at your *incorrect* quantity, you would be surprised how forgiving the grading rubric can be.

3. *Have the last laugh with a well-drawn graph.* There are some points that require an explanation (i.e., "Describe how . . ."). Not all free-response questions require a graph, but a garbled paragraph of explanation can be saved with a perfect graph that tells the reader you know the answer to the question. This does not work in reverse.

4. *If I say draw, you better draw, Tex.* There are what readers call "graphing points," and these cannot be earned with a well-written paragraph. For example, if you are asked to draw the monopoly scenario described above, certain points will be awarded for the graph and only the graph. A delightfully written and entirely accurate paragraph of text will not earn the graphing points. You also need to clearly label graphs. You might think that downward-sloping line is obviously a demand curve, but some of those graphing points will not be awarded if lines and points are not clearly, and accurately, identified. And please, *please*, draw your graph larger than a postage stamp. If the reader cannot clearly see the important aspects of the graph, you will not earn those points.

5. *Give the answer, not a dissertation.* There are some parts of a question where you are asked to simply "identify" something. For example, "Identify the price if this firm were a monopolist" or "Identify the area that corresponds to deadweight loss." This type of question requires a quick piece of analysis that can literally be answered in one word or number. That point will be given if you provide that one word or number whether it is the only word you write or the fortieth that you write. For example, you might be given a table that shows how a firm's output changes as it hires more workers. One part of the question asks you to identify the optimal number of workers that the firm should hire. Suppose the correct answer is 4. The point is given if you say "4," "four," and maybe even "iv." If you write a 500-word Magna Carta concluding with the word "four," you will get the point but will have wasted precious time. This brings me to . . .

6. *Welcome to the magical kingdom.* If you surround the right answer to a question with a paragraph of economic wrongness, you will usually get the point, so long as you say the magic word. The only exception is a direct contradiction of the right answer. For example, suppose that when asked to *identify* the optimal number of workers, you spend a paragraph describing how the workers are unionized and therefore are subject to a price ceiling and that the exchange rate between those workers and the production possibility frontier means the answer is four. You will get the point! You said they should hire four, and "four" were the magic words. However, if you say that the answer is four, but that it is also five and on Mondays it is seven, you have contradicted yourself and the point will not be given.

7. *Marginally speaking.* This point is made throughout the microeconomics review contained in this book, but it bears repeating here as a valuable test-taking strategy. In economics, anything that is optimal or efficient or rational or cost minimizing or profit maximizing can be answered by telling the reader that the marginal benefits must equal the marginal costs. Depending upon the situation, you might have to clarify that "marginal benefit" to the firm is "marginal revenue" or to the employer "marginal revenue product." If the question asks you *why* the answer is four, there is always a very short phrase that readers look for so that they may award the point. This answer often includes the appropriate marginal comparison.

8. *Identify, Illustrate, Define, Indicate, and Explain.* Each part of a free-response question includes a prompt that tells you what the reader will be looking for so that the points can be awarded. If the question asks you to "identify" something, you may need only one word or a short phrase to receive all the points. Writing a paragraph here will only waste your time. As mentioned, any reference to "illustrate" will require you to draw, or redraw, a graph to receive points. If the question asks you to "define" a concept, you will need to devote more time to providing your best definition of that concept. If you are prompted to "indicate" something, you must simply state what is expected to happen. For example, suppose you are told that a price floor has been installed in the market for soybeans and you are asked to indicate what will happen to deadweight loss. All you need to do to earn the point is indicate that deadweight loss will increase. You may also get the point if you clearly indicate, preferably with an arrow, in a graph of the soybean market that there is now an area of deadweight loss. The most time-intensive prompt is usually one that involves "explain." Suppose you are told that the government has eliminated the minimum wage. Then you are asked to explain how this will affect wages and employment in these labor markets. To give yourself the best chance at receiving all the points, your response must provide two parts. First, give a clear statement of what exactly will happen; second, explain why it is going to happen.

Here are some other things to keep in mind:

- The free-response section begins with a 10-minute reading period. Use this time well to jot down some quick notes to yourself so that when you actually begin to respond, you will have a nice start.
- The first parts of the free-response questions are the easiest parts. Spend just enough time to get these points before moving on to the more difficult sections.
- The questions are written in logical order. If you find yourself explaining Part C before responding to Part B, back up and work through the logical progression of topics.
- Abbreviations are your friends. You can save time by using commonly accepted abbreviations for economic variables and graphical curves, and you will get more adept at their use as your mastery improves. For example, in macroeconomics you can save some time by using "OMO" rather than "open market operation," and in microeconomics you can use "MRP" rather than "marginal revenue product."
- Show your work. In recent years, the exam has included more mathematical components that allow you to demonstrate that you know a particular economic concept by computing something. Virtually all these problems include the prompt "show your work," and you will *not* earn points if you have not set up the mathematical problem correctly and shown your work clearly. For example, suppose that price is $5 and 10 units are sold at this price; you are asked to compute total revenue and show your work. You know that total revenue ($P \times Q$) is obviously $50, but if you simply state that total revenue is $50, you will not earn the point, because you did not show your work. The simple fix for this is to write: $TR = P \times Q = \$5 \times 10 = \$50$. Point earned!

STEP **4**

Review the Knowledge You Need to Score High

CHAPTER 5

Fundamentals of Economic Analysis

IN THIS CHAPTER

Summary: If there are two concepts that you should have down pat, they are (1) scarce resources require decision makers to make decisions that involve costs and benefits and (2) these decisions are best made when the additional benefits of the action are exactly offset by the additional costs of the action. This chapter presents material that, at least on the surface, appears to be "Econ-lite." Some readers might make the mistake of simply glossing over it on the way to meatier topics. I urge you to take the time to reinforce these early concepts, for they should, like a bad commercial jingle, stick in your subconscious throughout your preparation for the AP exam.

Key Ideas
- ✪ Scarcity
- ✪ Opportunity Cost
- ✪ Marginal Analysis
- ✪ Cost-Benefit Analysis
- ✪ Production Possibilities
- ✪ Functions of Economic Systems

5.1 Scarce Resources

Main Topics: *Economic Resources, Scarcity, Trade-Offs, Opportunity Cost, Cost-Benefit Analysis, Marginal Analysis*

Economic Resources

Economics is the study of how people, firms, and societies use their scarce productive resources to best satisfy their unlimited material wants.

Resources, or factors of production, are commonly separated into four groups:

- *Labor.* Human effort and talent, physical and mental. This can be augmented by education and training (human capital).
- *Land* or *natural resources.* Any resource created by nature. This may be arable land, mineral deposits, oil and gas reserves, or water.
- *Physical capital.* Manmade equipment like machinery as well as buildings, roads, vehicles, and computers.
- *Entrepreneurial ability.* The effort and know-how to put the other resources together in a productive venture.

Scarcity

All of the above resources are scarce, or in limited supply. Since productive resources are scarce, it makes sense that the production of goods and services must be scarce.

Example:

Sometimes it is easier to see this if you look at the production of something familiar, like the production of a term paper:

- *Labor.* Your hours of research, writing, and rewriting. As we all know, these hours are scarce, or limited to the number of waking hours in the day.
- *Land/natural resources.* Paper (trees) and electricity (rivers, coal, natural gas, wind, solar). Not only are these in scarce supply, but your ability to acquire these resources is also limited by your income, which is a result of using some of your scarce labor hours to work for a wage.
- *Capital.* Your computer, printer, desk, pens and pencils, and the library and sources within it.
- *Entrepreneurial ability.* The skill it takes to compile the research into a coherent, thoughtful, and articulate piece of academic work.

Trade-Offs

The fact that we are faced with scarce resources implies that individuals, firms, and governments are constantly faced with trade-offs.

Individuals

Consumers choose between housing arrangements (Do I rent an apartment or buy a home?), transportation options, grocery store items, and many other daily purchases. Workers and students must choose from a wide range of employment opportunities. (Do I pick up an extra shift? Do I pursue my MBA or PhD?)

Firms

For the firm, decisions are often centered upon which good or service can be provided, how much should be produced, and how to go about producing those goods and services.

A local restaurant considers whether or not to stay open later on Saturday night. A steel company must decide whether to open a steel plant in Indiana or Indonesia.

Governments

Every society, in one form or another, places many tough decisions in the hands of government, both local and national. Not surprisingly, local government is faced with issues that are likely to have an immediate impact on the lives of local citizens. (Should we use tax revenues to pave potholes in the streets or buy a new city bus?) At the national level, not all citizens would feel the impact immediately, but the stakes are likely much higher. (Should we open protected wilderness areas to oil and gas exploration? Should we impose a tariff on imported rice?)

Regardless of the decision maker—individual, firm, or government—the reality of scarce resources creates a trade-off between the opportunity that is taken and the opportunity that was not taken and thus forgone. The value of what was given up is called the **opportunity cost**.

Opportunity Cost

At the most basic level, the opportunity cost of doing something is all that you sacrifice to do it. In other words, if you use a scarce resource to pursue activity X, the opportunity cost of activity X is activity Y, the next best use of that resource. In the next section of this chapter, we will discuss costs in a little more detail.

> **Example:**
> You have one scarce hour to spend between studying for an exam or working at a coffee shop for $8 per hour. If you study, the opportunity cost of studying is $8.

"Pay close attention here; this is a very common mistake."
—Hillary, AP Student

> **Example:**
> You have one scarce hour to spend between studying for an exam or working at a coffee shop for $8 per hour or mowing your uncle's lawn for $10 per hour. If you choose to study, what is the opportunity cost of studying?

> *Be careful!* A common mistake is to add up the value of *all* your other options ($18), but this misses an important point. In this scenario, and in many others, you have one hour to allocate to one activity, thus giving up the others. By choosing to study, you really only gave up one thing: mowing the lawn *or* serving cappuccinos, not both.

> The opportunity cost of using your resource to do activity X is the value the resource would have in its *next best alternative use.* Therefore, the opportunity cost of studying is $10, the better of your two alternatives.

> *At this point, you might be wondering, "Does everything have a dollar figure attached to it? Can't we just enjoy something without slapping a price tag on it?"*

This is an excellent question, and the concept can often be a difficult point to explain. If you have one scarce hour and you could either work at the coffee shop for $8 or take a restful nap, the opportunity cost of working is the nap, which certainly has value. How can we place a dollar value on the nap? Maybe you are giving serious thought to taking the nap, but your employer at the coffee shop really needs you to work. Maybe your employer offers you $10 to forgo the nap and come to work. After some consideration, you still choose the nap. Surely there is a price (the wage) that would be high enough to entice you to come to work at the coffee shop. If your employer offered you just enough to compensate you for the nap you gave up, you have found the value that you placed on the nap.

Cost-Benefit Analysis

Many people, even those who aren't studying economics (gasp!), make decisions by weighing the costs of an action against the benefits of that action. This process is called **cost-benefit analysis**. For example, Melanie is thinking about buying a ticket to an outdoor music festival. There are many questions that she must answer before making a decision to buy, or not to buy, the ticket. Can she afford the cost of the ticket? If she takes some time off from her job, how much in earnings will she give up? Will the musical performers live up to expectations? Will the weather be nice or is it likely to be stormy and ruin the experience? These questions address the costs and the benefits of attending the festival. Let's explore the costs first.

Total Cost

The total cost of doing something is the value of all things given up to do that thing. These costs can come in two categories: explicit and implicit.

Explicit Costs

The explicit costs of a decision are the direct out-of-pocket expenses of making that decision. In the case of the music festival, Melanie would need to add up all of the money she would pay to attend. These explicit costs would typically include the cost of the ticket, gas for her car, food or drink she would buy while there, and any shirts or other souvenirs she expects to purchase. But as the previous section of the book describes, there are other costs involved.

Implicit Costs

The implicit costs of making a decision is the value of the next best thing you could have done. For example, if Melanie is taking Friday off from her job so that she can go to the festival, any lost wages would be an implicit cost of the decision to attend. We will talk more about explicit and implicit costs in Chapter 8 when we discuss firms that incur costs in producing their goods and services.

When we add up all of the explicit and implicit costs of a decision, like attending the music festival, we have the total cost of that decision.

Total Benefit

The total benefit of a decision really depends upon the person making the decision and their personal evaluation of how much enjoyment they expect to receive. One way to conduct this evaluation is to ask yourself, "What is the absolute most money I would pay to take this action?" In the case of the music festival, Melanie would look at the performers, the venue, and maybe the weather forecast, and determine the highest dollar value she would ever consider paying to attend. Economists also describe this maximum price as a person's **willingness to pay**.

The Decision

So, should Melanie attend the music festival? If she is making this decision using cost-benefit analysis, she will carefully add up all of the costs of attending, and then evaluate her willingness to pay for attending and compare it to the total costs. She will choose to attend if her total benefit (willingness to pay) is greater than or equal to her total cost. If it is not, then she will not make the decision to attend.

- When making a decision, a person will choose something—let's call it Z—if the total benefit of Z is greater than or equal to the total cost of Z.

- If the total cost of Z is greater than the total benefit of Z, a person will not choose Z.

Marginal Analysis

Another way of making decisions is to weigh the costs and benefits of doing, or consuming, "the next one." You have one cup of coffee and are deciding whether to have another (the next one). You have studied five hours for an economics exam and need to decide if it is in your best interest to study another hour (the next one).

These decisions are said to be made at the margin. The next cup of coffee brings with it *additional* benefits to the consumer, but comes at *additional* costs. The rational consumer weighs the additional benefits against the additional costs.

Marginal: "the next one," or "additional," or "incremental."

This concept is seen throughout economics and we cover it throughout this book, but let's briefly look at **marginal analysis** from a consumer's point of view.

Marginal cost (MC): The additional cost incurred from the consumption of the next unit of a good or service.

Marginal benefit (MB): The additional benefit received from the consumption of the next unit of a good or service. Another way of measuring marginal benefit is to ask yourself, "How much would I pay for the next unit of this good?"

> **Example:**
>
> The soda machine down the hall charges me $1 for every can of pop. The decision to buy another soda is another example of marginal analysis. If I expect to receive at least $1 in additional benefit, or if I am willing to pay $1 or more to have it, buying another soda is a rational decision. This decision can be seen in Figure 5.1.

Figure 5.1

So how many sodas will I consume in a typical day? For each of the first three sodas, my MB > $1, the marginal cost of the next soda. The fourth soda provides me with exactly $1 in marginal benefit, so I find it exactly worth my while to buy it. The fifth soda is not bought because the MC > MB. Notice that my MB declines as I consume more sodas. This is a fairly predictable relationship, since I am likely to enjoy my first soda of the day more than my fifth.

Rule:

Do something if the marginal benefits ≥ marginal costs of doing it.

Stop doing something when the marginal benefits = marginal costs of doing it.

Never do something when the marginal benefits < marginal costs of doing it.

You will find this to be true in consumption, production, hiring, and many other economic decisions.

5.2 Production Possibilities

Main Topics: *Production Possibilities Curve, Resource Substitutability, Law of Increasing Costs, Comparative Advantage and Specialization, Efficiency, Growth*

Production Possibilities Curve

To examine production and opportunity cost, economists find it useful to create a simplified model of an individual, or a nation, that can choose to allocate its scarce resources between the production of two goods or services. For now we assume that those resources are being fully employed and used efficiently.

Example:

The owner of a small bakery can allocate a fixed amount of labor (the chef and her helpers), capital (mixers, pans, and ovens), natural resources (raw materials), and her entrepreneurial talent toward the production of pastries and pizza crusts.

The **production possibilities** table (Table 5.1) lists the different combinations of pastries and crusts that can be produced with a fixed quantity of scarce resources.

Table 5.1 Bakery Production Possibilities

PASTRIES	PIZZA CRUST
0	10
1	8
2	6
3	4
4	2
5	0

If the chef wishes to produce one more pastry, she must give up two pizza crusts. If she wishes one more crust, she must give up one-half of a pastry.

In other words:

The opportunity cost of a pastry is two crusts.
The opportunity cost of a pizza crust is one-half of a pastry.

We can graphically depict Table 5.1 in a **production possibility curve.** Each point on the curve represents some maximum output combination of the two products. Some refer to this curve as a **production possibility frontier** because it reflects the outer limit of production. Any point outside the frontier (e.g., 4, 8) is currently unattainable and any point inside the frontier (e.g., 1, 2) fails to use all the bakery's available resources in an efficient way. We talk more about efficiency at the end of this section.

So here you might wonder, "Why is there a limit to the production of these goods? In other words, why doesn't the frontier just expand to allow an unlimited amount of either?"

Over the course of time, the frontier is believed to expand. But at any given point in time, we must confront the scarcity problem again. The resources used to produce these goods are scarce, and thus, the production frontier is going to act as a binding constraint. The concept of economic growth is introduced in this chapter and also discussed in the coverage of macroeconomics, but for the time being, the frontier looks like Figure 5.2.

Figure 5.2

The opportunity cost of each good is also apparent in the slope of the production possibility curve itself. We ignore the fact that the curve slopes downward and simply focus on its magnitude, or absolute value.

- The slope of the curve, 2 in our case, measures the opportunity cost of the good on the x-axis.
- The inverse of the slope, ½ in our case, measures the opportunity cost of the good on the y-axis.

Notice that with a straight line, the opportunity cost of producing more of each good is always a constant. Is this realistic?

Resource Substitutability

Suppose our bakery chef is currently producing 10 pizza crusts and zero pastries. But today she decides that she should produce one pastry and eight crusts. In Figure 5.2, this decision appears fairly straightforward.

What we often forget is that resources must be reallocated from pizza crust production to pastry production. Labor, capital, and natural resources must be removed from crust production and moved into pastry production.

Perhaps some of the capital (i.e., pans) in the bakery are better suited to pizza crust production than pastry production. Certainly raw materials like chocolate and frosting are not very useful for pizza crust production but are extremely valuable to pastry production.

The same could be said for individual laborers. Maybe the entrepreneur herself was trained as a French pastry chef and can make pizza crusts but not as well as she can make éclairs. The fact that these resources are better suited to the production of one good, and less easily adaptable to the production of the other good, gives us the concept of . . .

Law of Increasing Costs

The **law of increasing costs** tells us that the more of a good that is produced, the greater its opportunity cost. This reality gives us a production possibility curve that is concave, or *bowed outward*, as seen in Figure 5.3.

Figure 5.3

Now as the bakery produces more pastries, the opportunity cost (slope) begins to rise. Of course, the same is happening if the chef chooses to produce more crusts. Because resources are not perfectly adaptable to alternative uses, our production possibility curve is unlikely to be linear and will probably become steeper as production moves downward along the curve.

Comparative Advantage and Specialization

I went to the dentist's office the other day. For 30 minutes the dental hygienist took an x-ray, and then cleaned and flossed my teeth. When she was done, the dentist popped in, peeked at her handiwork, studied my x-ray, and sent me on my way with a new toothbrush. Why did my dentist let the hygienist do all the cleaning and flossing, when she is perfectly capable of doing the task? Because the dentist's scarce time resource is better used performing tasks like oral surgery. The opportunity cost of the dentist flossing my teeth is the revenue earned from a procedure that only she is qualified to perform. Forgoing the revenue from the oral surgery is avoided by assigning the cleaning tasks to the hygienist, whose specialty is oral hygiene but not oral surgery.

The law of increasing costs tells us that it becomes more costly to produce a good as you produce more of it. This reality prompts us to find other, less expensive ways to get our hands on additional units. The concepts of **specialization** and **comparative advantage** describe the way that individuals, nations, and societies can acquire more goods at lower cost.

> **Example:**
> Suppose our bakery, which can produce both pizza crust and pastries, shares the local market with a pizza parlor. The pizza parlor can also produce pastries, but it might rather produce pizza crusts. Each firm would like to produce more goods at lower cost. Table 5.2 shows the production possibilities of these two firms and the opportunity costs of producing more of each good. To make things simpler, we assume that both businesses have access to the same economic resources.

Table 5.2 Production Possibilities and Opportunity Costs

BAKERY		PIZZA PARLOR	
Pastries	Crusts	Pastries	Crusts
10	0	5	0
0	5	0	10
OPPORTUNITY COSTS		OPPORTUNITY COSTS	
1 pastry costs	1 crust costs	1 pastry costs	1 crust costs
½ crust	2 pastries	2 crusts	½ pastry

Because the bakery can produce more pastries than the pizza parlor, the bakery has **absolute advantage** in pastry production. The pizza parlor has absolute advantage in crust production. Simply being able to produce more of a good does not mean that the firm produces that good at a lower opportunity cost.

Both producers could produce pastries, but the bakery can produce pastries at lower opportunity cost (0.5 crusts versus 2 crusts). The bakery is said to have **comparative advantage** in the production of pastries. Likewise, the table illustrates that the pizza parlor has the comparative advantage in pizza crusts (0.5 pastries versus 2 pastries). These producers can, and indeed should, **specialize** by producing only pastries at the bakery and only crusts at the pizza parlor. Because these firms are specializing and producing at lower cost, not only do they benefit by earning more profit, but consumers across town also benefit from purchasing goods at lower prices.

In microeconomics, the principle of comparative advantage explains why the pediatrician delivers the babies while the electrician wires the house and not the other way around. In macroeconomics, this principle is the basis for showing how nations can gain from free trade. We explore trade and trade barriers among nations in the last chapter. To see the microeconomics gains from specialization, we do a game called "before and after."

Before. Each firm devotes half of its resources to pastry production and half to crust production.

Total citywide pastry production = 5 + 2.5 = 7.5
Total citywide crust production = 2.5 + 5 = 7.5

After. Each firm specializes in the production of the good for which it has comparative advantage.

Total citywide pastry production = 10 + 0 = 10
Total citywide crust production = 0 + 10 = 10

Figure 5.4 shows both production possibility frontiers and how a combination of 10 crusts and 10 pastries (specialization) was previously unattainable and is superior to when each firm produced at the midpoint (50/50) of their individual frontiers.

Another Way of Determining Comparative Advantage

The previous example showed how a comparison of the opportunity cost of producing two outputs (pizza crusts and pastries) can determine which firm, or nation, has the comparative advantage in production of those goods. Another way of figuring out comparative advantage is to compare how many *inputs* must be sacrificed to produce different outputs.

Let's shift gears and talk about two nations that can produce both chocolate and kazoos. The table below Figure 5.4 shows how many hours of work (inputs) must be used to produce one pound of chocolate and one box of kazoos.

"Know the different ways of showing comparative advantage. This is a potential free-response question."
—AP Teacher

Figure 5.4

	HOURS TO PRODUCE 1 POUND OF CHOCOLATE	HOURS TO PRODUCE 1 BOX OF KAZOOS
Taiwan	5	1
Brazil	2	4

If Taiwan were to produce one pound of chocolate, it would take five hours, so the opportunity cost of chocolate is the five boxes of kazoos that could have been produced with those five hours of labor. On the other hand, if Brazil were to produce one pound of chocolate, it would take two hours of work, making the opportunity cost of chocolate one-half of a box of kazoos that would have taken four hours of work to complete. Since it only costs Brazil one-half of a box of kazoos to make one pound of chocolate, Brazil has comparative advantage in making chocolate.

We can quickly see that Taiwan has the comparative advantage in making kazoos. If Taiwan were to produce one box of kazoos, it would cost one-fifth of a box of chocolate. Alternatively, if Brazil produced a box of kazoos, it would cost the nation two pounds of chocolate.

If these nations were to trade based on comparative advantage, Brazil would export chocolate to Taiwan, and Taiwan would export kazoos to Brazil.

- If firms and individuals produce goods based upon their comparative advantage, society gains more production at lower cost.

Efficiency

If not all available resources are being used to their fullest, the economy is operating at some point inside the production possibility frontier. This is clearly inefficient. But even if the economy is operating at some point on the frontier, who is to say that it is the point that is most desired by the citizens? If it does not happen to be the point that society most wants, we are also facing an inefficient situation.

In this production possibility model, there are two types of efficiency:

Productive efficiency. The economy is producing the maximum output for a given level of technology and resources. All points on the production possibilities frontier are productively efficient.

Allocative efficiency. The economy is producing the optimal mix of goods and services. By optimal, we mean that it is the combination of goods and services that provides the most net benefit to society. If society is allocatively efficient, it is operating at the best point on the frontier.

How do we determine which point is the best point? Remember how I determined the optimal number of sodas to consume every day? Suppose we could measure, society-wide, the marginal social benefit (MSB) received from the consumption of pizza crusts. Like my MB for sodas, the MSB for crusts is falling as more crusts are consumed. We already know that the marginal social cost (MSC) of producing pizza crusts increases. The marginal social cost of producing and marginal social benefit of consuming more pizza crusts are illustrated in Figure 5.5.

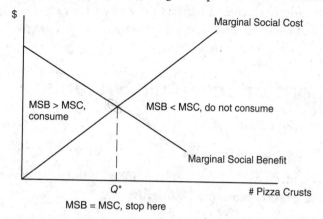

Figure 5.5

The allocatively efficient amount of pizza crusts is Q^*, the quantity where the MSB of the next crust is exactly equal to the MSC of producing it. If we produce anything beyond this point, we have created a situation where the MSC of producing it exceeds our MSB of consuming it. Clearly we should devote those resources to other goods that we desire to a greater degree and that are produced at a lower marginal social cost. Later in this book, we will see other examples of market outcomes that do produce the allocatively efficient quantity of a good or service. When this happens, we call it a **market failure**.

Growth

At a given point in time, the bakery (or a nation's economy) cannot operate beyond the production frontier. However, as time passes, it is likely that firms and nations experience economic growth. This results in a production possibilities frontier that moves outward, expanding the set of production and consumption.

Economic growth, the ability to produce a larger total output over time, can occur if one or all of the following occur:

- An increase in the quantity of resources. For example, the bakery acquires another oven.
- An increase in the quality of existing resources. For example, the chef acquires the best assistants in the city.
- Technological advancements in production. For example, electric mixers versus hand mixers.

Figure 5.6 illustrates economic growth for the bakery.

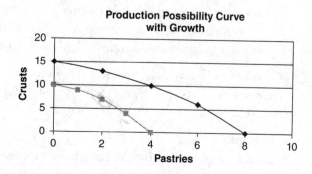

Figure 5.6

Notice that the frontier has not increased proportionally. The maximum number of crusts that could possibly be produced has increased by 50 percent, while the maximum number of pastries has increased by 100 percent.

Economic growth almost always occurs in this way. For example, technological advancements in wireless technology have certainly increased the nation's capacity to produce cell phones and tablet computers but has not likely measurably increased our capacity to produce tomatoes.

5.3 Functions of Economic Systems

Main Topic: *Market Systems*

Market Systems

> *"This concept, although an easy one, is a definite MC question. Don't miss it."*
> —Adam,
> AP Student

In the twenty-first century, most industrially advanced nations have gravitated toward a **market economy—capitalism.**

Keys to a Market System
- *Private Property.* Individuals, not government, own most economic resources. This private ownership encourages innovation, investment, growth, and trade.

  Example:
  If the state owned the bakery's ovens, mixers, and even the building itself, how much of an incentive would our entrepreneur have to maintain the equipment, the inventory, or even the quality of the product? Knowing that the state could take these resources with very little notice, our chef might just do the bare minimum, and if this situation happened all over town, the local economy would languish.

- *Freedom.* Individuals are free to acquire resources to produce goods and services and free to choose which of their resources to sell to others so that they may buy their own goods and services.

  Example:
  The bakery can freely use its resources to produce rolls, pastries, croissants, and anything else it believes leads to profitability. Of course, this freedom is limited by legal constraints. The bakery cannot sell illegal drugs from the back door, and the chef is not free to offer open-heart surgery with her bagels.

- *Self-Interest and Incentives.* Individuals are motivated by self-interest in their use of resources. Entrepreneurs seek to maximize profit while consumers seek to maximize happiness. With these incentives, goods are sold and bought.

  Example:
  Our bakery owner, motivated by profit, seeks to offer products that appeal to her customers. Customers, seeking to maximize their happiness, consume these bakery products only if they satisfy their personal tastes and wants.

- *Competition.* Buyers and sellers, acting independently, and motivated by self-interest, freely move in and out of individual markets. Again, the issue of incentives is powerful. A new firm, eager to compete in a market, only enters that market if profits are available.

  Example:
  Competition implies that prices are determined in the marketplace and not controlled by individual sellers, buyers, or the government. Our bakery owner employs labor at the going market wage, which is determined in the

competitive local labor market. She offers baked products at the going price, which is determined in the competitive local market for those goods.

- *Prices.* Prices send signals to buyers and sellers, and resource allocation decisions are made based upon this information. Prices also serve to ration goods to those consumers who are most willing and able to pay those prices. Prices coordinate the decentralized economic activity of millions of individuals and firms in a way that no one central economic figure can hope to achieve. Prices, not just for goods and services but also for labor and other resources, are the delivery mechanism for the previous incentives—profit for the firm and happiness for the consumer.

Example:

As the price of labor, relative to capital, changes, the bakery chef might be motivated to readjust her employment of assistants. Changes in the relative price of her products might prompt consumers to readjust their purchasing decisions.

› Review Questions

1. Economics is best described as

    (A) the study of how scarce material wants are allocated between unlimited resources.
    (B) the study of how scarce labor can be replaced by unlimited capital.
    (C) the study of how decision makers choose the best way to satisfy their unlimited material wants with a scarce supply of resources.
    (D) the study of how unlimited material wants can best be satisfied by allocating limitless amounts of productive resources.
    (E) the study of how capitalism is superior to any other economic system.

2. A student decides that, having already spent three hours studying for an exam, she should spend one more hour studying for the same exam. Which of the following is most likely true?

    (A) The marginal benefit of the fourth hour is certainly less than the marginal cost of the fourth hour.
    (B) The marginal benefit of the fourth hour is at least as great as the marginal cost of the fourth hour.
    (C) Without knowing the student's opportunity cost of studying, we have no way of knowing whether or not her marginal benefits outweigh her marginal costs.
    (D) The marginal cost of the third hour was likely greater than the marginal cost of the fourth hour.
    (E) The marginal benefit of the third hour was less than the marginal cost of the third hour.

The island nation of Beckham uses economic resources to produce tea and crumpets. Use the following production possibilities frontier for questions 3 to 4.

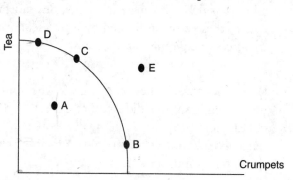

3. Economic growth is best represented by a movement from

    (A) A to B.
    (B) B to C.
    (C) C to D.
    (D) D to E.
    (E) E to A.

4. The shape of this PPF tells us that

    (A) economic resources are perfectly substitutable from production of tea to production of crumpets.
    (B) citizens prefer that an equal amount of tea and crumpets be produced.
    (C) the opportunity cost of producing crumpets rises as more crumpets are produced.
    (D) the opportunity cost of producing crumpets is constant along the curve.
    (E) the opportunity cost of producing tea falls as you produce more tea.

5. Ray and Dorothy can both cook and can both pull weeds in the garden on a Saturday afternoon. For every hour of cooking, Ray can pull 50 weeds and Dorothy can pull 100 weeds. Based on this information,

   (A) Ray pulls weeds, since he has absolute advantage in cooking.
   (B) Dorothy pulls weeds, since she has absolute advantage in cooking.
   (C) Dorothy cooks, since she has comparative advantage in cooking.
   (D) Ray cooks, since he has comparative advantage in cooking.
   (E) Dorothy pulls weeds, since she has comparative advantage in cooking.

〉 Answers and Explanations

1. **C**—It is important to remember that society has a limitless desire for material wants, but satisfaction of these wants is limited by scarce economic resources. Economics studies how to solve this problem in the best possible way.

2. **B**—If we observe her studying for the fourth hour, then it must be the case that the $MB \geq MC$ of studying for that next hour. If we observe her putting her books away and doing something else, the opposite must be true.

3. **D**—Economic growth is an outward expansion of the entire PPF. A movement from the interior to the frontier (A to B) is not growth; it just tells us that some unemployed resources (A) are now being used to their full potential (B).

4. **C**—When the PPF is concave (or bowed outward) it is an indicator of the law of increasing costs. This is a result of economic resources not being perfectly substitutable between tea and crumpets. A baking sheet used to bake crumpets might be quite useless in producing tea leaves.

5. **D**—For Ray, the opportunity cost of cooking is 50 weeds, while Dorothy's opportunity cost of cooking is 100 unpulled weeds. Ray does not pull weeds because he has comparative advantage in cooking. Dorothy does not cook because she has comparative advantage in weed pulling.

〉 Rapid Review

Economics: The study of how people, firms, and societies use their scarce productive resources to best satisfy their unlimited material wants.

Resources: Called factors of production, these are commonly grouped into the four categories of labor, physical capital, land or natural resources, and entrepreneurial ability.

Scarcity: The imbalance between limited productive resources and unlimited human wants. Because economic resources are scarce, the goods and services a society can produce are also scarce.

Trade-offs: Scarce resources imply that individuals, firms, and governments are constantly faced with difficult choices that involve benefits and costs.

Opportunity cost: The value of the sacrifice made to pursue a course of action.

Cost-benefit analysis: The process of weighing all of the costs of an action against all of the benefits of that action.

Total cost: The sum of the explicit and implicit costs of an action, or decision, being considered.

Explicit cost: The out-of-pocket costs of an action being considered.

Implicit cost: The cost of an action being considered, measured by the value of the next-best forgone alternative.

Total benefit: The sum of all expected enjoyment, as measured by willingness to pay, of an action being considered.

Marginal: The next unit or increment of an action.

Marginal social benefit: The additional benefit that society receives from the consumption of the next unit of a good or service.

Marginal social cost: The additional cost that society incurs from the production of the next unit of a good or service.

Marginal analysis: Making decisions based upon weighing the marginal benefits and costs of that action. The rational decision maker chooses an action if the $MB \geq MC$.

Production possibilities: Different quantities of goods that an economy can produce with a given amount of scarce resources. Graphically, the trade-off between the production of two goods is portrayed as a production possibility curve or frontier (PPC or PPF).

Production possibility curve or frontier (PPC or PPF): A graphical illustration that shows the maximum quantity of one good that can be produced, given the quantity of the other good being produced.

Law of increasing costs: The more of a good that is produced, the greater the opportunity cost of producing the next unit of that good.

Absolute advantage: This exists if a producer can produce more of a good with the same quantity of resources, or the same quantity of goods with fewer resources, than all other producers.

Comparative advantage: A producer has comparative advantage if it can produce a good at lower opportunity cost than all other producers.

Specialization: When firms focus their resources on production of goods for which they have comparative advantage, they are said to be specializing.

Productive efficiency: Production of maximum output for a given level of technology and resources. All points on the PPF are productively efficient.

Market failure: A market outcome for which the quantity produced is not allocatively efficient ($MSB \neq MSC$) and either too many or too few units are produced.

Allocative efficiency: Production of the combination of goods and services that provides the most net benefit to society. The optimal quantity of a good is achieved when the MSB = MSC of the next unit. This only occurs at one point on the PPF.

Economic growth: This occurs when an economy's production possibilities increase. It can be a result of more resources, better resources, or improvements in technology.

Market economy (capitalism): An economic system based upon the fundamentals of private property, freedom, self-interest, and prices.

CHAPTER 6

Demand, Supply, Market Equilibrium, and Welfare Analysis

IN THIS CHAPTER

Summary: A thorough understanding of the way in which the market system determines price and quantity pays dividends both in microeconomics and macroeconomics. In the absence of government intervention and/or externalities, the competitive market also provides the most efficient outcome for society.

Key Ideas

✪ Demand
✪ Supply
✪ Equilibrium
✪ Consumer and Producer Surplus

6.1 Demand

Main Topics: *Law of Demand, Income and Substitution Effects, The Demand Curve, Quantity Demanded Versus Demand, Determinants of Demand*

For many years now, you have understood the concept of demand. On the surface, the concept is rather simple: people tend to purchase fewer items when the price is high than they do when the price is low. This is such an intuitively appealing concept that your typical consumer cares little about the rationale and still manages to live a happy life. As someone knee-deep in reviewing to take the AP Microeconomics exam, you need to go "behind the scenes" of demand. Intuition will take you only so far; you need to know the underlying theory of what is perhaps the most widely understood, and sometimes misunderstood, economic concept.

Law of Demand

Let's get this part out of the way. The **law of demand** is commonly described as follows: *Holding all else equal (ceteris paribus), when the price of a good rises, consumers decrease their quantity demanded for that good.* In other words, there is an inverse, or negative, relationship between the price and the quantity demanded of a good.

"*Holding all else equal*"? Economic models—demand is just one of many such models—are simplified versions of real behavior. In addition to the price, there are many factors that influence how many units of a good consumers purchase. In order to predict how consumers respond to changes in one variable (price), we must assume that all other relevant factors are held constant. Say we observed that last month the price of orange juice fell, consumer incomes rose, the price of apple juice increased, and consumers bought more orange juice. Was this increased orange juice consumption because the price fell, because incomes rose, or perhaps because apple juice became more expensive? Maybe it increased for all these reasons. Maybe for none of these reasons. It is impossible to isolate and measure the effect of one variable (i.e., orange juice prices) on the consumption of orange juice if we do not control (hold constant) these other external factors. At the heart of the law of demand is a consumer's willingness and ability to pay the going price. If the consumer becomes more willing, or more able, to consume a good, then either the price has fallen or one of these external factors has changed. We spend more time on these demand "determinants" a little later in this chapter.

Income and Substitution Effects

One of the important factors behind the scenes of the law of demand is the economic mantra "*only relative prices matter.*" I'm sure you have heard the stories from your parents or grandparents about how the price of a cup of coffee back in the good old days was just a nickel. Today you might get the same coffee for $1.75. These prices are simply **money** (or **absolute**, or **nominal**) **prices**, and when it comes to a demand decision, a money price alone is near useless. However, if you think about the money price in terms of (1) what other goods $1.75 could buy or (2) how much of your income is absorbed by $1.75, then you're talking **relative** (or **real**) **prices**. These are what matter. The number of units of any other good Y that must be sacrificed to acquire the first good X, measures the relative price of good X.

Example:

Let's keep things simple and say that you divide your $10 daily income between apple fritters at today's prices of $1 each and chocolate chip bagels at $2 each. These are the money prices of your labor and of these two yummy snacks.

Table 6.1 Money vs. Relative Prices

	MONEY PRICE		RELATIVE PRICE		SHARE OF INCOME	
	Today	Tomorrow	Today	Tomorrow	Today	Tomorrow
Fritter	$1	$2	1/2 bagel	1 bagel	1/10	1/5
Bagel	$2	$2	2 fritters	1 fritter	1/5	1/5

Today at the price of $1, the relative cost of a fritter is one-half of a bagel (see Table 6.1). Relative to your income, it amounts to one-tenth of your budget.

Tomorrow, when the price doubles to $2 per fritter, two things happen to help explain, and lay the foundation for, the law of demand:

1. The relative price of a fritter has risen to one bagel, and the relative price of a bagel has fallen from two fritters to one fritter. Since fritters are now *relatively more expensive,* we would expect you to consume more bagels and fewer fritters. This is known as the **substitution effect**.
2. Relative to your income, the price of a fritter has increased from one-tenth to one-fifth of your budget. In other words, if you were to buy only fritters, today you can purchase 10 but tomorrow the same income would only buy you 5. This lost purchasing power is known as the **income effect**.

- **Substitution effect.** The change in quantity demanded resulting from a change in the price of one good relative to the price of other goods.
- **Income effect.** The change in quantity demanded resulting from a change in the consumer's purchasing power (or real income).

When the price of fritters increased, both of these effects caused our consumer (you) to decrease the quantity demanded, thus predicting a response consistent with the law of demand.

So at this point you might ask, "*How would a consumer react if the prices of fritters and bagels and daily income had all doubled?*"

Since the price of fritters, relative to the price of bagels, and relative to daily income, has not changed, the consumer is unlikely to alter behavior. This is why we say that only relative prices matter.

The Demand Curve

The residents of a small midwestern town love to quench their summer thirsts with lemonade. Table 6.2 summarizes the townsfolk's daily consumption of cups of lemonade at several prices, holding constant all other factors that might influence the overall demand for lemonade. This table is sometimes referred to as a **demand schedule**.

Table 6.2 Demand Schedule for Lemonade

PRICE PER CUP ($)	QUANTITY DEMANDED (CUPS PER DAY)
.25	120
.50	100
.75	80
1.00	60
1.25	40

The values in Table 6.2 reflect the law of demand: *Holding all else equal, when the price of a cup of lemonade rises, consumers decrease their quantity demanded for lemonade.* It is often quite useful to convert a demand schedule like the one above into a graphical representation, the **demand curve** (Figure 6.1).

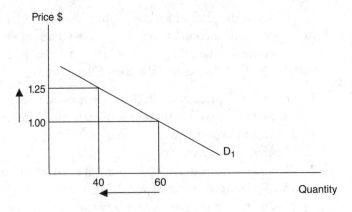

Figure 6.1

Quantity Demanded Versus Demand

The law of demand predicts a downward- (or negative-) sloping demand curve (Figure 6.1). If the price moves from $1 to $1.25 and all other factors are held constant, we observe a decrease in the *quantity demanded* from 60 to 40 cups. It is important to place special emphasis on "quantity demanded." If the price of the good changes and all other factors remain constant, the demand curve is held constant, and we simply observe the consumer moving along the fixed demand curve. If one of the external factors change, the entire demand curve shifts to the left or right.

Determinants of Demand

So, what are all of these factors that we insist on holding constant? These **determinants of demand** influence both the willingness and ability of the consumer to purchase units of the good or service. In addition to the price of the product itself, there are a number of variables that account for the total demand of a good like lemonade:

- Consumer income.
- The price of a substitute good such as iced tea.
- The price of a complementary good such as a Popsicle.
- Consumer tastes and preferences for lemonade.
- Consumer expectations about future prices of lemonade.
- Number of buyers in the market for lemonade.

- *Consumer Income*

Demand represents the consumer's willingness and ability to pay for a good. Income is a major factor in that "ability" to pay component. For most goods, when income increases, demand for the good increases. Thus, for these **normal goods**, increased income results in a graphical rightward shift in the entire demand curve. There are other **inferior goods**, fewer in number, where higher levels of income produce a decrease in the demand curve.

Example:

When looking to furnish a first college apartment, many students increase their demand for used furniture at yard sales. Upon graduation and employment in their first real job, new graduates increase their demand for new furniture and decrease their demand for used furniture. For them, new furniture is a normal good, while used furniture is an inferior good.

- An *increase in demand* is viewed as a *rightward shift* in the demand curve. There are two ways to think about this shift:
  a. At all prices, the consumer is willing and able to buy more units of the good. In Figure 6.2 you can see that at the constant price of $1, the quantity demanded has risen from two to three.
  b. At all quantities, the consumer is willing and able to pay higher prices for the good.
- Of course, the opposite is true of a *decrease in demand,* or *leftward shift* of the demand curve. In Figure 6.2 you can see that at the constant price of $1, the quantity demanded has fallen from two to one.

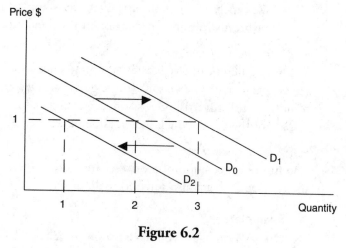

Figure 6.2

- *Price of Substitute Goods*

Two goods are substitutes if the consumer can use either one to satisfy the same essential function, therefore experiencing the same degree of happiness (utility). If the two goods are substitutes, and the price of one good *X* falls, the consumer demand for the substitute good *Y* decreases.

Example:

Mammoth State University (MSU) and Ivy Vine College (IVC) are considered substitute institutions of higher learning in the same geographical region. Ivy Vine College, shamelessly seeking to increase its reputation as an "elite" institution, increases tuition, while Mammoth State's tuition remains the same. We expect to see, holding all else constant, a decrease in quantity demanded for IVC degrees and an increase in the overall demand for MSU degrees. (See Figures 6.3 and 6.4.)

Figure 6.3

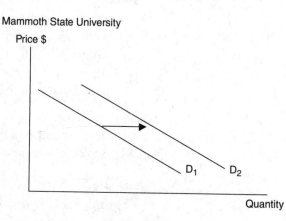

Figure 6.4

• *Price of Complementary Goods*

Two goods are complements if the consumer receives more utility from consuming them together than she would receive consuming each separately. I enjoy consuming tortilla chips by themselves, but my utility increases if I combine those chips with a complementary good like salsa or nacho cheese dip. If any two goods are complements, and the price of one good X falls, the consumer demand for the complement good Y increases.

Example:

College students love to order late-night pizza delivered to their dorm rooms. The local pizza joint decreased the price of breadsticks, a complement to the pizzas. We expect to see, holding all else constant, an increase in quantity demanded for breadsticks and an increase in the demand for pizzas.

• *Tastes and Preferences*

We have different internal tastes and preferences. Collectively, consumer tastes and preferences change with the seasons (more gloves in December, fewer lawn chairs), with fashion trends, or with advertising. A stronger preference for a good is an increase in the willingness to pay for the good, which increases demand.

• *Future Expectations*

The future expectation of a price change or an income change can cause demand to shift today. Demand can also respond to an expectation of the future availability of a good.

Example:

On a Wednesday, you have reason to believe that the price of gasoline is going to rise $.05 per gallon by the weekend. What do you do? Many consumers, armed with this expectation, increase their demand for gasoline today. We might predict the opposite behavior, a decrease in demand today, if consumers expect the price of gasoline to fall a few days from now.

Demand can also be influenced by future expectations of an income change.

Example:

One month prior to your college graduation day, you land your first full-time job. You have signed an employment contract that guarantees a specific salary, but you will not receive your first paycheck until the end of your first month on the job. This future expectation of a sizable increase in income often prompts consumers to increase their demand for normal goods now. Maybe you would start shopping for a car, a larger apartment, or several business suits.

Example:

For years, auto producers have been promising more alternative-fuel cars, but so far these cars are relatively difficult to find on dealership lots. Suppose the "Big 3" promise widespread availability of affordable electric and hydrogen fuel cell cars in the next 12 months. This expectation of increased availability in the future will likely decrease the demand for these cars today.

• *Number of Buyers*

An increase in the number of buyers, holding other factors constant, increases the demand for a good. This is often the result of demographic changes or increased availability in more markets.

Example:

When the Soviet Union fractured and the Russian government began allowing more foreign investment, corporations such as Coca-Cola, Apple, and

McDonald's found millions of new buyers for their products. Globally, the demand for colas, iPads, and burgers increased.

Example
As the average age of Americans has gradually increased, there are now more people above the age of 70 years old. This demographic change has caused an increase in the demand for prescription drugs, hip replacements, and other medical services.

6.2 Supply

Main Topics: *Law of Supply, Increasing Marginal Costs, The Supply Curve, Quantity Supplied Versus Supply, Determinants of Supply*

If there are three words that you need to have in your arsenal for the AP exams, they are "Demand and Supply," or "Supply and Demand" if you are the rebellious type. The previous section covered the demand half of this duo, and so it stands to reason that we should spend a little time studying the other side. Unlike demand, few of us have ever had up-close-and-personal experience as suppliers. Because you likely lack such personal experience with supply, it is helpful to put yourself in the shoes of someone who wishes to profit from the production and sale of a product. If something happens that would increase your chances of earning more profit, you increase your supply of the product. If something happens that will hurt your profit opportunities, you decrease your supply of the product.

Law of Supply

Drumroll, please. The **law of supply** is commonly described as follows: "*Holding all else equal (ceteris paribus), when the price of a good rises, suppliers increase their quantity supplied for that good.*" In other words, there is a direct, or positive, relationship between the price and the quantity supplied of a good.

Again, we insist on qualifying our law with the phrase "*holding all else equal.*" Similar to the *demand model,* the *supply model* is a simplified version of real behavior. In addition to the price, there are several factors that influence how many units of a good producers supply. In order to predict how producers respond to fluctuations in one variable (price), we must assume that all other relevant factors are held constant. Before we talk about these external supply determinants, let's examine what is happening behind the scenes of the law of supply.

Increasing Marginal Costs

The more you do something (e.g., a physical activity), the more difficult it becomes to do the next unit of that activity. Anyone who has run laps around a track, lifted weights, or raked leaves in the yard understands this. If you were asked to rake leaves, as more hours of raking are supplied, it becomes physically more and more difficult to rake the next hour. We also include the opportunity cost of the time involved in the raking, and you surely know that time is precious to a student. If you have a paper to write or an exam to cram for, raking leaves for an hour comes at a dear cost. In terms of forgone opportunities, the marginal cost of raking leaves rises as you postpone that paper or study session.

When we discussed production possibilities in Chapter 5, we addressed a key economic concept: as more of a good is produced, the greater is its marginal cost.

- As suppliers increase the quantity supplied of a good, they face rising marginal costs.
- As a result, they only increase the quantity supplied of that good if the price received is high enough to at least cover the higher marginal cost.

The Supply Curve

A small town has a thriving summer sidewalk lemonade stand industry. Table 6.3 summarizes the daily quantity of cups of lemonade offered for sale at several prices, holding constant all other factors that might influence the overall supply of lemonade. This table is sometimes referred to as a **supply schedule**.

Table 6.3 Supply Schedule for Lemonade

PRICE PER CUP ($)	QUANTITY SUPPLIED (CUPS PER DAY)
.25	40
.50	60
.75	80
1.00	100
1.25	120

> "Make sure on the AP test to include all labels, especially arrows." —Adam, AP Student

The values in this table reflect the law of supply: *"Holding all else equal, when the price of a cup of lemonade rises, suppliers increase their quantity supplied for lemonade."* Remember those profit opportunities? If kids can sell more cups of lemonade at a higher price, they will do so. It is often quite useful to convert a supply schedule like the one in Table 6.3 into a graphical representation, the **supply curve** (Figure 6.5).

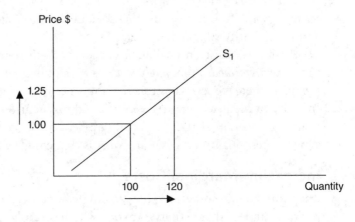

Figure 6.5

Quantity Supplied Versus Supply

> "This is an important distinction to make." —AP Teacher

The law of supply predicts an upward- (or positive-) sloping supply curve (Figure 6.5). When the price moves from $1 to $1.25, and all other factors are held constant, we observe an increase in the *quantity supplied* from 100 cups to 120 cups. Just as with demand, it is important to place special emphasis on "quantity supplied." When the price of the good changes, and all other factors are held constant, the supply curve is held constant; we simply observe the producer moving along the fixed supply curve. If one of the external factors changes, the entire supply curve shifts to the left or right.

Determinants of Supply

Lemonade producers are willing and able to supply more lemonade if something happens that promises to increase their profit opportunities. In addition to the price of the product itself, there are a number of variables, or **determinants of supply**, that account for the total supply of a good like lemonade:

- The cost of an input (e.g., sugar) to the production of lemonade
- Technology and productivity used to produce lemonade
- Taxes or subsidies on lemonade
- Producer expectations about future prices
- The price of other goods that could be produced
- The number of lemonade stands in the industry

- *Cost of Inputs*

If the cost of sugar, a key ingredient in lemonade, unexpectedly falls, it has now become less costly to produce lemonade, and so we should expect producers all over town, seeing the profit opportunity, to increase the supply of lemonade at all prices. This results in a graphical rightward shift in the entire supply curve.

- An *increase in supply* is viewed as a *rightward shift* in the supply curve. There are two ways to think about this shift:

  1. At all prices, the producer is willing and able to supply more units of the good. In Figure 6.6 you can see that at the constant price of $1, the quantity supplied has risen from two to three.

  2. At all quantities, the marginal cost of production is lower, so producers are willing and able to accept lower prices for the good.

- Of course, the opposite is true of a *decrease in supply*, or *leftward shift* of the supply curve. In Figure 6.6 you can see that at the constant price of $1, the quantity supplied has fallen from two to one.

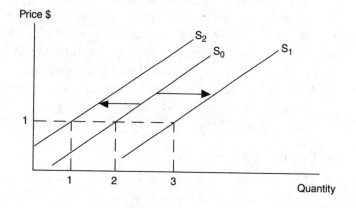

Figure 6.6

- *Technology or Productivity*

A technological improvement usually decreases the marginal cost of producing a good, thus allowing the producer to supply more units, and is reflected by a rightward shift in the supply curve. If kids all over town began using electric lemon squeezers rather than their sticky bare hands, the supply of lemonade would increase.

- *Taxes and Subsidies*

> "Remember, the tax goes to the government and is NOT included in the profit."
> —Hillary, AP Student

A per-unit tax is treated by the firm as an additional cost of production and would therefore decrease the supply curve, or shift it leftward. Mayor McScrooge might impose a 25-cent tax on every cup of lemonade, decreasing the entire supply curve. A subsidy is essentially the anti-tax, or a per-unit gift from the government because it lowers the per-unit cost of production.

- *Price Expectations*

A producer's willingness to supply today might be affected by an expectation of tomorrow's price. If it were the 2nd of July and lemonade producers expected a heat wave and a 4th of July parade in two days, they might hold back some of their supply today and hope to sell it at an inflated price on the holiday. Thus, today's quantity supplied at all prices would decrease.

- *Price of Other Outputs*

Firms can use the same resources to produce different goods. If the price of a milkshake were rising and profit opportunities were improving for milkshake producers, the supply of lemonade in a small town would decrease and the quantity of supplied milkshakes would increase.

- *Number of Suppliers*

When more suppliers enter a market, we expect the supply curve to shift to the right. If several of our lemonade entrepreneurs are forced by their parents to attend summer camp, we would expect the entire supply curve to move leftward. Fewer cups of lemonade would be supplied at each and every price.

6.3 Market Equilibrium

Main Topics: *Equilibrium, Shortage, Surplus, Changes in Demand, Changes in Supply, Simultaneous Changes in Demand and Supply*

Demanders and suppliers are both motivated by prices, but from opposite camps. The consumer is a big fan of low prices; the supplier applauds high prices. If a good were available, consumers would be willing to buy more of it, but only if the price is right. Suppliers would love to accommodate more consumption by increasing production but only if justly compensated. Is there a price and a compatible quantity where both groups are content? Amazingly enough, the answer is a resounding "maybe." Discouraged? Don't be. For now we assume that the good is exchanged in a free and competitive market, and if this is the case, the answer is "yes." We explore the "maybes" in a later chapter.

Equilibrium

The market is in a state of **equilibrium** when the quantity supplied equals the quantity demanded at a given price. Another way of thinking about equilibrium is that it occurs at the quantity where the price expected by consumers is equal to the price required by suppliers. So if suppliers and demanders are, for a given quantity, content with the price, the market is in a state of equilibrium. If there is pressure on the price to change, the market has not yet reached equilibrium. Let's combine our lemonade tables from the earlier sections in Table 6.4.

Table 6.4 Combining Demand and Supply Schedules

PRICE PER CUP ($)	QUANTITY DEMANDED (CUPS PER DAY)	QUANTITY SUPPLIED (CUPS PER DAY)	$Q_d - Q_s$	SITUATION	PRICE SHOULD
.25	120	40	80	Shortage	Rise
.50	100	60	40	Shortage	Rise
.75	80	80	0	Equilibrium	Be Stable
1.00	60	100	−40	Surplus	Fall
1.25	40	120	−80	Surplus	Fall

At a price of 75 cents, the daily quantity demanded and quantity supplied are both equal to 80 cups of lemonade. The equilibrium (or market clearing) price is therefore 75 cents per cup. In Figure 6.7 the equilibrium price and quantity are located where the demand curve intersects the supply curve. Holding all other demand and supply variables constant, there exists no other price where $Q_d = Q_s$.

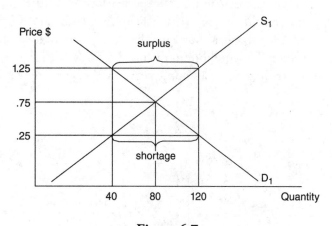

Figure 6.7

Shortage

A **shortage** exists at a market price when the quantity demanded exceeds the quantity supplied. This is why a shortage is also known as **excess demand**. At prices of 25 cents and 50 cents per cup, you can see the shortage in Figure 6.7. Remember that consumers love low prices so the quantity demanded is going to be high. However, suppliers are not thrilled to see low prices and therefore decrease their quantity supplied. At prices below 75 cents per cup, lemonade buyers and sellers are in a state of **disequilibrium**. The disparity between what the buyers want at 50 cents per cup and what the suppliers want at that price should remedy itself. Thirsty demanders offer lemonade stand owners prices slightly higher than 50 cents and, receiving higher prices, suppliers accommodate them by squeezing lemons. With competition, the shortage is eliminated at a price of 75 cents per cup.

Surplus

A **surplus** exists at a market price when the quantity supplied exceeds the quantity demanded. This is why a surplus is also known as **excess supply**. At prices of $1 and $1.25 per cup, you can see the surplus in Figure. 6.7. Consumers are reluctant to purchase as much lemonade as suppliers are willing to supply and, once again, the market is in disequilibrium. To entice more consumers to buy lemonade, lemonade stand owners offer slightly discounted cups of lemonade and buyers respond by increasing their quantity demanded. Again, with competition, the surplus would be eliminated at a price of 75 cents per cup.

- Shortages and surpluses are relatively short-lived in a free market as prices rise or fall until the quantity demanded again equals the quantity supplied.

Changes in Demand

"Explain your logic every time you shift a curve, no matter what!"
—Jake, AP Student

While our discussion of market equilibrium implies a certain kind of stability in both the price and quantity of a good, changing market forces disrupt equilibrium, either by shifting demand, shifting supply, or shifting both demand and supply.

Increase in Demand

About once a winter a freak blizzard hits southern states like Georgia and the Carolinas. You can bet that the national media show video of panicked southerners scrambling for bags of rock salt and bottled water. Inevitably a bemused reporter tells us that the price of rock salt has skyrocketed to $17 per bag. What is happening here? In Figure 6.8, the market for rock salt is initially in equilibrium at a price of $2.79 per bag. With a forecast of a blizzard, consumers expect a lack of future availability for this good. This expectation results in a feverish increase in the demand for rock salt and, at the original price of $2.79, there is a shortage. The market's cure for a shortage is a higher equilibrium price. (Note: The equilibrium quantity of rock salt might not increase much, since blizzards are short-lived and the supply curve might be nearly vertical.)

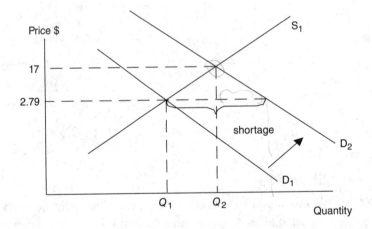

Figure 6.8

Decrease in Demand

The most recent recession was damaging to the automobile industry. When average household incomes fell in the United States, the demand for cars, a normal good, decreased. Manufacturers began offering deeply discounted sticker prices, zero-interest financing, and other incentives to reluctant consumers so that they might purchase a new car. In Figure 6.9 you can see that the original price of a new car was $18,000. Once the demand for new cars fell, there was a surplus of cars on dealer lots at the original price. The market cure for a surplus is a lower equilibrium price; therefore, fewer new cars were bought and sold.

- When demand increases, equilibrium price and quantity both increase.
- When demand decreases, equilibrium price and quantity both decrease.

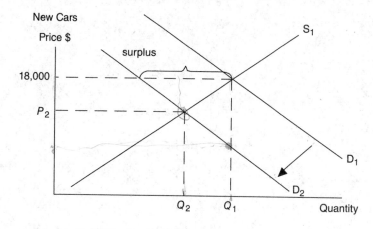

Figure 6.9

Changes in Supply

Increase in Supply

Advancements in computer technology and production methods have been felt in many markets. Figure 6.10 illustrates how, because of better technology, the supply of laptop computers has increased. At the original equilibrium price of $4,000, there is now a surplus of laptops. To eliminate the surplus, the market price must fall to P_2 and the equilibrium quantity must rise to Q_2.

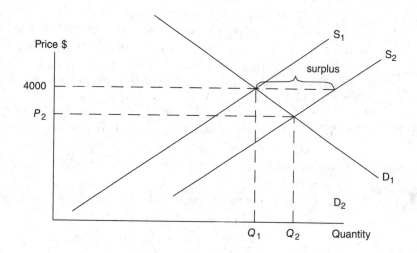

Figure 6.10

Decrease in Supply

Geopolitical conflict in the Middle East usually slows the production of crude oil. This decrease in the global supply of oil can be seen in Figure 6.11. At the original equilibrium price of $60 per barrel, there is now a shortage of crude oil on the global market. The market eliminates this shortage through higher prices and, at least temporarily, the equilibrium quantity of crude oil falls.

- When supply increases, equilibrium price decreases and quantity increases.
- When supply decreases, equilibrium price increases and quantity decreases.

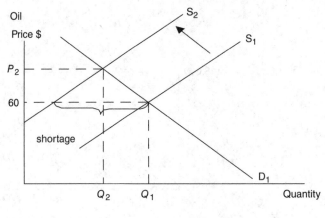

Figure 6.11

Simultaneous Changes in Demand and Supply

When both demand and supply change at the same time, predicting changes in price and quantity becomes a little more complicated. An example should illustrate how you need to be careful.

An extremely cold winter results in a higher demand for energy such as natural gas. At the same time, environmental safeguards and restrictions on drilling in protected wilderness areas have limited the supply of natural gas. An increase in demand, by itself, creates an increase in both price and quantity. However, a decrease in supply, by itself, creates an increase in price and a decrease in quantity. When these forces are combined, we see a double whammy on higher prices. But when trying to predict the change in equilibrium quantity, the outcome is uncertain and depends upon which of the two effects is larger.

One possible outcome is shown in Figure 6.12, where the initial equilibrium outcome is labeled E_1. A relatively large increase in demand with a fairly small decrease in supply results in more natural gas being consumed. The new equilibrium outcome is labeled E_2.

The other possibility is that the increase in demand is relatively smaller than the decrease in supply. This is seen in Figure 6.13 and, while the price is going to increase again, the equilibrium quantity is lower than before.

- When both demand and supply are changing, one of the equilibrium outcomes (price or quantity) is predictable and one is ambiguous.
- Before combining the two shifting curves, predict changes in price and quantity for each shift, by itself.
- The variable that is rising in one case and falling in the other case is your ambiguous prediction.

"Use different colored pens when drawing multiple curves on a single graph. This helps keep things clear when you shift many curves at a time." —Jake, AP Student

Figure 6.12

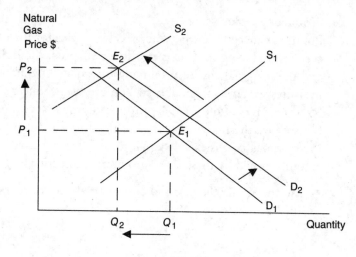

Figure 6.13

6.4 Welfare Analysis

Main Topics: *Total Welfare, Consumer Surplus, Producer Surplus*

Total Welfare

The competitive market, free of government and externalities, produces an equilibrium outcome that provides the maximum amount of total welfare for society. Society consists of all consumers and all producers and, in the marketplace, each party seeks the other so that they can make an acceptable transaction at the going market price. Each party expects to gain in these transactions. **Total welfare** is the sum of two measures of these gains: consumer surplus and producer surplus. Some textbooks, perhaps even the one you have used, refer to this sum of consumer and producer surplus as "total surplus."

Consumer Surplus

You know that great feeling you get when you pay a price that is lower than you expected, or is lower than you were willing to pay? That's **consumer surplus**, the difference between your willingness to pay and the price you actually pay. The market demand curve, at each quantity, measures society's marginal benefit, or willingness to pay (the price). You can see consumer surplus in Figure 6.14. At a price of $5, three units of the good are purchased. The first two units receive some amount of consumer surplus because the willingness to pay exceeds $5. The consumer of the third unit pays a price exactly equal to his willingness to pay so he earns no consumer surplus. Total consumer surplus is the total amount earned by these three consumer transactions.

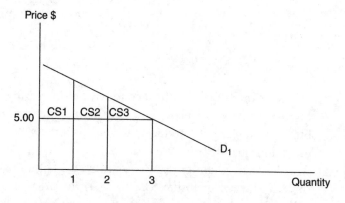

Figure 6.14

Producer Surplus

Producers are ecstatic when they receive a price for their product that is above the marginal cost of producing it. This is **producer surplus**, the difference between the price received and the marginal cost of producing the good. The market supply curve, at each quantity, measures society's marginal cost. You can see producer surplus in Figure 6.15. At a price of $5, three units of the good are produced. The first two units earn producer surplus because $5 is above the marginal cost. The third unit earns no additional producer surplus, since the marginal cost is exactly equal to the price received. Total producer surplus is the total amount earned by these three producer transactions.

- The area under the demand curve and above the market price is equal to total consumer surplus.

Figure 6.15

- The area above the supply curve and below the market price is equal to total producer surplus.

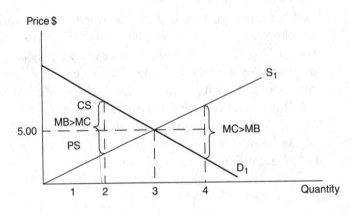

Figure 6.16

So, is market equilibrium conducive to increasing total welfare for society? Combining Figures 6.14 and 6.15 completes the market pictured in Figure 6.16. We see that the combined consumer and producer surplus, or total welfare, is greatest at the equilibrium price of $5 and quantity of three units.

At a lesser quantity (e.g., two units), the combined area is smaller than at a quantity of three. At greater quantities (i.e., $q = 4$) the price of $5 exceeds MB, so consumer surplus is being lost. If this weren't bad enough, the MC exceeds the price at $q = 4$, so producer surplus is being lost. Thus, if total welfare is falling at quantities less than three and at quantities greater than three, total welfare must be maximized at the market equilibrium quantity of three and price of $5.

A little bit of math can be a big help! Although the AP Microeconomics exam does not allow you to use a calculator, there are times when you will be required to do mathematical computations to earn points. In recent years, free-response questions have asked students to compute the area of consumer or producer surplus. It's really as simple as computing the area of a triangle: ½ × base × height. Typical exam questions will provide enough information for you to see the dimensions of the triangle (base and height) and then perform the multiplication. Let's see how this is done in the following graph.

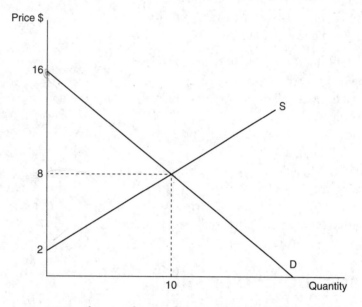

Suppose you were given this graph on a free-response question. Could you identify and compute the areas of consumer and producer surplus? It's important to remember that the consumer surplus is the area of the triangle below the demand curve and above the market price, whereas producer surplus is the area of the triangle above the supply curve and below the market price. Of course, both of these areas also depend on the equilibrium quantity, which will be the same for both triangles. Using the numbers from the graph, we compute as follows:

Consumer surplus = ½ × (10 units wide) × ($8 high) = $40

Producer surplus = ½ × (10 units wide) × ($6 high) = $30

You can now handle any similar questions on your exam.

⟩ Review Questions

1. When the price of pears increases, we expect the following:

(A) Quantity demanded of pears rises.
(B) Quantity supplied of pears falls.
(C) Quantity demanded of pears falls.
(D) Demand for pears falls.
(E) Supply of pears rises.

2. If average household income rises and we observe that the demand for pork chops increases, pork chops must be

(A) an inferior good.
(B) a normal good.
(C) a surplus good.
(D) a public good.
(E) a shortage good.

3. Suppose that aluminum is a key production input in the production of bicycles. If the price of aluminum falls, and all other variables are held constant, we expect

   (A) the demand for aluminum to rise.
   (B) the supply of bicycles to rise.
   (C) the supply of bicycles to fall.
   (D) the demand for bicycles to rise.
   (E) the demand for bicycles to fall.

4. The market for denim jeans is in equilibrium, and the price of polyester pants, a substitute good, rises. In the jean market

   (A) supply falls, increasing the price and decreasing the quantity.
   (B) supply falls, increasing the price and increasing the quantity.
   (C) demand falls, increasing the price and decreasing the quantity.
   (D) demand rises, increasing the price and increasing the quantity.
   (E) supply and demand both fall, causing an ambiguous change in price but a definite decrease in quantity.

5. The apple market is in equilibrium. Suppose we observe that apple growers are using more pesticides to increase apple production. At the same time, we hear that the price of pears, a substitute for apples, is rising. Which of the following is a reasonable prediction for the new price and quantity of apples?

   (A) Price rises, but quantity is ambiguous.
   (B) Price falls, but quantity is ambiguous.
   (C) Price is ambiguous, but quantity rises.
   (D) Price is ambiguous, but quantity falls.
   (E) Both price and quantity are ambiguous.

6. The competitive market provides the best outcome for society because

   (A) consumer surplus is minimized, while producer surplus is maximized.
   (B) the total welfare is maximized.
   (C) producer surplus is minimized, while consumer surplus is maximized.
   (D) the difference between consumer and producer surplus is maximized.
   (E) the total cost to society is maximized.

› Answers and Explanations

1. **C**—If the price of pears rises, either quantity demanded falls or quantity supplied rises. Entire demand or supply curves for pears can shift but only if an external factor, not the price of pears, changes.

2. **B**—When income increases and demand increases, the good is a normal good. Had the demand for pork chops decreased, they would be an inferior good.

3. **B**—This is a determinant of supply. If the raw material becomes less costly to acquire, the marginal cost of producing bicycles falls. Producers increase the supply of bicycles. Recognizing this as a supply determinant allows you to quickly eliminate any reference to a demand shift.

4. **D**—When a substitute good becomes more expensive, the demand for jeans rises, increasing price and quantity.

5. **C**—Increased use of pesticides increases the supply of apples. If the price of a substitute increases, the demand for apples increases. Combining these two factors predicts an increase in the quantity of apples but an ambiguous change in price. *To help you see this, draw these situations in the margin of the exam.*

6. **B**—When competitive markets reach equilibrium, no other quantity can increase total welfare (consumer + producer surplus). Total welfare is maximized at that point.

› Rapid Review

Law of demand: Holding all else equal, when the price of a good rises, consumers decrease their quantity demanded for that good.

All else equal: To predict how a change in one variable affects a second, we hold all other variables constant. This is also referred to as the "ceteris paribus" assumption.

Absolute (or money) prices: The price of a good measured in units of currency.

Relative prices: The number of units of any other good Y that must be sacrificed to acquire the first good X. Only relative prices matter.

Substitution effect: The change in quantity demanded resulting from a change in the price of one good relative to the price of other goods.

Income effect: The change in quantity demanded that results from a change in the consumer's purchasing power (or real income).

Demand schedule: A table showing quantity demanded for a good at various prices.

Demand curve: A graphical depiction of the demand schedule. The demand curve is downward sloping, reflecting the law of demand.

Determinants of demand: The external factors that shift demand to the left or right.

Normal goods: A good for which higher income increases demand.

Inferior goods: A good for which higher income decreases demand.

Substitute goods: Two goods are consumer substitutes if they provide essentially the same utility to the consumer. A Honda Accord and a Toyota Camry might be substitutes for many consumers.

Complementary goods: Two goods are consumer complements if they provide more utility when consumed together than when consumed separately. Cars and gasoline are complementary goods.

Law of supply: Holding all else equal, when the price of a good rises, suppliers increase their quantity supplied for that good.

Supply schedule: A table showing quantity supplied for a good at various prices.

Supply curve: A graphical depiction of the supply schedule. The supply curve is upward sloping, reflecting the law of supply.

Determinants of supply: One of the external factors that influences supply. When these variables change, the entire supply curve shifts to the left or right.

Market equilibrium: Exists at the only price where the quantity supplied equals the quantity demanded. Or, it is the only quantity where the highest price consumers are willing to pay is exactly the lowest price producers are willing to accept.

Shortage: Also known as *excess demand,* a shortage exists at a market price when the quantity demanded exceeds the quantity supplied. The price rises to eliminate a shortage.

Disequilibrium: Any price where quantity demanded is not equal to quantity supplied.

Surplus: Also known as *excess supply,* a surplus exists at a market price when the quantity supplied exceeds the quantity demanded. The price falls to eliminate a surplus.

Total welfare: The sum of consumer surplus and producer surplus. The free market equilibrium provides maximum combined gain to society. This is also called total surplus.

Consumer surplus: The difference between your willingness to pay and the price you actually pay. It is the area below the demand curve and above the price.

Producer surplus: The difference between the price received and the marginal cost of producing the good. It is the area above the supply curve and under the price.

CHAPTER 7

Elasticity, Microeconomic Policy, and Consumer Theory

IN THIS CHAPTER

Summary: It is critical to remember that behind the faceless supply and demand curves are individuals making decisions. These decisions are made with the rational decision maker's best interests at the top of the agenda but are influenced by many variables. This chapter begins by focusing on how sensitive consumer decisions are to external forces and how policies might affect the market and influence those choices. It concludes by analyzing the theory behind how consumers make choices to maximize their happiness.

Key Ideas
- ✪ Price Elasticity of Demand
- ✪ Income Elasticity
- ✪ Cross-Price Elasticity
- ✪ Price Elasticity of Supply
- ✪ The Impact of Taxes and Subsidies
- ✪ The Impact of Price Controls
- ✪ Tariffs and Quotas
- ✪ Utility Maximization

7.1 Elasticity

Main Topics: *Price Elasticity of Demand, Determinants of Elasticity, Total Revenue and Elasticity, Income Elasticity, Cross-Price Elasticity of Demand, Price Elasticity of Supply*

Studying the economic concept of elasticity is much like a corporate executive workshop, the topic of which is "Sensitivity Training." When we observe a consumer's purchase decision, say for good X, change in response to a change in some external variable (the price of good X or her income), **elasticity** helps us measure the sensitivity of her consumption to that external change. We also examine the sensitivity of suppliers of good X to a change in the price of good X. We use basic mathematical relationships to measure elasticity, but it is useful to remember that all elasticity formulas measure sensitivity to a change.

Price Elasticity of Demand

The law of demand tells us that: "*All else equal, when the price of a particular good falls, the quantity demanded for that good rises.*" But what it fails to answer for us is "by how much"? Will it be a relatively large increase in quantity demanded or will it be almost negligible? In other words, we would like to measure how sensitive consumers are to a change in the price of this good.

Price Elasticity of Demand Formula

$$E_d = (\%\Delta \text{ in quantity demanded of good X})/(\%\Delta \text{ in the price of good X})$$

Note: The law of demand ensures that E_d is negative, but for ease of interpretation, economists usually ignore the fact that price elasticity of demand is negative and simply use the absolute value. The greater this ratio, the more sensitive, or responsive, consumers are to a change in the price of good X.

Range of Price Elasticity

Economists like to classify things. It's a sickness, but it is usually done for a reason. (You do need to know these for the exam.) For example, we classify price elasticities based upon how sizable the reaction of consumers is to a change in the price. Rather than describing consumers as "really responsive" or "really, really responsive" or "super-duper responsive," we classify consumer responses as elastic or inelastic. The examples that follow should clarify things.

Example:

The price of a laptop computer increases by 10 percent, and we observe a 20-percent decrease in quantity demanded. Using the above formula:

$$E_d = (-20\%)/(+10\%) = -2, \text{ or simply } E_d = 2$$

- If $E_d > 1$, demand is said to be "**price elastic**" for good X. The responsiveness of the consumer exceeded, in percentage terms, the initial change in the price.

Example:

The price of a package of chewing gum increases by 10 percent, and we observe a 5-percent decrease in quantity demanded. Using the above formula:

$$E_d = (5\%)/(10\%) = .5$$

- If $E_d < 1$, demand is said to be "**price inelastic**" for good X. The initial change in the price exceeded, in percentage terms, the responsiveness of the consumer.

Example:

The price of oranges increases by 5 percent, and the quantity demanded decreases by 5 percent. Using our elasticity formula:

$$E_d = (5\%)/(5\%) = 1$$

- If $E_d = 1$, demand is said to be "**unit elastic**" for good X. The initial change in the price is exactly equal to, in percentage terms, the responsiveness of the consumer.

When describing or calculating elasticity measures, you *must* use percentage changes.

Elasticity on the Demand Curve

Take a very simple demand curve for cheeseburgers: $P = 6 - Q_d$, and plot this demand curve in Figure 7.1.

Figure 7.1

Table 7.1 summarizes changes in price, quantity demanded, and price elasticity at each point on the demand curve.*

As you can see in Figure 7.1, the price elasticity of demand is not constant at points A through G on the demand curve. Specifically, as the price rises, E_d rises, telling us that consumers are more price sensitive at higher prices than they are at lower prices. This makes good intuitive sense. When the price is relatively low (e.g., point B), a 10-percent increase in price might be almost negligible to consumers. But if the original price is quite high (point F), then a 10-percent increase in the price is pretty drastic. In fact, if we divide the demand curve in half, you can see that above the midpoint (point D), demand is price elastic and below the midpoint, demand is price inelastic. At the midpoint, demand is unit elastic.

Table 7.1 Price Elasticity at Points Along Demand

POINT	PRICE PER CHEESEBURGER	QUANTITY DEMANDED OF CHEESEBURGERS	PRICE ELASTICITY (E_d)
A	0	6	= 0
B	1	5	= .2
C	2	4	= .5
D	3	3	= 1
E	4	2	= 2
F	5	1	= 5
G	6	0	= ∞

*Note: To calculate the elasticity at each point on the demand curve in Figure 7.1, I used an equivalent way of calculating percentage change. Your AP test may or may not include similar calculations, but you do need to know how elasticity changes along a demand curve.

The Midpoint Formula

Calculating the percentage change between two prices or quantities on a demand curve is not always easy; after all, the percentage change between two values depends on which of them is the initial value. For example, if a price increases from $100 to $125, this is a 25-percent increase. If the price falls from $125 to $100, this is a 20-percent decrease. The two prices on the demand curve are the same, but the percentage change between them depends on where we begin.

To avoid some of the difficulties of calculating these types of changes, we use what is known as the midpoint formula. Let's use P_1 and Q_1 to represent the first point on the demand curve and P_2 and Q_2 to represent the second point. The midpoint formula calculates the price elasticity of demand between those two points by using the average price (P_{avg}) and average quantity (Q_{avg}) between them. The midpoint formula is therefore

$$E_d = \left(\frac{\Delta Q_d}{\Delta P}\right) \times \left(\frac{P_{avg}}{Q_{avg}}\right)$$

Let's say that the initial price of a hypothetical product is $16, and 20 units are demanded. When the price rises to $20, quantity demanded falls to 10 units. The average price between these two points is $18, and the average quantity is 15 units. When we use the midpoint formula, we compute

$$E_d = \left(\frac{\Delta Q_d}{\Delta P}\right) \times \left(\frac{P_{avg}}{Q_{avg}}\right) = \left(\frac{10}{\$4}\right) \times \left(\frac{\$18}{15}\right) = 3.$$

Some recent AP Microeconomics exams have required the use of the midpoint formula, so it is important to be able to perform such calculations to maximize your free-response points.

Special Cases

If it is true that any increase in the price results in no decrease in the quantity demanded, then we are describing the special case where demand for the good is **perfectly inelastic.** Figure 7.2 shows the demand (D_0) for a life-saving pharmaceutical, for which there is no substitute, and without which the patient dies. The vertical demand curve tells us that no matter what percentage increase, or decrease, in price, the quantity demanded remains the same. Mathematically speaking, $E_d = 0$.

Figure 7.2

Figure 7.3

In the case where a decrease in the price causes the quantity demanded to increase without limits, then we have the special case where demand is **perfectly elastic** for that good. Figure 7.2 shows demand for a good (D_1), maybe one farmer's grain, which has many substitutes. A horizontal demand curve tells us that even the smallest percentage change in price causes an infinite change in quantity demanded. Mathematically speaking, $E_d = \infty$.

Comparing the vertical (perfectly inelastic) demand curve to the horizontal (perfectly elastic) demand curve allows us to draw an important generalization. As a demand curve becomes more vertical, the price elasticity falls and consumers become more price inelastic. The opposite generalization can be made as the demand curve becomes more horizontal. Figure 7.3 illustrates some general points about slope and elasticity.

- In general, the more vertical a good's demand curve (D_0), the more inelastic the demand for that good.
- The more horizontal a good's demand curve (D_1), the more elastic the demand for that good.
- Despite this generalization, be careful; elasticity and slope are *not* equivalent measures.

Determinants of Elasticity

Perfectly elastic and perfectly inelastic demand curves are usually reserved for the hypothetical example, but they illustrate that E_d differs across consumer goods. Your intuition is that consumers respond to a price change in different ways. A 10-percent increase in the price of a car might have a drastically different consumer response from what we observe from a 10-percent increase in the price of a college education, a package of mechanical pencils, or a hotel stay in Fort Lauderdale. Let's look at some general explanations for why elasticity differs.

1. Number of Good Substitutes

    If the price of good X increases, and many substitutes exist, the decrease in quantity demanded can be quite elastic. For this reason, we expect E_d of orange juice to be high, since there are many substitutes available to drinkers of fruit juice.

    Corollary. Oftentimes you hear of a good that is a "necessity" or a "frivolity." These adjectives are reiterating a relative lack of or a relative wealth of good substitutes.

    Example:
    The more narrowly the product is defined, the more elastic it becomes. If we narrow our focus from orange juice down to one brand of orange juice (e.g., Minute Maid),

the number of substitutes grows and we predict that so too does the price elasticity of demand for Minute Maid brand orange juice. Likewise, the demand for blue Chevrolet SUVs is more elastic than the demand for Chevrolet SUVs, which, in turn, is more elastic than the demand for all SUVs.

2. Proportion of Income

If the price of a good increases, the consumer loses purchasing power. If that good takes up a large proportion of the consumer's income, he greatly feels the pinch of the income effect, and his responsiveness might be significant. If the price of toothpicks increased by 10 percent, the typical household probably would not feel the lost purchasing power and E_d would be low. The opposite would be true if the price of food items increased by 10 percent.

Example:

A young full-time college student is purchasing her education by the credit-hour and supporting herself with a part-time job on the weekends and evenings. Since the student is living on a relatively small monthly income, if the price of a credit-hour increases, the response might be very elastic. The student might drop down to part-time status or drop out of college altogether so that she can save enough money to return next quarter.

3. Time

Consumers faced by a rising price are usually fairly resourceful in their ability to find a way of decreasing the quantity demanded of a good. The difficulty faced by consumers is that they might not have time, at least not initially, to find a substitute for the more expensive good. We expect price elasticity to increase as more time passes after the initial increase in the price.

Example:

If the price of gasoline rises, consumers driving large SUVs do not immediately switch to small cars and the E_d is low for gasoline. But given enough time, if the gas price remains high, the E_d for gasoline increases.

Total Revenue and Elasticity

Discussing price elasticity and making simple calculations is not just a delightful academic exercise for students. Knowing how sensitive consumers are to changes in price is important to those who benefit from selling goods to those consumers—the sellers. Sellers compute total revenues collected from selling goods. It is also important to note that the dollars spent by consumers is equal to the dollars received as revenue by sellers.

$$\text{Total revenue} = \text{Price} \times \text{Quantity demanded} = \text{Total spending}$$

A seller might think, "If I continue to raise the price, my total revenues must continue to rise." A student of microeconomics knows that this is flawed logic, because quantity demanded falls when the price rises, making the impact on total revenue uncertain.

$$\text{Here's what's happening: (Price}\uparrow) \times (\text{Quantity demanded}\downarrow)$$
$$= \text{Total revenue} \updownarrow$$

With price going up and quantity demanded going down, it's like a tug-of-war between two teams, with total revenue being pulled in the direction of the strongest team.

Whether or not the total revenue increases with a price increase depends upon whether or not the gain from the higher price offsets the loss from lower quantity demanded. Price elasticity is an excellent way to predict how total revenue changes with a price change. This is sometimes called the total revenue test. Table 7.2 extends our earlier table by adding a column for total revenue at points A through G.

Table 7.2 Total Revenue and Price Elasticity

POINT	PRICE PER CHEESEBURGER	QUANTITY DEMANDED OF CHEESEBURGERS	TOTAL = REVENUE $P \times Q_d$ = TOTAL SPENDING	PRICE ELASTICITY (E_d)
A	$0	6	$0	0
B	1	5	5	0.2
C	2	4	8	0.5
D	3	3	9	1
E	4	2	8	2
F	5	1	5	5
G	6	0	0	∞

As you can see, if the price rises in the inelastic range of the demand curve, total revenues rise. However, if the price continues to rise into the elastic range, total revenues begin to fall. Why? Maybe a reminder of what it means for demand to be elastic helps to predict which team wins the tug-of-war.

- Inelastic demand $E_d < 1$: % ΔQ_d < % ΔP, so total revenue increases with a price increase.
- Elastic demand $E_d > 1$: % ΔQ_d > % ΔP, so total revenue decreases with a price increase.
- Unit elastic demand $E_d = 1$: % ΔQ_d = % ΔP, so total revenue remains the same.

In Figures 7.4 and 7.5, we can graphically illustrate the connection between the demand curve, elasticity, and total revenue.

If we start at the top of the demand curve and begin to lower the price, Figure 7.5 clearly shows that total revenue rises until quantity demanded equals three, and then falls until we reach a quantity of six units demanded. If the price is falling and total revenue is rising, it must be the case that the quantity demanded is rising by a larger percentage than the percentage by which price is falling; an elastic response. And if the price continues to fall and total revenue is falling, it must be the case that the percentage increase in quantity demanded is smaller than the percentage by which the price is falling; an inelastic response. The quantity of three in Figure 7.4 represents the midpoint of this particular demand curve and allows us to divide the demand curve into the elastic half (above the midpoint price of $3) and the inelastic half (below $3). This will always be true of any linear demand curve.

Figure 7.4

Figure 7.5

- At prices above the midpoint of a linear demand curve, consumers have an elastic response to a small change in price.
- At prices below the midpoint of a linear demand curve, consumers have an inelastic response to a small change in price.

Income Elasticity of Demand

In the case of the **income elasticity**, it is a measure of how sensitive consumption of good X is to a change in a consumer's income.

$$E_I = (\% \Delta Q_d \text{ good X})/(\% \Delta \text{ income})$$

Example:

Jason's income rises 5 percent, and we see his consumption of fast-food meals rises 10 percent.

$$E_I = (10\%)/(5\%) = 2$$

So what do we make of this? First, because E_I is greater than zero, we can determine that fast-food meals are a **normal** good for Jason. Second, at least in this example, the consumption of fast-food meals is quite income elastic. A relatively small percentage increase in income causes a large—in fact, twofold—percentage increase in fast-food meals. Some refer to these goods as **luxuries**.

Example:

Jen's income rises 5 percent, and we observe her consumption of bread rises 1 percent.

$$E_I = (1\%)/(5\%) = .2$$

Once again, this measure would indicate that bread is a **normal** good, as more income prompts more bread consumption. However, the relatively small increase in consumption compared to the increase in income tells us that bread demand is relatively income inelastic. This makes sense; after all, how much more bread does one really wish to consume as his or her income rises? If Jen's income doubled, would she double, or more than double, her consumption of bread? These goods are often referred to as **necessities**.

Example:

Consumer income increases by 5 percent, and we observe consumption of packaged bologna decreases by 2 percent.

$$E_I = (-2\%)/(5\%) = -.4$$

Again, there are two important observations that can be made here. First, because consumption of bologna decreased with an increase in income, we can conclude that bologna, in this example, is an **inferior** good. Second, there is a relatively inelastic response in bologna consumption to a change in income.

- If $E_I > 1$, the good is normal and income elastic (a luxury).
- If $1 > E_I > 0$, the good is normal but income inelastic (a necessity).
- If $E_I < 0$, the good is inferior.

Cross-Price Elasticity of Demand

Consumers also change their consumption of good X when the price of a related good, good Y changes. The sensitivity of consumption of good X to a change in the price of good Y is called the **cross-price elasticity of demand**.

$$E_{x,y} = (\%\Delta \ Q_d \text{ good X})/(\%\Delta \text{ Price good Y})$$

Example:
The price of eggs increases by 1 percent, and the consumption of bacon falls 2 percent. The fact that bacon consumption fell when eggs became more expensive tells us that these goods are complementary goods.

$$E_{x,y} = (\%\Delta \ Q_d \text{ bacon})/(\%\Delta \text{ Price eggs}) = -2\%/1\% = -2$$

Example:
The price of Honda cars increases by 2 percent and consumption of Ford cars increases by 4 percent. Because Ford cars saw increased consumption when Honda cars got more expensive, the two goods are substitutes.

$$E_{x,y} = (\%\Delta \ Q_d \text{ Ford})/(\%\Delta \text{ Price Honda}) = 2\%/1\% = +2$$

- A cross-price elasticity of demand less than zero identifies complementary goods.
- A cross-price elasticity of demand greater than zero identifies substitute goods.

Price Elasticity of Supply

Now that we have addressed the sensitivity of consumer consumption of good X, let us discuss elasticity from the supplier's perspective. When the price of good X changes, we expect quantity supplied to change. The law of supply predicts that as the price of good X increases, so too does quantity supplied. But what we do not know is, "by how much?" The price elasticity of supply helps to measure this response.

Price Elasticity of Supply Formula

$$E_s = (\%\Delta \text{ in quantity supplied of good X})/(\%\Delta \text{ in the price of good X})$$

Note: The law of supply ensures that E_s is positive. The greater this ratio, the more sensitive, or responsive, suppliers are to a change in the price of good X.

The Element of Time

Perhaps the most important determinant of how price elastic suppliers are in a particular industry is the time that it takes suppliers to change the quantity supplied once the price of the good itself has changed. This flexibility, of course, is different for different types of producers.

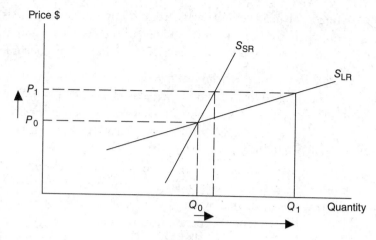

Figure 7.6

Example:

A local attorney produces hours of legal service in a small midwestern town from her small office. At the current market price, for an hour of legal advice, she works a 40-hour workweek with the help of one clerical employee. If the price of an hour of legal assistance rises by 10 percent in the local market, initially our attorney responds by working a few additional minutes each weekday evening and on Saturday, but the constraints of the calendar allow for only an increase of 5 percent in the hours that she supplies.

$$\text{Short-term } E_s = (5\%)/(10\%) = .5$$

If this higher price is maintained for a month or two, the attorney might ask her employee to work additional hours, thus allowing the small office to increase the quantity of hours supplied by 10 percent. And if the price continues to stay at the higher rate, she might expand the office and employ a junior associate and thus increase the hours supplied by 20 percent.

$$\text{Long-term } E_s = (20\%)/(10\%) = 2$$

Because suppliers, once the price of the good has changed, usually cannot quickly change the quantity supplied, economists predict that the price elasticity of supply increases as time passes. Figure 7.6 illustrates the short-term (S_{SR}) and long-term (S_{LR}) supply curves for our attorney. In general, the less steep the supply curve, the more elastic suppliers are in response to a change in the price.

7.2 Microeconomic Policy and Applications of Elasticity

Main Topics: *Excise Taxes, The Role the Supply Curve Plays in the Impact of an Excise Tax, Subsidies, Price Floors, Price Ceilings*

Excise Taxes

Government occasionally imposes an **excise tax** on the production of a good or service. Because it is a per-unit tax on production, the firm responds as if the marginal cost of producing each unit has risen by the amount of the tax. Graphically this results in a vertical shift in the supply curve by the amount of the tax. The reasons for this tax are usually twofold: (1) to increase revenue collected by the government and/or (2) to decrease consumption of a good that might be harmful to some members of society. For these reasons, tobacco is a good example of an excise tax. Can an excise tax on tobacco raise money for government? Can it deter people from smoking? Let's use our two extreme demand curves to see where these goals might, or might not, be achieved and how the price elasticity of demand plays a critical role on where the burden, or **incidence**, of the tax rests. Economists commonly express the incidence of the tax as the percentage of the tax paid by consumers, in the form of a higher price.

Demand Is Perfectly Inelastic

If the demand for cigarettes is perfectly inelastic ($E_d = 0$), then the demand curve (D_0) is vertical. With an untaxed supply (S_0) of cigarettes, the initial price of a pack of cigarettes is P_0 and Q_0 packs of cigarettes are consumed every day. If a per-unit tax of T is imposed on the producers of cigarettes, the supply curve shifts upward by T. *Be careful! This is not an "increase in supply"!* Because the demand is perfectly inelastic, the equilibrium quantity remains at Q_0, but the new price rises to $P_0 + T$. Total dollars spent on cigarettes increases from $P_0 \times Q_0$ to $(P_0 + T) \times Q_0$. The revenue collected by the government is equal to the area of the rectangle $T \times Q_0$.

Did our excise tax accomplish our goals? Since quantity remained constant, the tax did nothing to decrease the harmful effects of smoking in society and only increased tax revenues for the government. In fact, because the quantity demanded did not fall, this scenario creates the largest revenue rectangle collected by the government. Who paid the burden of the tax? In Figure 7.7, you can see that the entire tax was paid by consumers in the form of a new price exactly equal to the old price plus the tax.

Figure 7.7

Demand Is Perfectly Elastic

Figure 7.8 shows that if the demand for cigarettes is perfectly elastic ($E_d = \infty$), then the demand curve (D_0) is horizontal. With an untaxed supply (S_0) of cigarettes, the initial price of a pack of cigarettes is P_0 and Q_0 packs of cigarettes are consumed daily. The per-unit tax of T shifts the supply curve upward by T, but with a perfectly elastic demand curve, the equilibrium price of cigarettes does not change, while equilibrium quantity demanded falls to Q_1. Total spending by consumers falls to the area $P_0 \times Q_1$. Tax revenue for the government is a much smaller rectangle $T \times Q_1$.

Figure 7.8

Who paid for the tax in this case? Because the price of a pack of cigarettes did not increase after the tax, it was not the consumers. Each producer receives a price of P_0 but must then pay T to the government, so the net price received from each pack of cigarettes is $(P_0 - T)$. So the producer pays the entire share of the tax when demand is perfectly elastic. Compared to the perfectly inelastic scenario, the government collected much fewer tax revenue dollars, but the maximum decrease in harmful cigarette consumption is a definite plus.

With these two extreme cases as benchmarks, we can conclude that as demand is more inelastic, consumers pay a higher share of an excise tax. Government revenues from the excise tax increase with inelastic demand, but the goal of decreasing consumption sees only minimal success. Table 7.3 summarizes the effects of a higher excise tax and how these depend upon the price elasticity of demand.

Table 7.3 Price Elasticity of Demand and Tax Incidence

PRICE ELASTICITY OF DEMAND	GOVERNMENT REVENUE	DECREASE IN CONSUMPTION	INCIDENCE OF TAX PAID BY CONSUMERS	INCIDENCE OF TAX PAID BY SUPPLIERS
$E_d = \infty$	The least	The most	0%	100%
$E_d > 1$	Falling	Sizeable	Less than 50%	More than 50%
$E_d < 1$	Rising	Minimal	More than 50%	Less than 50%
$E_d = 0$	The most	Zero	100%	0%

Since cigarette demand is usually inelastic, significant improvements in the health of consumers is probably not the primary outcome of higher excise taxes, although they would seem to be effective revenue-generating devices. Ironically, although the tax is actually imposed on suppliers of cigarettes, most of the burden of the tax falls upon consumers. Figure 7.9 illustrates an inelastic demand for cigarettes, before and after an excise tax.

The Role the Supply Curve Plays in the Impact of an Excise Tax

We have seen that the greater the price elasticity of demand, the smaller the portion of the tax paid by consumers. It is also true that the price elasticity of supply plays a role in determining how much a tax will cause the price to increase and therefore helps to determine which group, consumers or producers, pays a higher burden of a tax.

Figure 7.9

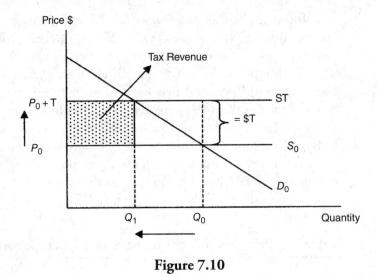

Figure 7.10

It again helps to see if we look at two extremes: a perfectly elastic supply curve and a perfectly inelastic supply curve.

A perfectly elastic, or horizontal, supply curve tells us that even a very small change in the price will cause an infinitely large change in the quantity supplied. A per-unit tax T imposed on suppliers causes this horizontal supply curve to shift upward by the amount of the tax. In Figure 7.10, you can see that the new equilibrium price is exactly T higher than the old price P_0, so consumers pay the entire burden of the tax. The equilibrium quantity decreases from Q_0 to Q_1, and the government collects tax revenue equal to $T \times Q_1$.

A perfectly inelastic, or vertical, supply curve illustrates the special case where any change in the price creates absolutely no change in quantity supplied. Figure 7.11 shows that in this case, the supply curve cannot vertically shift. At the equilibrium quantity Q_0, suppliers would like to charge a higher price than P_0, but any price above P_0 creates a surplus, and this surplus will clear only at the equilibrium price P_0. Therefore the firms must pay T to the government for each of the Q_0 units that are sold and consumers continue to pay the original price of P_0. In this special case, producers pay the entire burden of the tax because, after paying the tax, they receive only $(P_0 - T)$ on each unit. The government collects total revenue equal to $T \times Q_0$.

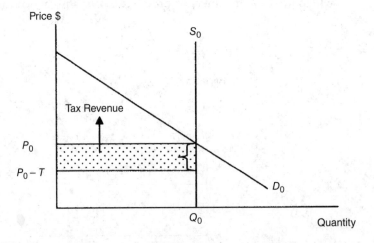

Figure 7.11

Table 7.4 summarizes the effects of a higher excise tax and how these depend upon the price elasticity of supply.

Table 7.4 Price Elasticity of Supply and Tax Incidence

PRICE ELASTICITY OF SUPPLY	GOVERNMENT REVENUE	DECREASE IN CONSUMPTION	INCIDENCE OF TAX PAID BY CONSUMERS	INCIDENCE OF TAX PAID BY PRODUCERS
$E_s = \infty$	The least	The most	100%	0%
$E_s > 1$	Falling	Sizeable	More than 50%	Less than 50%
$E_s < 1$	Rising	Minimal	Less than 50%	More than 50%
$E_s = 0$	The most	Zero	0%	100%

By now you are probably wondering, "How can I keep all of this straight?" If we consider the extreme cases of perfectly elastic and perfectly inelastic demand and supply curves, we can draw some general conclusions.

- As the price elasticity of demand falls, and the price elasticity of supply rises, the greater the consumer's share of a per-unit excise tax. Why? Because this describes a situation where the consumer response to a higher price is negligible and the producer's response is sizable. The group that has the best ability to respond to the higher post-tax price is going to make out better.
- Conversely, as the price elasticity of demand rises and the price elasticity of supply falls, the producer's share of a per-unit excise tax rises.

Loss to Society

KEY IDEA

There is also a cost to society when an excise tax is imposed on a competitive market. In the hypothetical soda market depicted in Figure 7.12, the equilibrium quantity is 100 and the equilibrium price is $1. At this point, the marginal benefit to society exactly equals the marginal cost and net benefit; total welfare (combined consumer and producer surplus) is the greatest. When a $1 excise tax is imposed, the price of sodas paid by consumers increases to $1.80, and the number (amount) of sodas consumed decreases to 80. After sellers pay the excise tax, the price they receive falls to $0.80. The government collects $80 = \$1 \times 80$ in tax revenue. With the tax, consumers and producers demand and supply 20 fewer units than

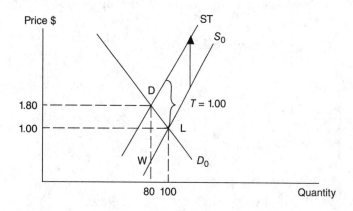

Figure 7.12

without the tax. For these 20 units that go unproduced, the marginal benefit to consumers exceeds the marginal costs to producers. The fact that these 20 units go unproduced and unconsumed results in an inefficient outcome. The triangle labeled DWL used to be earned by society in the form of consumer and producer surplus. With the excise tax, society loses this area; it goes to no one. Economists call this area **deadweight loss** (DWL), or the net benefit sacrificed by society when such a per-unit tax is imposed. In fact, with the numbers given, we can calculate the deadweight loss as the area of the triangle that is 20 units wide and $1 tall. Since the key to deadweight loss is a large decrease in quantity below the untaxed outcome, the area of deadweight loss to society increases as the demand or supply curves get more elastic.

Note: Taxes such as these are not the only sources of distortions away from market efficiency. For example, production often generates pollution (a negative externality), which creates a situation where harmful spillover costs are incurred by third parties. Left unregulated, these costs are not captured by the market price and the market will not produce the "correct" amount of a good. These sources of inefficiency, or market failures, are addressed in Chapter 11.

- Taxes create lost efficiency by moving away from the equilibrium market quantity where MB = MC to society.
- The area of deadweight loss (triangle DWL) increases as the quantity moves further from the competitive market equilibrium quantity.

Subsidies

A per-unit **subsidy** on good X has the opposite effect of an excise tax, because firms respond as if the subsidy has lowered the marginal cost of production, therefore resulting in a downward vertical shift in the supply curve for good X. *Be careful here! This is not a "decrease in supply"!* Since subsidies come from the government, they are certainly not designed as revenue-generating devices. Ideally, their primary goal is to support producers of a good or service that has significant benefit to society so that it can be produced in greater quantities and at lower prices to consumers. This form of positive externality is also explored in Chapter 11. Public university education is a common example of this type of subsidy.

Figure 7.13 illustrates the market for public university education where the demand (D_0) and unsubsidized supply (S_0) curves produce an equilibrium price P_0 (tuition) and quantity Q_0 (degrees earned). If government decides that provision of bachelor's degrees is a beneficial service to society, a per-student subsidy U is given to the public university system. The subsidy decreases tuition to P_1 and increases the number of undergraduate degrees received. Notice that the producers receive, after the subsidy, $(P_1 + U)$ for each student at the new quantity of Q_1. Like an excise tax, a subsidy distorts the market and creates deadweight loss. By creating an incentive for producers to increase production beyond the market quantity, producers end up producing "too many" units of the good. In the

"Taxes and subsidies are usually tested in both the multiple-choice section and as part of a free-response question."
—AP Teacher

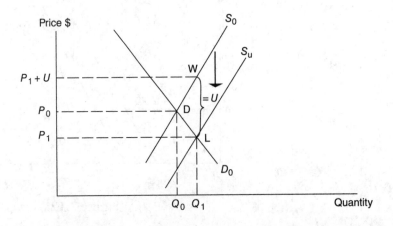

Figure 7.13

hypothetical example depicted in Figure 7.13, the deadweight loss is the area of the triangle labeled "DWL."

How does the price elasticity of demand factor into this outcome? If the demand for public university education is elastic, then a relatively small percentage decrease in the price of tuition creates a sizable percentage increase in the number of degrees earned by members of society. If demand is price inelastic, it takes a much larger percentage decrease in the price to achieve the same percentage increase in degrees earned.

Price Floors

In some cases, the market-determined equilibrium price P_0 is deemed "too low" by some members of society. Typically, suppliers who feel that the market price is not high enough to cover production costs and earn a decent living make this argument. If the government agrees with this argument, a **price floor** may be installed at some level above the equilibrium price. A price floor is a legal minimum price below which the product cannot be sold. Another example is a minimum wage in a market for labor. An effective price floor in the market for milk is seen in Figure 7.14. An ineffective price floor would be a price set below the equilibrium price. After all, a price floor sets a minimum legal price so if a price floor is set *below* equilibrium, the market would simply revert to the higher equilibrium price and the price floor would have no impact.

The resulting surplus of milk is not eliminated through the market, and the government usually agrees, as part of the price floor arrangement, to purchase the surplus milk. For consumers, the result of the policy is a higher price of milk (and other dairy products) at grocery stores, a decrease in milk consumption, and an increase in taxpayer-supported government spending. The amount of government spending to purchase the surplus is equal to $(P_F) \times$ surplus. If the price elasticities of demand or supply are large, the surplus, and resulting government spending, rises.

By providing an incentive for producers to produce beyond where MB = MC, the price floor policy causes efficiency to be lost. For gallons of milk above Q_0, MC > MB; there is an overallocation of resources to milk production. Quite simply, the policy produces a situation where "too much" milk is produced, and this is inefficient.

- A price floor is installed when producers feel the market equilibrium price is "too low."
- A price floor creates a permanent surplus at a price above equilibrium.
- If the government purchases the surplus, taxpayers eventually pay the bill.
- The more price elastic the demand and supply curves, the greater the surplus and the greater the government spending to purchase the surplus.
- The price floor reduces net benefit by overallocating resources to the production of the good.

Figure 7.14

Figure 7.15

Price Ceilings

For some goods and services, the market equilibrium price is judged to be "too high." Consumers who feel that the price is so high that it prevents a significant fraction of citizens from being able to consume a good, usually express this sentiment. If the government agrees with this argument, a **price ceiling** may be installed at a level below the equilibrium price. A price ceiling is a legal maximum price above which the product cannot be bought and sold. An effective price ceiling in the market for rental apartments (rent control) is seen in Figure 7.15. An effective price ceiling must be set below the equilibrium price. Because the price ceiling sets a legal maximum price, a ceiling set *above* the equilibrium price would quickly revert back to the market equilibrium outcome and have no impact.

The resulting shortage of rent-controlled apartments is not eliminated through the market, and this creates a sticky situation for low-income households, the group for which the policy was intended. Many suppliers completely remove their rental units from the market, converting them into office space or condominiums. Others attempt to increase profits by lowering levels of health and safety maintenance, or by charging exorbitant fees for a key to the apartment. For families lucky enough to find rent-controlled space, the result of this policy is certainly lower rents, but the shortage also tends to create an underground or "black" market for apartments where a vacant apartment might go to the highest bidder, regardless of financial need. If the price elasticities of demand or supply are large, the shortage, and the negative consequences of it, increase.

Again, this form of price control results in lost efficiency for society. When suppliers reduce their quantity supplied below the competitive equilibrium quantity, there is a situation where MB > MC, and we see an underallocation of resources in the rental apartment market. This policy, intended to help low-income families, creates a situation where "too little" of the good is produced.

- A price ceiling is installed when consumers feel the market equilibrium price is "too high."
- A price ceiling creates a permanent shortage at a price below equilibrium.
- The more price elastic the demand and supply curves, the greater the shortage.
- The price ceiling reduces net benefit by underallocating resources to the production of the good.

7.3 Trade Barriers

Main Topics: *Tariffs, Quotas*

The issue of free trade is hotly politicized. Proponents usually argue that free trade raises the standard of living in **both nations**, and most economists agree. Detractors argue that free trade, especially with nations that pay lower wages than those paid to domestic workers, costs domestic jobs in higher-wage nations. The evidence shows that in some industries, job losses have certainly occurred as free trade has become more prevalent. To protect domestic jobs, nations can impose trade barriers. Tariffs and quotas are among the most common of barriers.

Tariffs

In general, there are two types of tariffs. A **revenue tariff** is an excise tax levied on goods that are not produced in the domestic market. For example, the United States does not produce bananas. If a revenue tariff were levied on bananas, it would not be a serious impediment to trade, and it would raise a little revenue for the government. A **protective tariff** is an excise tax levied on a good that is produced in the domestic market. Though this tariff also raises revenue, the purpose of this tariff, as the name suggests, is to protect the domestic industry from global competition by increasing the price of foreign products.

Example:

The hypothetical domestic supply and demand for steel is pictured in Figure 7.16. The domestic price is $100 per ton and the equilibrium quantity of domestic steel is 10 million tons. Maybe other nations can produce steel at lower cost. As a result, in the competitive world market, the price is $80 per ton. At that price, the United States would demand 12 million tons but only produce 8 million tons, and so 4 million tons are **imported**. It is important to see that in the competitive (free-trade) world market, consumer surplus is maximized and no deadweight loss exists. You can see the consumer surplus as the triangle below the demand curve and above the $80 world price.

If the steel industry is successful in getting a protective tariff passed through Congress, the world price rises by $10, increasing the quantity of domestic steel supplied and reducing the amount of steel imported from 4 million to 2 million tons. A higher price and lower consumption reduces the area of consumer surplus and creates deadweight loss.

Figure 7.16

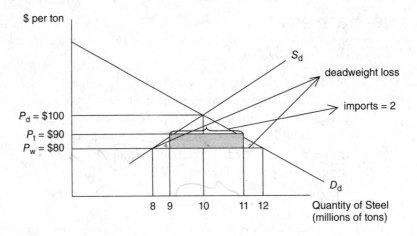

Figure 7.17

Economic Effects of the Tariff

- *Consumers pay higher prices and consume less steel.* If you are building airplanes or door hinges, you have seen an increase in your costs.
- *Consumer surplus has been lost.*
- *Domestic producers increase output.* Domestic steel firms are not subject to the tariff, so they can sell more steel at the price of $90 than they could at $80.
- *Declining imports.* Fewer tons of imported steel arrive in the United States.
- *Tariff revenue.* The government collects $10 × 2 million = $20 million in tariff revenue as seen in the shaded box in Figure 7.17. This is a transfer from consumers of steel to the government, not an increase in the total well-being of the nation.
- *Inefficiency.* There was a reason the world price was lower than the domestic price. It was more efficient to produce steel abroad and export it to the United States. By taxing this efficiency, the United States promotes the inefficient domestic industry and stunts the efficient foreign sector. As a result, resources are diverted from the efficient to the inefficient sector.
- *Deadweight loss now exists.*

Quotas

Quotas work in much the same way as a tariff. An **import quota** is a maximum amount of a good that can be imported into the domestic market. With a quota, the government only allows 2 million tons to be imported. Figure 7.18 looks much like Figure 7.17, only

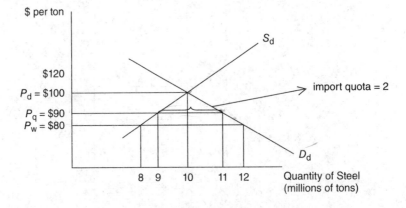

Figure 7.18

without revenue collected by government. So the impact of the quota, with the exception of the revenue, is the same: higher consumer prices and inefficient resource allocation.

Tariffs and quotas share many of the same economic effects.

- Both hurt consumers with artificially high prices and lower consumer surplus.
- Both protect inefficient domestic producers at the expense of efficient foreign firms, creating deadweight loss.
- Both reallocate economic resources toward inefficient producers.
- Tariffs collect revenue for the government, while quotas do not.

> "It is important to know the differences between tariffs and quotas."
> —Lucas, AP Student

7.4 Consumer Choice

Main Topics: *Utility; Unconstrained Consumer Choice; Diminishing Marginal Utility; Constrained Utility Maximization; Constrained Utility Maximization, Two Goods*

Utility

If you pull back the curtain on the law of demand to study how consumers behave, much insight can be gained. It's important to remember that people demand things because *those things make those people happy.* We choose to consume mundane items like electricity or crackers, or luxury items like trans-Atlantic flights and tickets to an NFL game, because they provide us with happiness. In economics, we call this happiness (or benefit, or satisfaction, or enjoyment) **utility**.

While in the course of a week, consumption of more and more pints of Cherry Garcia ice cream is likely to increase our **total utility**, it is probably safe to say that the first pint in a week provides more **marginal utility** than the second, third, or fourth pint. If you recall from Chapter 5, analysis of marginal changes is extremely important in modeling how individuals make decisions.

- Total utility (TU) is the total amount of happiness received from the consumption of a certain amount of a good.
- Marginal utility (MU) is the additional utility received (or sometimes lost) from the consumption of the *next* unit of a good.
- Mathematically speaking: $MU = \Delta TU/\Delta Q$ (this ΔQ is likely to equal 1 if you are consuming one additional unit at a time).

Example:

Table 7.5 summarizes the utility gained from consumption of successive cups of coffee in a typical morning at work. Some choose to measure utility in hypothetical "**utils**," but I like to think about these as "happy points."

As our coffee drinker (Joe) goes from zero to one cup of coffee, his total happiness from coffee drinking increases from zero to 20 happy points. The incremental, or marginal, change is also 20 points. The marginal utility is simply calculated as the difference between the totals as Joe consumes consecutive cups of coffee.

Unconstrained Consumer Choice

So how much coffee should our desk jockey consume in a typical morning? Assuming that he does not have to pay for each cup and can freely use the coffee machine, one might assume that Joe consumes unlimited amounts of coffee. Using Table 7.5 or Figure 7.19, you can easily see that total utility initially rises, peaks, and then begins to fall as more coffee is consumed. If Joe is a consumer who seeks to maximize happiness, and this seems

Table 7.5 Total and Marginal Utility

# CUPS (Q)	TOTAL UTILITY (TU) ("HAPPY POINTS")	MARGINAL UTILITY (MU)
0	0	—
1	20	20
2	35	15
3	45	10
4	50	5
5	45	−5
6	35	−10

a reasonable aim, he would not consume more than four cups of coffee, even if he were not asked to pay for each cup.

- Even if the monetary price of good X is zero, the rational consumer stops consuming good X at the point where total utility is maximized.

Diminishing Marginal Utility

In Figure 7.19 you can see a relationship between total utility and coffee consumption. There is the obvious rise, peak, and fall of total utility as the number of cups increases. But closer inspection reveals that, as more coffee is consumed, total utility rises at a slower and slower rate. Since marginal utility is the rate at which total utility changes, marginal utility must be falling.

The **law of diminishing marginal utility** says that in a given time period, the marginal utility from consumption of one more of that item falls. A graphical depiction of marginal utility, also the slope of total utility, is seen in Figure 7.20.

Constrained Utility Maximization

Now we require Joe to pay a price P_c for additional cups of coffee. With a fixed daily income and a price that must be paid, this individual is now a **constrained utility maximizer**. Joe must ask himself: "Does the next cup of coffee provide at least $\$P_c$ worth of additional happiness?" If Joe answers "yes" to this question for the first three cups of coffee, he maximizes his utility by stopping at three cups. If his answer is "no" to the fourth cup, he does not consume it.

Figure 7.19

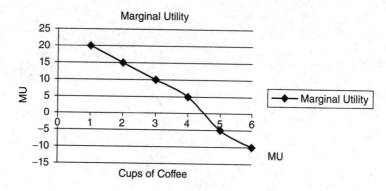

Figure 7.20

Does this sound familiar? It should, as it is another example of how a consumer never does something if the marginal benefit (in this case, utility) gained is exceeded by the marginal cost incurred.

- When required to pay a price, the utility-maximizing consumer stops consuming when MB = P.

- This MB also represents the highest price, or "willingness to pay," our consumer would be willing to pay for the next cup.

Demand Curve Revisited

Using the logic outlined above as an example, what would happen if the price of coffee fell? If Joe was facing a new lower price, you should expect that Joe would rationally increase his daily consumption of cups of coffee. Have you heard this behavior described before? Sure! It's the law of demand, and it has a tight connection to the law of diminishing marginal utility.

Imagine you are a consumer who has already paid for and consumed the first pint of ice cream this week. Would your willingness to pay for the second pint of ice cream be the same as your willingness to pay for the first pint? Doubtful, because the second pint does not provide the same marginal utility as the first. In order to entice you to purchase and consume additional pints of Cherry Garcia ice cream, the price must fall to compensate you for your falling marginal utility.

This law of diminishing marginal utility is the backbone of the law of demand. To convert the relationship between marginal utility and quantity consumed at any price, we might ask you how much you are willing to pay to consume successive pints of ice cream. Because of diminishing marginal utility, you offer to pay less for additional units. Thus, we can then construct your monthly demand curve for ice cream. Figure 7.21 illustrates how diminishing marginal utility from consumption of a good can be converted to a demand curve for that good.

Constrained Utility Maximization, Two Goods

"Learn the definitions first. This will make the logic much more obvious."
—David, AP Student

Economists see a consumer, constrained by income and prices, as living within a budget constraint. In a simple case where one good is consumed, the consumer maximizes utility by buying units of good X up to the point where the marginal utility of the last unit of good X is equal to the price. Most consumers allocate limited income between many goods and services, each with a price that must be paid. To see how a consumer maximizes utility in this situation, we consider a two-good case where, in addition to daily cups of coffee, Joe also purchases scones. We start with a "rule" and then proceed to solve a couple of problems.

Figure 7.21

Utility Maximizing Rule

Given limited income, consumers maximize utility when they buy amounts of goods X and Y so that the marginal utility per dollar spent is equal for both goods. Another way to think about it is that they seek the most "bang for their bucks." Mathematically, this **utility maximizing rule** is expressed:

$$MU_x/P_x = MU_y/P_y \text{ or } MU_x/MU_y = P_x/P_y$$

If the consumer has used all income and the above ratios are equal, they are said to be in equilibrium. Under this condition, no other combination of X and Y provides more total utility.

Example:

Joe has daily income of $20, each cup of coffee costs $P_c = \$2$, and each scone costs $P_s = \$4$. Table 7.6 provides us with Joe's marginal utility received in the consumption of each good.

Table 7.6 Marginal Utility for Two Goods

CUPS OF COFFEE	MU OF COFFEE	# OF SCONES	MU OF SCONES
1	10	1	30
2	8	2	24
3	6	3	20
4	4	4	16
5	2	5	14
6	1	6	8

- It is very important to remember that consuming more of one good causes the *marginal utility* to fall, but the *total utility* to rise.

In order to maximize Joe's utility, he seeks a combination of coffee and scones so that $MU_c/\$2 = MU_s/\$4$ and spends exactly his income of $20. Another way to solve this problem is to rearrange these ratios so that:

$$MU_c/MU_s = \$2/\$4 = .5$$

There are several combinations of coffee and scones in Table 7.6 where the ratio of marginal utilities is one-half. For example, Joe could consume one cup of coffee (MU = 10) and three scones (MU = 20) for a total utility of 84 (10 + 30 + 24 + 20). But this combination would only spend a total of $14, and surely Joe would be happier if he used all of his income.

- To find the total utility of consuming cups of coffee, sum up the marginal utility of each cup consumed. Do the same for scones to calculate total utility.

Another possibility is to consume two cups of coffee (MU = 8) with four scones (MU = 16). This does indeed spend exactly $20. The total utility of 108 confirms that Joe is happier with this combination of coffee and scones. There exists one other combination of goods that satisfies our rule: four cups of coffee (MU = 4) with six scones (MU = 8) expends too much money ($32) for Joe's income.

So according to our rule, Joe's utility maximizing decision would be to use his income of $20 to consume two cups of coffee and four scones. What if he decided to experiment and reallocate his consumption while still spending only $20 on coffee and scones? For example, four cups of coffee (MU = 4) and three scones (MU = 20) fails our rule, but Joe still is spending $20. On closer inspection, this is a poor decision because total utility falls to 102.

Example:

Now the price of a cup of coffee falls to $1. Joe needs to reexamine his utility maximizing combination of coffee and scones.

$$MU_c/MU_s = \$1/\$4 = .25$$

Again, there are three possibilities, but only one uses exactly $20 of income. If Joe buys four cups of coffee (MU = 4) and four scones (MU = 16), he spends exactly his income and receives total utility of 118. The combination of three cups of coffee and two scones does not use all of the income, and the combination of five cups of coffee and six scones exceeds the income constraint.

Connection Back to Demand Curves

Joe, as a utility-maximizing consumer, chooses two cups of coffee at a price of $2 and four cups of coffee at a price of $1. This sounds familiar! What Joe has done, simply by responding in a utility-maximizing way, is illustrate the law of demand. The two combinations of price and quantity demanded are two points on Joe's coffee demand curve. By connecting these points, we trace out his demand curve (Figure 7.22).

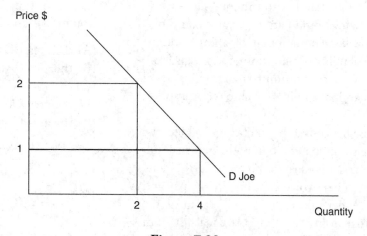

Figure 7.22

Individual and Market Demand Curves

We can take the individual decisions made by consumers like Joe and expand the analysis to build a market demand curve for coffee and other goods. This process is called **horizontal summation**. At every price, we would simply add the quantity demanded for all individual consumers.

- Utility-maximizing behavior of individuals creates individual demand curves.
- Summing the quantity demanded by individuals at each price creates market demand curves.

> Review Questions

1. If the price of corn rises 5 percent and the quantity demanded for corn falls 1 percent, then

   (A) $E_d = 5$ and demand is price elastic.
   (B) $E_d = 1/5$ and demand is price elastic.
   (C) $E_d = 5$ and demand is price inelastic.
   (D) $E_d = 1/5$ and demand is price inelastic.
   (E) $E_d = 5$ and corn is a luxury good.

2. A small business estimates price elasticity of demand for the product to be 3. To raise total revenue, owners should

   (A) decrease price as demand is elastic.
   (B) decrease price as demand is inelastic.
   (C) increase price as demand is elastic.
   (D) increase price as demand is inelastic.
   (E) do nothing; they are already maximizing total revenue.

3. Mrs. Johnson spends her entire daily budget on potato chips, at a price of $1 each, and onion dip at a price of $2 each. At her current consumption bundle, the marginal utility of chips is 12 and the marginal utility of dip is 30. Mrs. Johnson should

   (A) do nothing; she is consuming her utility-maximizing combination of chips and dip.
   (B) increase her consumption of chips until the marginal utility of chip consumption equals 30.
   (C) decrease her consumption of chips until the marginal utility of chip consumption equals 30.
   (D) decrease her consumption of chips and increase her consumption of dip until the marginal utility per dollar is equal for both goods.
   (E) increase her consumption of chips and increase her consumption of dip until the marginal utility per dollar is equal for both goods.

4. A consequence of a price floor is

   (A) a persistent shortage of the good.
   (B) an increase in total welfare.
   (C) a persistent surplus of the good.
   (D) elimination of deadweight loss.
   (E) an increase in quantity demanded and a decrease in quantity supplied.

Use the figure below to respond to the next two questions.

5. The competitive market equilibrium is at point C. If a per-unit excise tax is imposed on the production of this good, the deadweight loss is

   (A) the area BDE.
   (B) the area BADH.
   (C) the area GDH.
   (D) the area DAC.
   (E) the area GDAB.

6. The competitive market equilibrium is at point C. If a per-unit excise tax is imposed on the production of this good, the revenue collected by the government is

(A) the area BDE.
(B) the area BADH.
(C) the area GDH.
(D) the area DAC.
(E) the area GDAB.

› Answers and Explanations

1. **D**—You must know the formula for elasticity: $E_d = (\%\Delta Q_d)/(\%\Delta P) = 1/5$. Since $E_d < 1$, this is inelastic demand, and you can quickly eliminate any reference to elastic demand. Although calculators are not allowed on the AP exam, simple calculations can be made in the margins of your exam.

2. **A**—If you know your elasticity measures, you see that with $E_d = 3$, you can eliminate any reference to inelastic demand. Choice E is incorrect, as total revenue is maximized at the midpoint of the demand curve where $E_d = 1$. If $E_d > 1$, the firm increases total revenue by decreasing the price because the quantity demanded rises by a greater percentage than the fall in price.

3. **D**—Mrs. Johnson needs to find the combination of chips and dip where the ratio of marginal utility per dollar is equated. Currently, $MU_c/P_c = 12$ and $MU_d/P_d = 15$, so choice A is ruled out. Since she is receiving more "bang for her buck" from dip consumption, she increases dip consumption and therefore decreases chip consumption. MU_d falls and MU_c rises. She adjusts her spending until $MU_c/P_c = MU_d/P_d$.

4. **C**—Price floors are installed when the market equilibrium price is believed to be "too low." This price lies above the equilibrium price, decreasing Q_d and increasing Q_s, thus creating a surplus. Price controls worsen total welfare and create deadweight loss.

5. **D**—Deadweight loss is total welfare that used to be gained by society prior to the tax. When looking for deadweight loss, narrow your focus by comparing the quantity produced with and without the tax. The horizontal distance between Q_0 and Q_1 is the unattained output from the tax. The vertical distance between points D and A illustrates that MB > MC and is therefore an inefficient outcome.

6. **B**—Revenue collected by the government is equal to the per-unit tax multiplied by the new quantity. The vertical distance between supply curves is the tax.

› Rapid Review

Elasticity: Measures the sensitivity, or responsiveness, of a choice to a change in an external factor.

Price elasticity of demand (E_d): Measures the sensitivity of consumer quantity demanded for good X when the price of good X changes.

Price elasticity formula: $E_d = (\%\Delta Q_d)/(\%\Delta P)$. Ignore the negative sign.

Price elastic demand: $E_d > 1$ or the $(\%\Delta Q_d) > (\%\Delta P)$. Consumers are price sensitive.

Price inelastic demand: $E_d < 1$ or the $(\%\Delta Q_d) < (\%\Delta P)$. Consumers are not price sensitive.

Unit elastic demand: $E_d = 1$, meaning $(\%\Delta Q_d) = (\%\Delta P)$.

Perfectly inelastic: $E_d = 0$. In this special case, the demand curve is vertical and there is absolutely no response to a price change.

Perfectly elastic: $E_d = \infty$. In this special case, the demand curve is horizontal, meaning consumers have an instantaneous and infinite response to a price change.

Slope and elasticity: In general, the more vertical a good's demand curve, the more inelastic the demand for that good. The more horizontal a good's demand curve, the more elastic the demand for that good. Despite this generalization, be careful, as elasticities and slopes are *not* equivalent measures.

Determinants of elasticity: If a good has more readily available substitutes (luxuries versus necessities), it is likely that consumers are more price elastic for that good. If a high proportion of a consumer's income is devoted to a particular good, consumers are generally more price elastic for that good. When consumers have more time to adjust to a price change, their response is usually more elastic.

Total revenue: $TR = P \times Q_d$

Total revenue test: Total revenue rises with a price increase if demand is price inelastic and falls with a price increase if demand is price elastic.

Elasticity and demand curves: At the midpoint of a linear demand curve, $E_d = 1$. Above the midpoint demand is elastic and below the midpoint demand is inelastic.

Income elasticity: A measure of how sensitive consumption of good X is to a change in the consumer's income.

Income elasticity formula: $E_I = (\%\Delta Q_d \text{ good X})/(\%\Delta \text{ income})$

Luxury: A good for which the income elasticity is greater than one.

Necessity: A good for which the income elasticity is above zero but less than one.

Values of Income Elasticity: If $E_I > 1$, the good is normal and a luxury. If $1 > E_I > 0$, the good is normal and income inelastic (necessity). If $E_I < 0$, the good is inferior.

Cross-price elasticity of demand: A measure of how sensitive consumption of good X is to a change in the price of good Y.

Cross-price elasticity formula: $E_{x,y} = (\%\Delta Q_d \text{ good X})/(\%\Delta \text{ price Y})$

Values of cross-price elasticity of demand: If $E_{x,y} > 0$, goods X and Y are substitutes. If $E_{x,y} < 0$, goods X and Y are complementary.

Price elasticity of supply: Measures the sensitivity of quantity supplied for good X when the price of good X changes.

Price elasticity of supply formula: $E_s = (\%\Delta Q_s)/(\%\Delta P)$

Excise tax: A per-unit tax on production results in a vertical shift upward in the supply curve by the amount of the tax.

Incidence of Tax: The proportion of the tax paid by consumers in the form of a higher price for the taxed good is greater if demand for the good is inelastic and supply is elastic.

Deadweight Loss: The lost net benefit to society caused by a movement away from the competitive market equilibrium. Policies like excise taxes, subsidies, and price controls create lost welfare to society.

Subsidy: Has the opposite effect of an excise tax, as it has the effect of lowering the marginal cost of production, resulting in a downward vertical shift in the supply curve for good X.

Price floor: A legal minimum price below which the product cannot be sold. If a floor is installed at some level above the equilibrium price, it creates a permanent surplus.

Price ceiling: A legal maximum price above which the product cannot be sold. If a ceiling is installed at a level below the equilibrium price, it creates a permanent shortage.

Utility: Happiness, benefit, satisfaction, or enjoyment gained from consumption.

Total utility: Total happiness received from consumption of a number of units of a good.

Marginal utility: The incremental happiness received, or lost, when the consumer increases consumption of a good by one unit.

Utils: A unit of measurement often used to quantify utility. Also known as "happy points."

Law of diminishing marginal utility: In a given time period, the marginal (additional) utility from consumption of more and more of that item falls.

Constrained utility maximization: For a one-good case. Constrained by prices and income, a consumer stops consuming a good when the price paid for the next unit is equal to the marginal benefit received.

Utility maximizing rule: The consumer maximizes utility when they choose amounts of goods X and Y, with their limited income, so that the marginal utility per dollar spent is equal for both goods. Mathematically: $MU_x/P_x = MU_y/P_y$, or $MU_x/MU_y = P_x/P_y$.

Horizontal summation: The process of adding, at each price, the individual quantities demanded to find the market demand curve for a good.

Revenue tariff: An excise tax levied on goods not produced in the domestic market.

Protective tariff: An excise tax levied on a good that is produced in the domestic market so that it may be protected from foreign competition.

Import quota: A limitation on the amount of a good that can be imported into the domestic market.

CHAPTER > 8

The Firm, Profit, and the Costs of Production

IN THIS CHAPTER

Summary: The previous chapter focused on the choices made by consumers and how external forces and microeconomic policies affected those choices. The chapter concluded with the concept of constrained utility maximization and the utility maximizing rule. Also known as the consumer's equilibrium, this concept goes a long way toward explaining demand for goods and services. This chapter examines the same ideas for firms, who are assumed to maximize profit by hiring the perfect combination of production inputs at the lowest cost. First the firm is introduced, along with the importance of opportunity costs and the economic view of profits. Then the short-run production function and several principles that flow from production are introduced. The discussion then turns to the short-run costs of employing inputs and important principles associated with costs. In particular, these concepts provide the foundation for the supply curve. Lastly, the analysis is extended into the long run.

KEY IDEA

Key Ideas
- ✪ Economic Profit
- ✪ Short Run Versus Long Run
- ✪ Production in the Short Run
- ✪ Law of Diminishing Marginal Returns
- ✪ Costs in the Short Run
- ✪ Costs in the Long Run

8.1 Firms, Opportunity Costs, and Profits

Main Topics: *The Firm, Profit and Cost: When CPAs and Economists Collide, Short-Run and Long-Run Decisions*

The Firm

When we talk about consumers, it's very easy to imagine yourself in the leading role. However, when the conversation switches to the firm, it is often much more difficult to visualize what it is or who we are talking about. The firm can bring to mind many things to many different people. The firm can be an independent bookstore in your town, or it can be Barnes & Noble. It can be a street vendor selling hot dogs, or it can be Oscar Mayer. Regardless of the size of the business, a **firm** is defined as: "An organization that employs factors of production to produce a good or service that it hopes to profitably sell."

Profit and Cost: When CPAs and Economists Collide

Before we launch into a technical discussion of production and costs, we need to take care of, well, a technicality. The bottom line is that the accountant sees profit differently than does the economist.

Example:

Upon completion of her undergraduate double major in accounting and economics, Molly creates a firm that sells lemonade on a busy street corner in her small town. Selling cups of lemonade at $1 each, Molly sells 1,000 cups per month. The accountant and the economist in her agree (imagine a little devil and little angel on each shoulder—you can decide which is the CPA) that monthly total revenues (TR) = $1 × 1,000 cups = $1,000.

Molly's accounting textbooks clearly state that profit (π) is calculated by subtracting total production costs (TC) from total revenue. She rents a table from her parents at $75 per month; spends $300 per month on lemons, sugar, and cups; and purchases a monthly vendor's license at $25. These direct, purchased, out-of-pocket costs are referred to as accounting costs, or the firm's **explicit costs**.

$$\text{Accounting } \pi = \text{TR} - \text{explicit costs} = \$1,000 - 75 - 300 - 25$$
$$= \$600, \text{ a tidy profit!}$$

The economist on Molly's other shoulder disagrees. Are these the only costs of running the lemonade stand? What about the opportunity costs of resources not accounted for above? For example, Molly has chosen to give up a monthly salary of $1,000 at a bank. The economist knows that this opportunity cost must be subtracted from total revenue to better measure profitability. These indirect, nonpurchased, opportunity costs are called economic costs, or the firm's **implicit costs**.

$$\text{Economic } \pi = \text{TR} - \text{explicit costs} - \text{implicit costs} = \$1,000 - 75 - 300 - 25 - 1,000$$
$$= -\$400, \text{ a painful loss!}$$

Other implicit costs borne by many entrepreneurs include the interest given up when savings are liquidated, or rent forgone if the individual works out of a home or garage. Here's one way to try to keep the firm's explicit and implicit costs straight:

- Were the dollars paid to outside resource suppliers (employees, a landlord, a wholesale food store)? Did money actually change hands? **Explicit.**
- Were the resources supplied by the entrepreneur herself (salary or interest given up)? **Implicit.**

So Which Should I Use?

This is an excellent question. The "quickie" answer is to turn to the title page of this book, and use that method. Of course, as a student of economics, you must include implicit economic costs in calculating economic profit. But why? Well, it's more accurate. An adept student of economics knows that the cost of something goes beyond the price tag. A friend of mine in graduate school once said that "nothing is free; it is just nonpriced." If you visit your AP teacher's office, you might not have to pay to pass through the door, but you could be doing something else with your time. This is a nonpriced economic cost. Molly's labor and effort at the lemonade stand appear to be free; this is why an accountant does not include that effort in calculating profit. An economist knows that it is not free—it is just nonpriced. An economist tries to quantify that price by using the value of Molly's efforts in her next best alternative as the banker. Throughout this book, costs refer to economic costs, and profits refer to economic profits.

Short-Run and Long-Run Decisions

The short run is a time when at least one production input is fixed and cannot be changed to respond to a change in product demand. During the holiday season a local gift shop extends hours and increases the workers hired. Much more difficult to change is the total capacity of the shop. The capacity of the shop is fixed in the short run but can be altered with enough time. The amount of time required to change the plant size is known as the **long run**. In other words, all inputs are variable in the long run. See Table 8.1.

Table 8.1

	PLANT SIZE (CAPITAL)	FIXED COSTS	VARIABLE COSTS	ENTRY/EXIT OF FIRMS
Short Run	Fixed	Some	Some	No
Long Run	Variable	None	All	Yes

Example:

When Molly pays $25 for a monthly vendor's license on January 1, she is committed for a month. She cannot receive a refund if she fails to operate the lemonade stand, and she does not have to pay more if she works 24 hours a day all month. For Molly, the long run is one month. On the other hand, at any point in the month, Molly can choose to purchase more lemons, cups, or sugar, or employ assistants if she is selling more cups of lemonade. This is a short-run decision.

8.2 Production and Cost

Main Topics: Short-Run Production Functions, Law of Diminishing Marginal Returns, Short-Run Costs, Bridge over (Troubling) Economic Waters, Long-Run Costs, Economies of Scale

Short-Run Production Functions

How do economic resources like labor, capital, natural resources, and entrepreneurial talent become a cup of lemonade, or a ton of copper, or a 30-second television commercial? A **production function** is the mechanism for combining production resources with existing technology into finished goods and services. In other words, a production function takes inputs and creates output. In a production function that uses only labor (L) and capital (K):

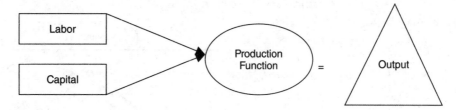

Fixed and Variable Inputs

The short run is a period of time too brief to change the plant capacity. This implies that some production inputs cannot be changed in the short run. These are **fixed inputs**. During the short run, firms can adjust production to meet changes in demand for their output. This implies that some inputs are **variable inputs**. Using only labor and capital, we assume that labor can be changed in the short run, but capital (i.e., the plant capacity) is fixed.

Short-Run Production Measures

By its very nature, production lends itself to be quantified, and as a result, you need to study these three production measures. To keep it simple, capital is assumed to be fixed while labor can be changed to produce more or less output.

1. **Total product of labor (TP_L)** is the total quantity, or total output, of a good produced at each quantity of labor employed.

2. **Marginal product of labor (MP_L)** is the change in total product resulting from a change in the labor input. $MP_L = \Delta TP_L/\Delta L$. If labor is changing one unit at a time, $MP_L = \Delta TP_L$.

3. **Average product of labor (AP_L)** is also a measure of average labor productivity and is total product divided by the amount of labor employed: $AP_L = TP_L/L$.

As you can see, MP_L and AP_L are both derived from TP_L. It is useful to see how these three measures are related with a numerical example.

Example:

In the production period of a month, Molly's lemonade stand combines variable inputs of her labor (and the raw materials) to the fixed inputs of her table and her license to operate. Molly adds employees to her stand (or we could call it the plant) and forecasts the change in production (cups per day) in Table 8.2.

Table 8.2

UNITS OF LABOR	TOTAL PRODUCT (TP_L)	MARGINAL PRODUCT (MP_L)	AVERAGE PRODUCT (AP_L)
0	0 cups		
1	5	5−0 = 5	5/1 = 5
2	15	10	7.5
3	30	15	10
4	40	10	10
5	45	5	9
6	40	−5	6.67
7	30	−10	4.29

As Molly employs more workers to the fixed plant capacity (the table on the corner), total product increases, eventually peaks, and then begins to fall. This production function can be seen in Figure 8.1.

Figure 8.1

Law of Diminishing Marginal Returns

"An important principle to know and understand."
—AP Teacher

Imagine what happens to the lemonade stand as Molly adds more and more workers. At first, tasks are divided. (For example, Josh squeezes the lemons; Molly adds the sugar; Kelli stirs.) Specialization occurs. The marginal productivity of successive workers is rising in the early stage of production, but at some point, adding more workers increases the total product by a lesser amount. Maybe the fourth worker is pouring the lemonade and stocking while the fifth is taking money and making change. Beyond the fifth worker, the table is too crowded with employees, cups are spilled, product is wasted, and total production actually falls. The marginal contribution of these workers is negative. This illustrates one of the most important production concepts in the short run, the **law of diminishing marginal returns**, which states that *as successive units of a variable resource are added to a fixed resource, beyond some point the marginal product falls.*

- Increasing marginal returns: MP_L increases as L increases.
- Diminishing marginal returns: MP_L decreases as L increases.
- Negative marginal returns: MP_L becomes negative as L increases.

Graphically Speaking

Marginal product is the incremental change in total product as one more unit of labor is added. Marginal product is the geometric slope of total product. In Figure 8.1, the total product curve is initially getting steeper as more labor is added. This is seen in Figure 8.2 as increasing marginal product. From the third to the fifth worker, the slope of total product is still positive, but it is becoming less steep. In Figure 8.2, marginal product from workers 3 to 5 is still positive but is falling. Beyond the fifth worker, total product is falling and thus has a negative slope. This turn of events is seen below when marginal product becomes negative.

Average product, also plotted below, initially rises, reaches a peak, and then begins to fall. So long as the marginal (next) worker adds production that is above the current average, they are pulling the average up. This is why we see AP_L rising so long as MP_L is above AP_L. If the marginal worker adds production that is below the current average, the worker pulls the average down. Thus, when MP_L is below AP_L, you see that AP_L is falling. Logically then, MP_L intersects AP_L at the peak of AP_L. Average product cannot be negative.

- If $MP_L > AP_L$: AP_L is rising.
- If $MP_L < AP_L$: AP_L is falling.
- If $MP_L = AP_L$: AP_L is at the peak.

Figure 8.2

Short-Run Costs

It is important to note that we have discussed production theory without including the nagging necessity of paying for our hired inputs. For every employed input, fixed or variable, a cost is incurred.

Total Costs

In the short run, there is at least one input that is fixed and so these costs are also fixed. All inputs that are variable incur variable costs.

1. **Total fixed costs (TFC)** are those costs that do not vary with changes in short-run output. They must be paid even when output is zero. These include rent on building or equipment, insurance, or licenses.

2. **Total variable costs (TVC)** are those costs that change with the level of output. If output is zero, so are total variable costs. They include payment for materials, fuel, power, transportation services, most labor, and similar costs.

3. **Total cost (TC)** is the sum of total fixed and total variable costs at each level of output:

$$TC = TVC + TFC$$

Table 8.3

TOTAL PRODUCT CUPS PER MINUTE	TOTAL FIXED COST (TFC)	TOTAL VARIABLE COST (TVC)	TOTAL COST (TC = TFC + TVC)
0	$6	$0	$6
1	$6	$5	$11
2	$6	$8	$14
3	$6	$13	$19
4	$6	$19	$25
5	$6	$26	$32
6	$6	$34	$40
7	$6	$43	$49

Figure 8.3

Table 8.3 summarizes Molly's costs of producing cups of lemonade per minute. Her total fixed costs are assumed to be $6 per minute, and total variable costs increase as production increases.

Figure 8.3 illustrates the three total cost functions. Total fixed cost is a constant at all levels of output. Total variable cost quickly rises at first, briefly slows, and then proceeds to increase at an increasing rate. Total cost is simply the sum of TFC and TVC at every level of output, and so it lies parallel to TVC. Thus, the vertical distance between TC and TVC is equal to TFC.

Table 8.4

TOTAL PRODUCT CUPS PER MINUTE	MARGINAL COST (MC)	AVERAGE FIXED COST (AFC)	AVERAGE VARIABLE COST (AVC)	AVERAGE TOTAL COST (ATC)
0				
1	$5	$6.00	$5.00	$11.00
2	$3	$3.00	$4.00	$7.00
3	$5	$2.00	$4.33	$6.33
4	$6	$1.50	$4.75	$6.25
5	$7	$1.20	$5.20	$6.40
6	$8	$1.00	$5.67	$6.67
7	$9	$0.86	$6.14	$7.00

Marginal and Average Costs

Similar to our discussion of production, we can derive marginal and per-unit measures of cost from the total cost functions. These are in Table 8.4.

1. **Marginal cost** is the additional cost of producing one more unit of output $MC = \Delta TC/\Delta Q$. Since TVCs are the only costs that change with the level of output, marginal cost is also calculated as $MC = \Delta TVC/\Delta Q$. If quantity is changing one unit at a time, $MC = \Delta TC = \Delta TVC$.

2. **Average fixed cost (AFC)** is total fixed cost divided by output: $AFC = TFC/Q$. It continuously falls as output rises.

3. **Average variable cost (AVC)** is total variable cost divided by output: AVC = TVC/*Q*.

4. **Average total cost (ATC)** is total cost divided by output ATC = TC/*Q*. Note that ATC = AFC + AVC.

Graphically Speaking

"It's all about the graphs . . . if you can see it, you got it." —Cleo, AP Student

If marginal product is the slope of total product, it should be no surprise that marginal cost is the slope of total cost, or total variable cost. We can see that marginal cost initially falls due to specialization but soon begins to rise as more output is produced. This is the law of increasing costs and is a direct result of the law of diminishing marginal returns to production. Both being U-shaped curves, average variable and average total costs initially fall, hit a minimum point, and begin to rise. Average total cost is vertically above AVC by the amount of AFC. Figure 8.4 illustrates this.

Marginal cost and average variable and average total cost are related in much the same way as marginal product is related to average product of labor. When the marginal cost of producing another cup of lemonade exceeds the current average cost, the average is rising. When the marginal cost of producing another cup of lemonade falls below the current average cost, the average is falling. Therefore, marginal cost equals average total cost at the minimum of ATC and equals average variable cost at the minimum of AVC.

When drawing a graph similar to the one in Figure 8.4, it is important that you show an upward-sloping MC curve intersecting AVC and ATC at the *minimum* of those U-shaped curves. You can lose free-response points for sloppy graphs that show MC intersecting AVC and ATC at a point that is not *clearly* the minimum point, or bottom of the U-shaped curves.

Figure 8.4

Here are three easy steps to drawing a clean graph that avoids any lost graphing points:

- Draw the upward-sloping curve and label it MC.
- Draw a downward-sloping curve that stops at the MC curve. Lift your pen from the paper. Trust me, if you try to draw the U in one smooth movement, you are more likely to lose this point.
- Beginning at the point where your downward-sloping curve intersects MC, draw an upward-sloping curve to complete the U-shaped ATC curve. You can repeat these steps to draw the AVC curve that lies below the ATC curve.

The mathematical relationship between total costs and per-unit (or average) costs is rather straightforward: divide the total dollars of cost by the output produced, and you get average dollars spent on a unit of output. These relationships can also be seen in a graph similar to the one in Figure 8.4, and recent free-response questions have tested these relationships by asking students to use an average-cost graph like the one in Figure 8.5 to identify a total cost concept.

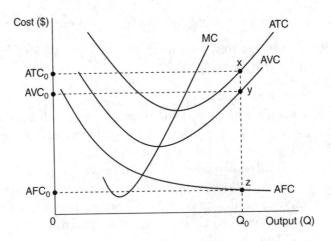

Figure 8.5

Suppose the firm is producing Q_0 units of output. How can we determine total cost (TC_0), total variable cost (TVC_0), and total fixed cost (TFC_0) from the information in Figure 8.5? Let's take the relationship between ATC and TC as an example. Remember that average total cost is computed as

$$ATC_0 = TC_0/Q_0$$

so $TC_0 = ATC_0 \times Q_0$. In Figure 8.5, TC_0 is the area of a rectangle with a width of Q_0 units and a height of ATC_0. Using the notation in the graph, this area would be identified by the area $0ATC_0xQ_0$. In a similar way, the TVC_0 would be identified by the area $0AVC_0yQ_0$, and TFC_0 by the area $0AFC_0zQ_0$.

If you know the relationships between total and per-unit costs, and you can identify the area in a graph like Figure 8.5, you are prepared to earn some valuable free-response points.

Bridge over (Troubling) Economic Waters

Many students think that production and cost concepts are two sets of theoretical topics. This separation creates the impression that "there's twice as much to remember." These students are surprised to find out that production and cost are closely connected.

Think about it from Molly's point of view. If the next worker employed has a high marginal product, then the marginal cost of producing that increased product must be quite low. When things are going well with production, they must be going well with cost. Try to see the concepts of production and cost not as two isolated bodies of theory but as two related sets of concepts that just need to be bridged. Let us try to build this bridge with a little algebra.

Marginal Product and Marginal Cost

$MC = \Delta TVC/\Delta Q$, and since the only variable input is labor being paid a fixed wage w,
$MC = w\Delta L/\Delta Q$ which can be modified as,
$MC = w/(\Delta Q/\Delta L) = w/MP_L$. MC and MP_L are inverses of each other!

- As MP_L is falling (diminishing marginal returns), MC is rising.
- As MP_L is rising (increasing marginal returns), MC is falling.
- When MP_L is highest, MC is lowest.

Average Product and Average Variable Cost

$AVC = TVC/Q$ and with the only variable input being labor paid a fixed wage w,
$AVC = wL/Q$ which can be modified as,
$AVC = w/(Q/L) = w/AP_L$. AVC and AP_L are inverses of each other!

Figure 8.6

Figure 8.7

- As AP_L is falling, AVC is rising.
- As AP_L is rising, AVC is falling.
- When AP_L is highest, AVC is lowest.

If we put smoother versions of our production and cost figures together, we can see these relationships in Figures 8.6 and 8.7.

Long-Run Costs

Since all inputs are variable in the long run, discussion of production levels isn't so much about output per hour or day; it's more a question of plant size or capacity. In the short run, the firm asks, "With our current plant size, how much must we produce today?" The long run is long enough to adjust the plant capacity, so the issue is really one of scale. The firm might ask itself, "At what scale do we want to operate?"

Long-Run Average Cost

I like to think of the firm's short-run average costs as a snapshot of the firm's ability to produce efficiently *at the fixed plant size*. Over time, the firm may grow and expand the plant size and begin to produce efficiently, but at the larger fixed plant size, giving us another snapshot. This process repeats itself as the firm expands or contracts and each time we receive another short-run snapshot of average cost. If we could put these short-run snapshots together into a kind of motion picture, we would see a more continuous long-run home movie of the firm's average costs. The example and Figure 8.8 illustrate the connection between short- and long-run average costs.

> "Make sure you know the definition for the Law of Diminishing Marginal Returns. It could appear in lots of different questions."
> —Cassie, AP Student

> "Make sure you can differentiate between long-run and short-run curves." —Kristy, AP Student

Example:

- In year one, Molly's firm operates at a "small" scale, producing on $SRAC_1$.
- In year two, Molly could expand and operate at a "medium" scale, producing on $SRAC_2$, but only if she can sell more than 100 gallons of lemonade. At quantities below 100, $SRAC_1 < SRAC_2$, so expansion would not be wise.
- In year three, Molly might expand to operate at a "large" scale and move to $SRAC_3$, but only if she can sell more than 250 gallons.
- Beyond the "large" scale exists a "grand" scale, but very quickly $SRAC_4 > SRAC_3$ and so this plant capacity actually begins to incur rising per-unit costs.

Each of these four short-run snapshots of average costs can be smoothed out into the home movie long-run average cost curve, which is composed of sections of each short-run average cost curve at each of the four plant sizes that Molly might choose for her firm. In Figure 8.8, the long-run average cost curve would lie along the segments a→b→c→d→e.

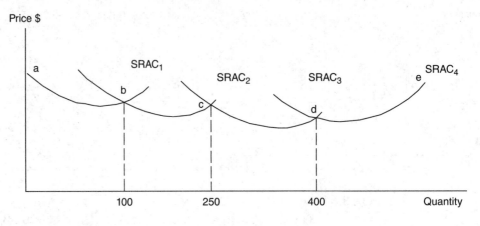

Figure 8.8

Economies of Scale

Construction of a smoother version of Figure 8.8 allows us to see more easily some important stages of the long-run average cost curves (Figure 8.9).

1. **Economies of scale** are advantages of increased plant size and are seen on the downward part of the LRAC curve. LRAC falls as plant size rises.
   a. Labor and managerial specialization is one reason for this.
   b. Ability to purchase and use more efficient capital goods also can explain economies of scale.
   c. The plant size that marks the lowest point on the long-run average cost curve is called **minimum efficient scale**. Because minimum efficient scale is associated with small per-unit costs, firms will do their best to expand the plant size to that level of output, and this has a big role in shaping what the industry looks like. If the minimum efficient scale represents a small plant size, the industry is likely to be populated with many small firms. However, if the minimum efficient scale represents a giant-sized firm, the industry almost assuredly includes just a small number of enormous companies.

2. **Constant returns to scale** can occur when LRAC is constant over a variety of plant sizes.

3. **Diseconomies of scale** are illustrated by the rising part of the LRAC curve and can occur if a firm becomes too large.
   a. Some reasons for this include distant management, worker alienation, and problems with communication and coordination.

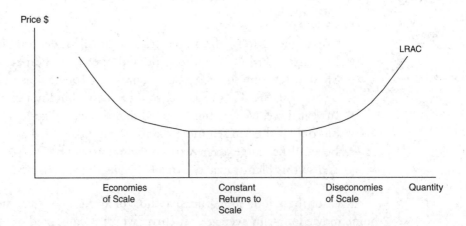

Figure 8.9

Another Bridge between Production and Cost

You might be thinking, "I've heard about scale economies, but my teacher was talking about production, not cost. I'm so confused!" You're right; it can be confusing when similar-sounding economic phrases are tossed around in seemingly different contexts. If you remember the "bridge" between costs and production, you might recall that when something is happening with regard to cost, a similar thing is happening in the production realm. They are very much connected in both the short run and the long run. Let's look at a quick example.

Remember that, in the long run, the firm can adjust all inputs to produce more or less output. Let's suppose that the firm initially has one unit of both labor (L) and capital (K), these inputs are producing one unit of output (Q), and the price of labor and capital is $1 each. With these input prices, the firm is spending a total of $2 ($1 for labor plus $1 for capital) in total cost (TC) and the average total cost (ATC) is also $2 (TC/Q). This is summarized in the first row of Table 8.5.

Table 8.5

QUANTITY OF LABOR (L)	QUANTITY OF CAPITAL (K)	OUTPUT PRODUCED (Q)	TOTAL COST (TC)	LONG-RUN AVERAGE TOTAL COST (LRAC) = TC/Q
1	1	1	$2	$2
2	2	4	$4	$1
4	4	8	$8	$1
8	8	12	$16	$1.33

In the second row of Table 8.5, let's see what happens if the firm doubles both labor and capital in the long run, and the output more than doubles (increases from one to four units). When this happens in the production function, the firm is said to experience **increasing returns to scale**. And notice what happens to long-run average total cost; it falls. This tells us that if the firm is experiencing increasing returns to scale in production (a good thing), they are also experiencing economies of scale in costs (also a good thing).

If we double our inputs again, and output exactly doubles, it is said that the firm has **constant returns to scale** in production. In this case, long-run average total costs remain at $1, and this is also described as constant returns to scale in costs. This is seen as the horizontal region of the LRAC curve.

Finally, if we double our inputs one last time, and output increases by less than double (not a desired outcome), we say that the firm has **decreasing returns to scale** in production. When this happens, the long-run average total costs increase to $1.33. Once again we see that if something bad is happening in production, something undesirable is happening with long-run average costs; they are rising.

Table 8.6 summarizes these long-run production and cost concepts in a way that might help you see that they are not really different.

Table 8.6

WHEN ALL INPUTS ARE DOUBLED AND...	OUTPUT INCREASES BY...	WE CALL THIS...	AT THE SAME TIME, LRAC IS...	AND WE CALL THIS...
More than double	Increasing returns to production	falling	Economies of scale
Exactly double	Constant returns to scale in production	horizontal	Constant returns to scale
Less than double	Decreasing returns to scale in production	rising	Diseconomies of scale

❭ Review Questions

1. Which of the following is most likely an example of production inputs that can be adjusted in the long run, but not in the short run?

   (A) Amount of wood used to make a desk.
   (B) Number of pickles put on a sandwich.
   (C) The size of a McDonald's kitchen.
   (D) Number of teachers' assistants in local high schools.
   (E) The amount of electricity consumed by a manufacturing plant.

2. The law of diminishing marginal returns is responsible for

   (A) AVC that first rises, but eventually falls, as output increases.
   (B) AFC that first rises, but eventually falls, as output increases.
   (C) MP that first falls, but eventually rises, as output increases.
   (D) MC that first falls, but eventually rises, as output increases.
   (E) ATC that first rises, but eventually falls, as output increases.

3. Which of the following cost and production relationships is inaccurately stated?

   (A) $AFC = AVC - ATC$
   (B) $MC = \Delta TVC / \Delta Q$
   (C) $TVC = TC - TFC$
   (D) $AP_L = TP_L / L$
   (E) $MC = w / MP_L$

4. If the per-unit price of labor, a variable resource, increases, it causes which of the following?

   (A) An upward shift in AFC.
   (B) An upward shift in MP_L.
   (C) A downward shift in ATC.
   (D) An upward shift in MC.
   (E) A downward shift in AFC.

Use the following figure to respond to questions 5 and 6.

5. The curves labeled W, X, Y, Z refer to which respective cost functions?

   (A) MC, AVC, ATC, and AFC.
   (B) MC, TC, TVC, and AFC.
   (C) MC, ATC, AVC, and AFC.
   (D) MC, ATC, AVC, and TFC.
   (E) ATC, AVC, AFC, and MC.

6. At the q_3 level of output,

   (A) $AFC = \$d_2 - \$d_1$.
   (B) $MC = \$d_2$.
   (C) $TVC = \$d_2$.
   (D) $ATC = \$d_3$.
   (E) $AFC = \$d_3 - \$d_2$.

❭ Answers and Explanations

1. **C**—The short run is a period of time too short to increase the plant size. All other choices involve decisions that could increase production almost immediately, with no change in the size of the facility. Increasing the size of a McDonald's kitchen takes quite some time and represents an increase in the total capacity of the kitchen to produce.

2. **D**—The law of diminishing marginal returns says that MP_L eventually falls as you add more labor to a fixed plant. This question tests you on the important connection between production and cost. Remember that we derived this "bridge" and found that $MC = w / MP_L$. So when MP_L is initially rising, MC is falling. Eventually when MP_L is falling, MC is rising. Choices A, B, and E are just flat wrong. All three average costs begin by falling. AFC continues to fall, but AVC and ATC eventually rise.

3. **A**—AFC plus AVC equals ATC. If you do the subtraction, AFC = ATC − AVC, making choice A the only incorrect statement. If you have studied your production and cost relationships, you recognize that choices B, C, D, and E are all stated correctly.

4. **D**—When labor is more expensive, the MC of producing the good increases, so the MC curve shifts upward. The price of a variable input has increased, so easily rule out any reference to fixed costs. Because of the inverse relationship between marginal cost and marginal product of labor, a higher wage shifts MP_L downward.

5. **C**—You must be familiar with the graphical representation of marginal and average cost functions.

6. **A**—The vertical distance between ATC and AVC is AFC at any level of output.

› Rapid Review

The firm: An organization that employs factors of production to produce a good or service that it hopes to profitably sell.

Accounting profit: The difference between total revenue and total explicit costs.

Economic profit: The difference between total revenue and total explicit and implicit costs.

Explicit costs: Direct, purchased, out-of-pocket costs paid to resource suppliers outside the firm. Also referred to as *accounting costs*.

Implicit costs: Indirect, nonpurchased, or opportunity costs of resources provided by the entrepreneur. Also called *economic costs*.

Short run: A period of time too short to change the size of the plant, but many other, more variable resources can be adjusted to meet demand.

Long run: A period of time long enough to alter the plant size. New firms can enter the industry and existing firms can liquidate and exit.

Production function: The mechanism for combining production resources, with existing technology, into finished goods and services. Inputs are turned into outputs.

Fixed inputs: Production inputs that cannot be changed in the short run. Usually this is the plant size or capital.

Variable inputs: Production inputs that the firm can adjust in the short run to meet changes in demand for their output. Often this is labor and/or raw materials.

Total Product of Labor (TP_L): The total quantity, or total output, of a good produced at each quantity of labor employed.

Marginal Product of Labor (MP_L): The change in total product resulting from a change in the labor input. $MP_L = \Delta TP_L/\Delta L$, or the slope of total product.

Average Product of Labor (AP_L): Total product divided by labor employed: $AP_L = TP_L/L$.

Law of diminishing marginal returns: As successive units of a variable resource are added to a fixed resource, beyond some point the marginal product declines.

Total fixed costs (TFC): Costs that do not vary with changes in short-run output. They must be paid even when output is zero.

Total variable costs (TVC): Costs that change with the level of output. If output is zero, so are total variable costs.

Total cost (TC): The sum of total fixed and total variable costs at each level of output: TC = TVC + TFC.

Marginal cost (MC): The additional cost of producing one more unit of output. $MC = \Delta TC/\Delta Q = \Delta TVC/\Delta Q$ or the slope of total cost and total variable cost.

Average fixed cost (AFC): Total fixed cost divided by output: $AFC = TFC/Q$.

Average variable cost (AVC): Total variable cost divided by output: $AVC = TVC/Q$.

Average total cost (ATC): Total cost divided by output. $ATC = TC/Q = AFC + AVC$.

Relationship between MP_L and MC: If labor is the variable input being paid a fixed wage (w), MC and MP_L are inverses of each other. $MC = w/(\Delta Q/\Delta L) = w/MP_L$.

Relationship between AP_L and AVC: In the simplified case where labor is the variable input being paid a fixed wage (w), AVC and AP_L are inverses of each other. $AVC = w/(Q/L) = w/AP_L$.

Economies of scale: The downward part of the LRAC curve where LRAC falls as plant size increases. This is the result of specialization, lower cost of inputs, or other efficiencies from larger scale.

Minimum efficient scale: The plant size at which the LRAC first reaches its minimum point.

Constant returns to scale: Occurs when LRAC is constant over a variety of plant sizes.

Diseconomies of scale: The upward part of the LRAC curve where LRAC rises as plant size increases. This is usually the result of the increased difficulty of managing larger firms, which results in lost efficiency and rising per-unit costs.

Increasing returns to scale in production: The long-run outcome when output more than doubles from a doubling of all inputs.

Constant returns to scale in production: The long-run outcome when output exactly doubles from a doubling of all inputs.

Decreasing returns to scale in production: The long-run outcome when output less than doubles from a doubling of all inputs.

CHAPTER 9

Market Structures, Perfect Competition, Monopoly, and Things Between

IN THIS CHAPTER

Summary: Chapter 7 presented the relationship between product demand, elasticity, and total revenue. Chapter 8 introduced the concept of economic profit and presented the theory behind production and costs. This chapter puts revenue and cost together to examine how a firm chooses the profit-maximizing level of output and price of the product. But this profit-maximizing decision depends very much upon the structure in which the firm operates. At one extreme there are many perfectly competitive firms, each too small to have a measurable impact on market price, much less each other. At the other extreme there is one firm, a monopolist, that absolutely controls the industry price and output. In between are various shades of each extreme, some closer to monopoly, and some closer to perfect competition. It is important to realize that there is no "representative" industry, or market structure, so we focus on four general models and study how firms in these structures determine price and output. In addition to the extremes of perfect competition and monopoly, we cover the models of monopolistic competition and oligopoly. This chapter also introduces you to some basic game theoretic models.

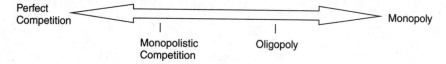

Perfect Competition — Monopolistic Competition — Oligopoly — Monopoly

Key Ideas

KEY IDEA

✪ Perfect Competition
✪ Monopoly
✪ Monopolistic Competition
✪ Oligopoly

9.1 Perfect Competition

Main Topics: *Structural Characteristics of Perfect Competition, Demand for the Firm, Profit Maximization, Short-Run Profit and Loss, Decision to Shut Down, Long-Run Adjustment*

Structural Characteristics of Perfect Competition

Each market structure is defined by structural characteristics. These characteristics determine, among other things, how the profit-maximizing price and quantity are set in the short run, as well as how profits might be maintained in the long run. Perfect competition is typically described by four characteristics:

- *Many small independent producers and consumers.* Each firm is too small to have an impact on market price. No one firm can drive up the price by restricting supply, or drive down the price by flooding the market with output. No one consumer can, by changing the amount of the good that he consumes, impact the price.
- *Firms produce a standardized product.* There exist no real differences between one firm's output and the next.
- *No barriers to entry or exit.* There exist no significant obstacles to the entry of new firms into, or the exit of existing firms out of, this industry. Profitability, or lack thereof, determines whether the industry is expanding or contracting.
- *Firms are "price takers."* This characteristic is actually a result of the first three. Because all firms are too small to affect the price, they must accept the market price and produce as much as they wish at that price. Even if they *could* change the price, they would not do so. To see this, suppose that the market determined the competitive price of barley is $5. If farmer Katie increased the price to $5.01, she would now be the high-price supplier of barley, with thousands of competitors producing an identical product at a lower price; Katie is likely to lose all of her customers. If she lowers her price to $4.99, she would seemingly clean up her competition. But, remember, the price-taking characteristic tells us that Katie can sell all she wants at the market price of $5. If you can sell all you want at $5, why would Katie sell even one unit at $4.99?

> "In order to keep the different types of firms straight, make a table including the firm's definition, what kind of product they produce, barriers, and how they control price. It is the best way to study."
> —Kristy, AP Student

All four of the characteristics of perfect competition are rarely found in today's industries, but agricultural commodities are usually regarded as approximately perfectly competitive.

Demand for the Firm

Each perfectly competitive firm produces a standardized, or homogenous, product. Because each firm's output is such a small share of the total market supply, the demand for each firm's output is perfectly elastic. Perfectly competitive firms have no effect on the market price; they simply produce as much as they can at the going price. This implies a horizontal demand curve for their product. This does *not* imply that the market demand curve is

Figure 9.1

horizontal. If the market price of barley falls, quantity demanded rises. Figure 9.1 illustrates the difference between market demand (D) and the demand for one firm's product (d).

Profit Maximization

Let's get one thing straight. When we say firms *maximize* economic profit, this means they are not going to settle for anything less than the highest possible difference between total revenue and total economic cost. If an additional dollar of profit is to be earned, they take that opportunity. If the maximum profit possible is actually zero, or even negative dollars, they accept this short-run outcome. There are two equivalent ways to maximize economic profit.

The Method of "Totals"
The perfectly competitive firm cannot change the price; it can only adjust output. To maximize profit, the firm selects the output to maximize:

Economic profit (π) = Total revenue − Total economic cost

An example should help to illustrate how a firm goes about maximizing profit.

Example:
A carrot farmer operates in a perfectly competitive market. The going price for a bushel of carrots is $11. Table 9.1 summarizes how total revenue, total cost, and profit differ at various levels of output. Because it is the short run, there exist $16 of fixed costs. All costs reflect the explicit and implicit costs of hiring a resource.

Table 9.1

DAILY BUSHELS OF CARROTS (q)	PRICE (P)	TOTAL REVENUE (TR)	TOTAL COST (TC)	PROFIT (π)
0	$11	$0	$16	−$16
1	$11	$11	$22	−$11
2	$11	$22	$27.50	−$5.50
3	$11	$33	$34	−$1
4	$11	$44	$42	$2
5	$11	$55	$53	$2
6	$11	$66	$65	$1

Because the firm is a price taker, the level of output does not affect the going price. Total costs rise as production increases, a concept seen in the previous chapter. As a profit maximizer, our carrot farmer would choose to produce five bushels per day and earn $2 in daily economic profit. Note, when there are two quantities that produce the same amount of profit, like four and five bushels, we select the larger of the two quantities. This method of profit maximization is much like trial and error and is a bit cumbersome. Let's explore an equivalent and easier way.

The Method of "Marginals"
Throughout this book we have seen illustrations of marginal analysis, and this situation is no different. You'll recall that rational decision making implies the following:

- If MB > MC, do more of it.
- If MB < MC, do less of it.
- If MB = MC, stop here.

Since the only decision to be made by the perfectly competitive firm is to choose the optimal level of output, the firm's rule is as follows:

- **Choose the level of output where MR = MC.**

Table 9.2 can be modified to show the marginal revenue and marginal cost of selling additional bushels of carrots.

Table 9.2

DAILY BUSHELS OF CARROTS (q)	PRICE (P)	TOTAL REVENUE (TR)	TOTAL COST (TC)	PROFIT (o)	MARGINAL REVENUE (MR)	MARGINAL COST (MC)
0	$11	$0	$16	−$16		
1	$11	$11	$22	−$11	$11	$6
2	$11	$22	$27.50	−$5.50	$11	$5.50
3	$11	$33	$34	−$1	$11	$6.50
4	$11	$44	$42	$2	$11	$8
5	$11	$55	$53	$2	$11	$11
6	$11	$66	$65	$1	$11	$12

Notice that in perfect competition, the price is equal to marginal revenue. This is fairly simple if you recall the assumptions of the model. Farmers can sell as much as they want at the market price. If a farmer sells one more bushel, total revenue increases by the price of the bushel, $11 in this case. Sell another bushel; earn another marginal revenue of $11. Price is also equivalent to **average revenue** (AR), or total revenue per unit. These relationships can be seen in Figure 9.2.

- $MR = \Delta TR/\Delta Q = P \times \Delta Q/\Delta Q = P$
- $AR = TR/Q = P \times Q/Q = P$
- $P = MR = AR$ = Demand for the firm's product
- Total revenue ($P \times q$) equal to $55 can be seen as the area of the rectangle with a height of $P = \$11$ and width of $q_e = 5$.

Figure 9.2

Short-Run Profit and Loss

To maximize profit, the firm must choose the level of output (q_e) where MR = MC. But how can we use Figure 9.2 to identify these profits? A little algebra goes a long way.

π = TR − TC = $P \times q_e$ − TC. If you divide both terms by quantity and remember that TC/q = Average total cost (ATC), you have

$$\pi = q_e \times (P - \text{ATC})$$

The term (P − ATC) is the per-unit difference between what the firm receives from the sale of each unit and the average cost of producing it, or profit per unit. When you multiply this per-unit profit by the number of units (q_e) produced, you have total profit. Table 9.3 and Figure 9.3 incorporate the ATC into our carrot farmer's profit-maximizing decision table.

Table 9.3

DAILY BUSHELS OF CARROTS (q)	PRICE (P)	TOTAL COST (TC)	AVERAGE TOTAL COST (ATC)	(P − ATC)	PROFIT (Π) = q × (P − ATC)
0	$11	$16			−$16
1	$11	$22	$22	−$11	−$11
2	$11	$27.50	$13.75	−$2.75	−$5.50
3	$11	$34	$11.33	−$.33	−$1
4	$11	$42	$10.50	$.50	$2
5	$11	$53	$10.60	$.40	$2
6	$11	$65	$10.83	$.17	$1

Profit Rectangles and Flying Monkeys

Everyone remembers *The Wizard of Oz* and the critical instructions that the people of Munchkinland gave Dorothy and Toto as they set off to find the Wizard: "Follow the yellow brick road." And when Dorothy, Toto, and friends stayed on the yellow brick road,

Figure 9.3

they were fine. Whenever they ignored these cautionary words and left the yellow brick road, bad things happened—the scariest being the arrival of the flying monkeys. The flying monkeys tore the Scarecrow limb from limb and set the Scarecrow's straw innards on fire. Very bad things happen when you leave the yellow brick road.

When you find the profit-maximizing level of production, q_e, you are locating the yellow brick road for this firm. *Never* leave this level of output or bad things happen. Finding q_e is the first step in calculating profit with a "profit rectangle." The area of the shaded rectangle is 5 bushels wide, multiplied by 40 cents high. In our case, the price $11 in Figure 9.3 is above the average total cost $10.60, so we have positive economic profits of $2. This does not always occur in the short run. Another look at our per-unit equation tells us:

- If $P >$ ATC, $\pi > 0$.
- If $P <$ ATC, $\pi < 0$.
- If $P =$ ATC, $\pi = 0$.

Short-Run Losses

While firms would love to maintain the above scenario where $P >$ ATC and positive economic profits are made, it might not always turn out that way. Due to a failure of the Bugs Bunny diet fad, the market for carrots suffers a dramatic decrease in demand. Plummeting demand decreases the market price to $6.50 per bushel, and firms must readjust their profit-maximizing output decision.

As seen in Table 9.4, at the much lower price of $6.50, the firm now finds that MR = MC at an output of three bushels per day. Not surprisingly, the opportunity for positive economic profit has been eliminated. The profit-maximizing, or loss-minimizing, output of three bushels provides the best possible scenario for the firm; but that scenario involves economic losses of $14.50. The rectangle can still be seen in Figure 9.4, where average total cost is $11.33 per bushel.

Table 9.4

DAILY BUSHELS OF CARROTS (Q)	PRICE (P)	TOTAL REVENUE (TR)	TOTAL COST (TC)	PROFIT (π)	MARGINAL REVENUE (MR)	MARGINAL COST (MC)
0	$6.50	$0	$16	−$16		
1	$6.50	$6.50	$22	−$15.50	$6.50	$6
2	$6.50	$13	$27.50	−$14.50	$6.50	$5.50
3	*$6.50*	*$19.50*	*$34*	*−$14.50*	*$6.50*	*$6.50*
4	$6.50	$26	$42	−$16	$6.50	$8
5	$6.50	$32.50	$53	−$20.50	$6.50	$11
6	$6.50	$39	$65	−$26	$6.50	$12

- Many AP students lose points because they incorrectly locate and label profit. When you are finding the profit/loss rectangle, it is important to remember the following.

- Find q_e where $P =$ MR = MC. Once you have found q_e, never leave it.
- Find ATC vertically at q_e. If you move downward, $\pi > 0$. If you move upward, $\pi < 0$.
- Move horizontally from ATC to the y-axis to complete the rectangle, and clearly label it as positive or negative.

One Carrot Farmer

Loss = 3 × ($6.50 − $11.33)
= −$14.50

MC

ATC

11.33
6.50

d = P = MR = AR

$q_e = 3$

Quantity

Figure 9.4

Decision to Shut Down

KEY IDEA

Firms obviously do not enjoy producing at a loss and desperately hope that the market price improves so that profits are possible. However, if firms are incurring losses, they must decide whether it is economically rational to operate at all. The decision to shut down, or produce zero, in the short run is sometimes the optimal strategy. To see why, consider what happens when a firm begins to produce. When a perfectly competitive firm decides to produce any level of output greater than zero, two things happen:

"This has great potential to be asked on both sections of the exam."
—AP Teacher

1. It collects total revenue (TR) $= P \times q_e$.
2. It incurs variable costs (TVC). Of course, the firm also incurs total fixed costs, but it incurs those costs anyway, regardless of the level of output.

If the firm, by producing in the short run, can collect total revenues that at least exceed the total variable costs, then it continues to produce, even at a loss. However, if producing output incurs more variable cost than revenue collected, why bother? Shut down, hope for better times, and suffer losses equal to TFC. This comparison provides us a decision rule for shutting down in the short run:

TIP

- If TR $\geq$ TVC, the firm produces q_e where MR = MC.
- If TR $<$ TVC, the firm shuts down and $q = 0$.

The Shutdown Point

We can see the shutdown point in Figure 9.5 by converting the above decision rule into a per-unit comparison. Dividing total revenue and total variable cost by q tells us to shut down if $P <$ AVC. This is the identical decision rule; it is just a per-unit comparison of revenue and variable cost:

TIP

- If $P \geq$ AVC, the firm produces q_e where MR = MC.
- If $P <$ AVC, the firm shuts down and $q = 0$.

In Figure 9.5, there are four prices shown:

- PH is the highest price. At q_h, the firm earns enough total revenue to cover all costs. $\pi > 0$.
- PM is the middle price. At q_m, the firm's TR exceeds TVC but only covers part of the TFC. $\pi < 0$.
- PD is the shutdown price. At q_d, the firm's TR just covers TVC and the firm is at the shutdown point. If price falls any lower, the firm does not produce.
- PL is the lowest price. At q_1, the firm's TR cannot even cover TVC, and so the firm shuts down, producing $q = 0$. $\pi = -$TFC.

Figure 9.5

Short-Run Supply

As you can see in Figure 9.5, when the price fluctuates between PH and PD, the firm finds a new profit-maximizing quantity where P = MR = MC. If price increases, quantity supplied increases. If price decreases, quantity supplied decreases. This is a restatement of the law of supply. This movement upward and downward along the marginal cost curve implies that MC serves as the supply curve for the perfectly competitive firm. The only exception is when the price falls below the shutdown point (minimum of AVC) and the firm quickly decides to produce nothing. The market supply curve is simply the horizontal summation of all firms' MC curves.

- The MC curve above the shutdown point serves as the supply curve for each perfectly competitive firm.
- The market supply curve is therefore the horizontal sum of all of the MC curves: $S = \Sigma MC$.

Long-Run Adjustment

The short run is a period of time too brief for firms to change the size of their plants. This means that it is also too short for existing firms to exit the industry in bad times and too short for new entrepreneurs to enter the industry in good times. The "free entry and exit" characteristic of perfect competition assures us that in the long run, we can expect to see firms either exiting or entering, depending upon whether profits or losses are being made in the short run. We'll first examine the case where short-run positive profits are made in the carrot industry. Then we'll look at the situation where short-run losses are incurred.

- In most of the past AP Microeconomics exams, free-response questions have appeared that test the students' knowledge of perfect competition and the difference between the short- and long-run equilibria.

Short-Run Positive Profits

Figure 9.6 illustrates the perfectly competitive carrot industry where the market price is above average total cost. Firms are earning positive short-run profits, as illustrated by the shaded rectangle.

So what next? Well, many entrepreneurs on the outside of this market are attracted by the positive short-run profits being made by carrot producers. Given sufficient time (i.e., the long run), these new firms enter the market. With more carrot producers, the market supply curve shifts outward, driving down the price. As the price falls, the profit rectangle gets smaller and smaller until it actually disappears. At the point where $P = MR = MC = ATC$, each carrot farmer is now breaking even with $\pi = 0$. Would the next potential carrot farmer enter the market? Unlikely, as the entry of one more firm pushes the price down just enough to where losses are actually incurred. Thus,

Figure 9.6

this breakeven point is described as the long-run equilibrium. The market quantity has increased, and each firm produces less at the lower price. Figure 9.7 illustrates the movement toward the long-run equilibrium.

Figure 9.7

- Entry of new firms attracted by economic $\pi > 0$.
- Increase in market supply.
- A decrease in the market price to P_{LR}.
- Profits fall to the breakeven point, $P_{LR} = MR = MC = ATC$ and economic $\pi = 0$.
- Market quantity increases.
- Individual producer output falls.
- Many FRQs ask you to draw perfect competition with side-by-side graphs of the market and the typical firm. In addition to knowing perfect competition inside and out, you must be very careful to follow all instructions in the prompt. For example, questions often say, "Label output in the market Q_m and output for the typical firm Q_f." Following these instructions exactly can prevent unnecessary errors that will cost you easy graphing points.

What's So Great About Breaking Even?

Remember there is a distinction between accounting profit and economic profit. Economic profit subtracts the next best opportunity costs of your resources from total revenue. If you are still breaking even after subtracting what you might have earned in all of those other opportunities, you can't feel cheated. In other words, you are making a fair rate of return on your invested resources and you have no incentive to take them elsewhere. Sure, you would like to earn more than zero economic profit (aka "**normal profit**"), but the characteristics of perfect competition rule this out in the long run.

Short-Run Losses

Figure 9.8 illustrates short-run losses with a price below ATC but above the shutdown point. The long-run adjustment story might sound familiar, only with market forces moving in the opposite direction.

Figure 9.8

Again, we should ask "What next?" Some existing firms in this market begin to exit the industry. With fewer carrot producers, the market supply curve shifts leftward, driving up the price. As the price rises, the loss rectangle gets smaller and smaller until again it disappears. At the point where $P_{LR} = MR = MC = ATC$, each remaining carrot farmer is now breaking even with $\pi = 0$. Would another carrot farmer exit the market? Possibly, but the exit of one more firm bumps up the price just enough so that a small positive profit is earned, prompting one firm to enter and get us back to the breakeven point. Arrival at the breakeven point is once again the long-run equilibrium. The market quantity has decreased, but each surviving firm produces more at the higher price. Figure 9.9 illustrates the movement toward the long-run equilibrium.

The long-run adjustment to short-run losses can be summarized as:

- Exit of existing firms prompted by economic $\pi < 0$.
- Decrease in market supply.
- An increase in the market price to P_{LR}.
- Profits increase to the breakeven point, $P_{LR} = MR = MC = ATC$ and economic $\pi = 0$.
- Market quantity decreases.
- Individual producer output rises.

The U.S. Carrot Market

One Carrot Producer

Figure 9.9

Table 9.5 provides a summary of the four possible short-run scenarios and resulting long-run adjustments to the perfectly competitive equilibrium, which always ends in the same place.

Table 9.5

WHEN THE SHORT RUN ...	THE FIRM PRODUCES WHERE ...	SHORT-RUN ECONOMIC PROFITS ARE ...	IN THE LONG RUN ...	THE LONG-RUN OUTCOME IS ...
$P > \text{ATC}$	$\text{MR} = \text{MC}$	Positive	Firms enter	$P_{LR} = \text{MR} = \text{MC} = \text{ATC}$ and $\pi = 0$
$P = \text{ATC}$	$\text{MR} = \text{MC}$	Zero, break even	No entry or exit	$P_{LR} = \text{MR} = \text{MC} = \text{ATC}$ and $\pi = 0$
$\text{AVC} < P < \text{ATC}$	$\text{MR} = \text{MC}$	Negative $0 > \pi > -\text{TFC}$	Firms exit	$P_{LR} = \text{MR} = \text{MC} = \text{ATC}$ and $\pi = 0$
$P < \text{AVC}$	Zero, shut down	Negative $(= -\text{TFC})$	Firms exit	$P_{LR} = \text{MR} = \text{MC} = \text{ATC}$ and $\pi = 0$

Are There Variations on This Story and Do I Need to Know Them?

The answer to these questions are yes, and maybe. Throughout this section we have made an assumption that entry and exit of firms has no impact on the cost curves of firms in the market. In other words, we have been assuming a **constant cost industry**. Recent AP Microeconomics exams have made references to constant cost industries and (maybe) caused unnecessary confusion for test takers. It is always possible that future exams will refer to constant, increasing, or decreasing cost industries, so you should probably become familiar with these terms. A quick explanation and you will not be one of the confused.

Suppose that entry of new firms into a profitable carrot market increases the demand for key resources like land, labor, and capital. Increased demand for these resources might increase the cost of employing those resources. When this happens, the cost curves for firms in the carrot industry start to shift upward. This situation is described as an **increasing cost industry**. Graphing this situation gets sticky, but if you follow the logic, you will be fine. The entry of new firms drives down the price of the output *and* increases the cost curves, so the profit is eliminated more quickly than with our constant cost industry. Fewer firms eventually enter this version of the carrot market, and the new long-run price is higher than it is in a constant cost industry.

A **decreasing cost industry** is one in which the entry of new firms actually decreases the price of key inputs and causes the cost curves to shift downward. This might occur because producers of the key inputs expand production and experience economies of scale and lower per-unit costs. Since the entry of new firms lowers the price of the output *and* decreases the cost curves, it takes longer for the profit to be eliminated than in our constant cost industry. More firms can eventually enter this market, and the new long-run price is lower than it would be in a constant cost industry.

9.2 Monopoly

Main Topics: *Structural Characteristics of Monopoly, Monopoly Demand, Profit Maximization, Efficiency Analysis, Price Discrimination*

Structural Characteristics of Monopoly

Since monopoly is the very opposite of perfect competition in the range of market structures, we can expect that the structural characteristics are also quite different.

- *A single producer.* This is pretty self-explanatory, but a strict definition of monopoly requires that there are no other firms in the industry.
- *No close substitutes.* Consumers cannot find a similar product in other markets.
- *Barriers to entry.* Perhaps the most important characteristic of monopoly is that there exists something that prevents rival firms from entering the market to provide competition to the monopolist and choice to consumers.
- *Market power.* This is the result of the first three characteristics. With no competition and barriers to entry, the unregulated monopolist has **market power**, or monopoly price-setting ability.

Again, it is rare to find a firm that satisfies all of the characteristics of monopoly, but the De Beers firm holds a near monopoly on global diamond production. The only gas station or bank in a small town might also act as a local monopolist.

Barriers to Entry

If there were no barrier to entry, a monopolist earning positive economic profits would be history and this chapter would be done. So before moving on to the behavior of monopoly, let's talk a little more about this necessary condition for the existence of monopoly.

- *Legal barriers.* In your local television market, only one firm is given the right to broadcast on a specific frequency. There might be only one firm given the right to sell liquor in a small community. There are patents, trademarks, and copyright laws to protect inventions and intellectual property. These legal protections do not provide for absolute monopoly, for there are often viable substitutes available to consumers.
- *Economies of scale.* In Chapter 8, this concept was introduced. As a firm grows larger in the long run, average total costs fall, providing the larger firm a cost advantage over smaller firms. If extensive economies of scale exist, an industry could evolve into one with only one enormous producer. A **natural monopoly** is a case where economies of scale are so extensive that it is less costly for one firm to supply the entire range of demand. Power plants are a good example of natural monopoly within a local area.
- *Control of key resources.* If a firm controlled most of the available resources in the production of a good, it would be very difficult for a competitor to enter the market. For example, if a

producer of granulated sugar wanted to monopolize the market, the firm might wish to control all of the sugarcane plantations.

Monopoly Demand

The perfectly competitive firm is a price taker and faces perfectly elastic demand for the product. The firm sells all it wants at the going market price; this decision does not affect the market price. The monopolist is the only provider of that good, making the demand for the product the market demand for that product. The monopolist must pay attention to the law of demand, which means that if it wishes to sell more, the monopolist must decrease the price.

Demand, Price, and Marginal Revenue

Price exceeds marginal revenue because the monopolist must lower price to boost sales. The added revenue from selling one more unit is the price of the last unit less the sum of the price cuts that must be taken on all prior units of output. For example, the demand curve for the monopolist's product is $P = 7 - Q_d$.

The monopolist begins at a price of $6 and sells one unit of the good (see Table 9.6). A price cut to $5 results in one more unit sold, so total revenue increases by $5 on this second unit. However, the first unit, previously sold at $6, must also now be sold at $5, which costs the firm $1 in total revenue. With $5 gained ($P$) from the second and $1 lost in total revenue from the first unit, the net or marginal increase (MR) in total revenue is $4 for the second unit. Graphically we can see the revenue effect of selling the second unit in Figure 9.10.

Chapter 7 examined the effect that price elasticity of demand (E_d) has on total revenue. Demand is elastic above the midpoint of a linear demand curve like the one in Figure 9.10, so cuts in price increase total revenue. Demand is inelastic below the midpoint; further cuts in price decrease total revenue. At the midpoint, total revenue is maximized and demand is unit elastic. Recognizing this connection, the price-making monopolist is going to avoid the inelastic portion of the demand curve and operate at some point to the left of the midpoint. Figure 9.11 combines demand, marginal revenue, and the total revenue function. You can see that when total revenue is at the maximum, marginal revenue is zero and further price cuts decrease total revenue, making marginal revenue negative.

Table 9.6

P	Q	TR	MR
7	0	0	
6	1	6	6
5	2	10	4
4	3	12	2
3	4	12	0
2	5	10	-2
1	6	6	-4
0	7	0	-6

Figure 9.10

- Demand is horizontal, and $P = \text{MR}$ in perfect competition.
- Demand is downward sloping, and $P > \text{MR}$ in monopoly.
- The monopolist operates in the elastic (or upper) range of demand.

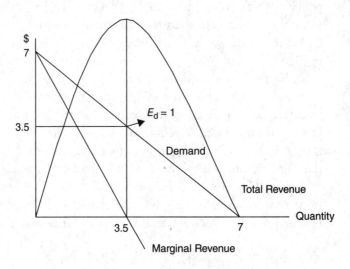

Figure 9.11

Profit Maximization

While demand looks different for the monopolist, the mechanism for maximizing profit is the same for both the monopolist and the perfectly competitive firm. **The firm must set output at the level where MR = MC. At this level of output (Q_m), the monopolist sets the price (P_m) from the demand curve.** Profit is found in the same way by creating the profit rectangle with average total cost. This is seen in Figure 9.12.

The positive monopoly profits illustrated in Figure 9.12 are likely, due to the entry barrier, to last into the long run. Though $\pi > 0$ is usually the case for a monopoly firm, you might imagine a case where demand plummets, or perhaps production costs increase, to the point where $P < \text{ATC}$ and losses are incurred. In the event of persistent losses, we expect the monopolist to exit the industry.

"Understand the profit max rule well. It will help you throughout economics."
—Nick,
AP Student

Figure 9.12

- Find Q_m where MR = MC. Once you have found Q_m, never leave it.
- Find P_m vertically from the demand curve above MR = MC.
- Find ATC vertically at Q_m. If you move downward, $\pi > 0$. If you move upward, $\pi < 0$.
- Move horizontally from ATC to the y-axis to complete the rectangle and clearly label it as positive or negative.

Efficiency Analysis

We refer to efficiency in a couple of different sections of this book, and now that we have compared perfect competition to monopoly, it is time for another discussion. **Allocative efficiency** is achieved when the market produces a level of output where the marginal cost (MC) to society exactly equals the marginal benefit (P) received by society. Total welfare to society is maximized at this outcome, so any movement away from this level of output results in deadweight loss. **Productive efficiency** is achieved if society has produced a level of output with the lowest possible cost. In perfect competition, the long-run market outcome achieves both of these criteria for efficiency. Figure 9.13 illustrates the competitive and

Figure 9.13

monopoly outcomes. Allocative efficiency exists because P_c = MR = MC at Q_c, and productive efficiency exists because firms produce at minimum ATC, once entry or exit has occurred in the long term.

On the other hand, the monopolist produces at a quantity Q_m where P_m > MR = MC. This result tells us that consumers would like to consume more of the product; but the monopolist does not produce as much as consumers want. This is an example of market failure, a concept introduced back in Chapter 5. Failing to achieve allocative efficiency creates the deadweight loss (DWL) shown in Figure 9.13. The monopoly output is not at the point where ATC is minimized; thus the monopolist is not productively efficient. A profit earned by the monopolist is a transfer of consumer surplus from consumers to the firm. To see what happens to output, price, profit, and efficiency after a tax has been imposed, see one of the practice FRQs later in this book.

- $Q_m < Q_c$.
- $P_m > P_c$.
- P_m > MC so monopoly is not allocatively efficient.
- Deadweight loss exists with monopoly.
- P_m > minimum ATC so monopoly is not productively efficient.
- π_m > 0 is a transfer of lost consumer surplus from consumers to the firm.

Price Discrimination

Though the name implies a nasty stereotype, **price discrimination** is the selling of the same good at different prices to different consumers. Successful price discrimination is possible if three conditions exist:

1. The firm has monopoly pricing power.

2. The firm is able to identify and separate groups of consumers.

3. The firm is able to prevent resale between consumers.

Common examples of price discrimination include the following:

- Child and senior discounts at the movie theater or restaurants
- Airline tickets that are bought three weeks in advance compared to tickets bought one hour in advance
- Coupons that separate price-sensitive consumers (those who use the coupon) from those who are less price sensitive
- A lower per-unit price paid by consumers who buy items in large quantities (like a case of soda) than those paid by consumers who buy in lesser quantities (like a six-pack of soda, or one can from a vending machine)

The airline industry is clearly not perfectly competitive, so there must be a degree of monopoly pricing power. The firm creates groupings based upon when consumers purchase tickets. The photo identification requirement for all passengers is an important security measure, but it also prevents the resale of a low-priced ticket to a consumer who is willing to pay a higher price. If resale were possible, the pricing system might break down. It should not surprise you that price discrimination allows firms to earn more profit than if they charged a single price.

Perfect Price Discrimination

Imagine a monopoly shop that sells a certain kind of gadget, but there is something odd about the way these gadgets are priced. When a customer walks into the shop, a sign above the door flashes a number that only the shopkeeper can see; this number is the highest price this particular customer is willing to pay (WTP) for a gadget. Because each customer has a different budget, and different tastes and preferences, each customer has a different WTP. The shopkeeper, knowing the customer's willingness to pay, charges a price exactly equal to this customer's WTP. For example, if Becky's WTP is $8, that's the price she would be charged for a gadget. If Jamaal's WTP is $9.50, that's the price he would be charged.

This unique kind of price discrimination is called **perfect price discrimination** and is seen in Figure 9.14. The demand curve and marginal revenue are now the same ($P = MR$), and the firm will continue selling gadgets until the marginal revenue from the last sale is equal to the marginal cost of a gadget. There is no single equilibrium price, because each customer was charged a different price. There are two other key outcomes to see here. First, because each customer pays a price exactly equal to their WTP, there is no consumer surplus; the monopolist takes all of it as producer surplus. Second, because the last unit sold is the one for which $P = MC$, this outcome is allocatively efficient.

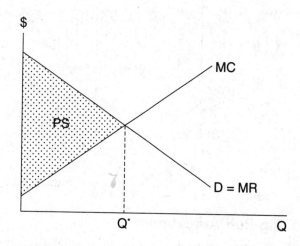

Figure 9.14

9.3 Monopolistic Competition

Main Topics: *Structural Characteristics, Short-Run Profit Maximization, Long-Run Adjustment*

Structural Characteristics

Sharing some of the characteristics of both perfect competition and monopoly, the market structure of monopolistic competition provides a description of many modern industries.

- *Relatively large number of firms.* Rather than the thousands of perfectly competitive firms, in monopolistic competition there are perhaps dozens, each with a fairly small share of the total market.
- *Differentiated products.* This characteristic makes monopolistic competition stand out as different from the perfectly competitive market structure and gives firms their ability to set the price above the competitive level.
- *Easy entry and exit.* There are very few barriers to entry in monopolistic competition, perhaps the largest being the need to provide sufficient marketing to differentiate a new firm's product from that of the existing rivals.

The market for shoes closely fits the description of monopolistic competition. While all shoes serve the same basic purpose, to cover and protect the feet, a running shoe, a hiking boot, and a flip-flop are very different and are made by many firms in the global market. The book publishing and local restaurant markets are also described as monopolistically competitive.

Short-Run Profit Maximization

Like the monopoly, the firm in monopolistic competition faces a downward-sloping demand curve for its differentiated product. Because there are many similar substitutes available to consumers, the demand is fairly elastic. In a recurring theme for profit-maximizing behavior, the firm sets Q_{mc} where MR = MC and sets the price from the demand curve. Figure 9.15 illustrates a monopolistically competitive firm that is earning positive short-run economic profits.

Figure 9.15

Long-Run Adjustment

With easy entry and exit into the monopolistically competitive industry, short-run positive profits like those in Figure 9.15 are not going to last for long. As new firms enter this industry, the market share of all existing firms begins to fall. Graphically we see this as a leftward shift in the demand curve. As the price begins to fall, the profit rectangle begins to shrink. Entry stops when profits are zero and P_{mc} = ATC, or when the demand curve is just tangent to ATC. This adjustment is seen in Figure 9.16.

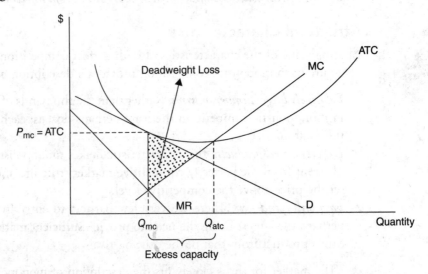

Figure 9.16

"What About Advertising to Maintain Profits?"

Because easy entry of competitors drives profits down to breakeven levels, monopolistically competitive firms typically engage in extensive amounts of advertising to slow down, and even reverse, declining market share. This advertising is realistically only a short-run "fix," as there is no reason to believe that barriers to entry suddenly emerge to prevent the eventual return to breakeven profit levels.

Efficiency and Excess Capacity

In long-run monopolistic competition, the firm earns $\pi = 0$, a characteristic shared by the perfectly competitive firm. But because of the differentiated products, $P > MR = MC$, allocative efficiency is not achieved. The deadweight loss is the shaded area in Figure 9.16. Though the firms are breaking even, they are not operating at the minimum of ATC; productive efficiency is also not achieved. The difference between the monopolistic competition output Q_{mc} and the output at minimum ATC is referred to as **excess capacity**. Excess capacity is underused plant and equipment that is the result of producing at an output less than that which minimizes ATC. The market is overpopulated with firms, each producing enough to break even in the long run, but so many firms means that each produces below full capacity.

- $Q_{mc} < Q_c$.
- $P_{mc} > P_c$.
- $P_{mc} > MC$ so monopolistic competition is not allocatively efficient.
- Deadweight loss exists, but not as much as with monopoly.
- $P_m > $ minimum ATC so monopolistic competition is not productively efficient.
- $\pi_{mc} = 0$ in the long run.
- Excess capacity is $Q_{atc} - Q_{mc}$.

9.4 Oligopoly

Main Topics: *Structural Characteristics, Industry Concentration, Game Theory and the Prisoner's Dilemma, Is Every Game a Prisoner's Dilemma?, Collusive Pricing*

Oligopoly markets are typically further from perfect competition than the monopolistic market structure, although there is no one model of oligopoly. A couple of oligopoly models are presented, but keep in mind that if one little assumption is relaxed, the predictions of the model can be radically different. For the AP exam, you will likely face only these basics.

Structural Characteristics

You can see from these characteristics that oligopoly shares more common ground with monopoly, but these are flexible enough to describe many different and diverse industries:

- *A few large producers.* Can it get more vague than this? Think of the American auto industry, with the "Big 3" producers, or cell phone providers, an industry dominated by four huge firms. If the distribution of market share in an industry is top-heavy with a few large firms, the industry is described as oligopolistic.
- *Differentiated or standardized product.* Oligopoly industries can come in both flavors. Crude oil is a fairly standard product, but it is very much an oligopoly of large producers. Automobiles, beer, and soft drinks are also oligopoly markets, but with more differentiated products.
- *Entry barriers.* If these industries were fairly easy to enter, we would not see them dominated by a few huge producers.
- *Mutual interdependence.* Because a few large producers control these industries, the action of one firm (price setting or advertising) is likely to affect the others and prompt

a response. A good example of this is your local gasoline market. This is very much an oligopoly; when one gas station lowers prices by one cent per gallon, the others usually quickly follow.

Industry Concentration

How does an industry become classified as an oligopoly? Economists have tried to get more specific than a "few large producers" by developing ways to measure how much market share is held by, or concentrated in, the largest of the firms. One way to gauge how powerful the largest of firms might be is to sum up the market share of the top 4, or 8, or 12 firms and create a **concentration ratio**. If the top four firms in the breakfast cereal industry have a combined market share of 85 percent, we say that the four-firm concentration ratio is 85. Some economists use a four-firm concentration ratio of 40 percent or greater as a rough guideline for identifying an oligopolistic industry. We predict that as this concentration ratio increases, the degree of monopoly price-setting power increases.

Game Theory and the Prisoner's Dilemma

Imagine a case where a two-firm oligopoly (a duopoly) engages in a daily pricing decision. Each firm knows that if it sets a price higher than the rival's, it loses sales. Likewise, if it sets a price below the rival's, it steals sales. This noncollusive model of pricing, called the **prisoner's dilemma,** emerges from the following scenario that any fan of *Law and Order* quickly recognizes.

Example:

A college professor suspects two students (Jack and Diane) of cheating on a take-home final exam, but she cannot prove guilt with enough certainty to fail both students in the course or expel them from the school. Without a confession, she will give each student a D in the course. With a confession from one student but not the other, she can reward the confessor with a B. The professor brings both students, one at a time, into her office and gives each the following deal:

- If you remain silent and do not confess, and your classmate implicates you, I will expel you from school and give your friend a B.
- If you confess to cheating and implicate your silent classmate, I will pass you with a B and expel your friend from school.

These options are depicted in the following matrix:

		JACK'S CHOICES	
		Confess	Stay Silent
DIANE'S CHOICES	Confess	D: Fail the course J: Fail the course	D: Gets a B J: Expelled from school
	Stay Silent	D: Expelled from school J: Gets a B	D: Gets a D J: Gets a D

Diane doesn't know what Jack is going to do when he is in the professor's office. But whatever Jack's decision, Diane should confess. She might be thinking that Jack is going to confess. If so, she confesses because staying silent will get her expelled from school. Maybe she thinks that Jack is going to stay silent. If true, the choice is between a B and a D in the course. Diane would be wise to confess. For Diane, confessing is a **dominant strategy** because no matter what Jack does, confession is always better than staying silent. Likewise, for Jack, the dominant strategy is to confess.

The outcome of the game (both students confess) is called a "**Nash equilibrium**" after the late Dr. John Nash, a mathematician at Princeton, who won the Nobel Prize in Economics in 1994. The premise is quite simple: the outcome of the game is a Nash equilibrium if each player's strategy maximizes his or her payoff, given the strategies used by the rival players. In other words, Jack's decision to confess ensures his best outcome, *given he knows that Diane is also going to confess.* And the same is true of Diane's decision. In other words, the decision to confess is the best response to what the other player is going to do.

This is certainly a dilemma, because if Jack and Diane could only agree to give the professor the silent treatment, they would both walk away with a D, which is much better than failing the course or expulsion from school. Without such a binding agreement, cheating on the pact would be quite tempting, maybe even fairly predictable.

Example:

The owners of two gas stations operate on opposite corners of a busy intersection. Every morning each owner goes out to the sign and sets the price of gasoline, either high or low. Consumers are concerned only about the lowest price of gas. The following matrix summarizes the daily revenues for each station:

		STATION X	
		Price High	Price Low
STATION Y	Price High	X: $2,000 Y: $2,000	X: $3,000 Y: $500
	Price Low	X: $500 Y: $3,000	X: $1,000 Y: $1,000

Can you see the dilemma? Both stations would love to set a high price of gas so that they could earn $2,000 in daily revenue. But if the rival were to set the low price, the high price station would be stuck with $500 while the other station cleans up with $3,000. Since both firms recognize that pricing low is the dominant strategy, both earn only $1,000 every day. This outcome, where both firms set the low price, is the Nash equilibrium. A collusive agreement might emerge.

Use of the previous game matrices assumes that both players in the game make simultaneous choices. Many games involve a series of stages where one player moves first. The second player observes the choice made by the first and then reacts to it. These sequential games are typically seen as a game tree rather than a game matrix.

Let's convert the previous game to a sequential game where gas station X gets to move first, as shown in Figure 9.17. Station Y sees the choice of station X and then sets the price high or low. Payoffs are given at the end of the tree.

Can you see how this game will play out? Gas station X knows that its rival, station Y, still has a dominant strategy of setting a low price. No matter what the initial decision of station X, station Y would always see that a low price beats a high price. Because station X knows this about its rival, it will select a low price at the beginning of the game. In 2007, the AP Microeconomics exam included simple game theory on the free-response section for the very first time. Since 2007, this area of microeconomics has been repeatedly tested, and I predict that the degree of difficulty will gradually increase.

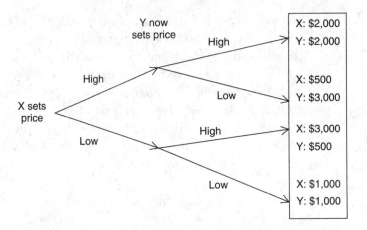

Figure 9.17

Is Every Game a Prisoner's Dilemma?

Absolutely not. Several recent AP Microeconomics exams have included FRQs that are not simple examples of a prisoner's dilemma.

Example:

Suppose there are two hamburger stands in town, Stinky's and Sloppy's, and each firm sells what it considers to be the best burger in town. Both burger stands are considering a move to offer hot dogs on the menu, or they could do nothing and continue to offer only burgers. The following payoff matrix shows payoffs as daily profits for Stinky's, followed by daily profits for Sloppy's.

		SLOPPY'S CHOICES	
		Burgers Only	*Add Hot Dogs*
STINKY'S CHOICES	*Burgers Only*	$500, $300	$400, $400
	Add Hot Dogs	$600, $200	$500, $100

In this game, Stinky's has a dominant strategy of adding hot dogs to the menu. No matter what Sloppy's does, Stinky's earns more money by making this choice. However, Sloppy's does not have a dominant strategy. If Stinky's were to offer only burgers, Sloppy's should add hot dogs ($400 is better than $300). But if Stinky's were to add hot dogs to its menu, Sloppy's should continue to offer only burgers ($200 is better than $100).

So where is the dominant strategy? Sloppy's will recognize that Stinky's is going to add hot dogs to the menu, so Sloppy's will respond by maintaining a burgers-only menu. The Nash equilibrium combination of payoffs is $600 for Stinky's and $200 for Sloppy's. This is not a prisoner's dilemma, because there is no alternative outcome that would, with prior collusion, increase profits for *both* firms.

Collusive Pricing

Explicit **collusive** behavior between direct competitors is an illegal business practice, but it does happen (surprise!) from time to time. More common is a kind of tacit, or understood, collusion. Two competitors over time figure out that repeated attempts to undercut the price of their rivals is counterproductive. Eventually they understand that if both set the price high, both firms win. When one cheats on this "understanding," the other inflicts punishment with a retaliatory price cut.

Cartels are more organized forms of collusive oligopoly behavior. Cartels are groups of firms that create a formal agreement not to compete with each other on the basis of price, production, or other competitive dimensions. The general idea of the cartel is that rather than act independently to maximize individual profits, they collectively operate as a monopolist to maximize their joint profits. Each cartel member agrees to a limited level of output, and this results in a higher cartel price. Joint profits are maximized and distributed to each member.

In addition to the pesky illegality of forming cartels, these entities face three challenges that are completely unrelated to the Attorney General:

1. Difficulty in arriving at a mutually acceptable agreement to restrict output. Have you ever tried to order pizza or binge-watch a TV series with more than two other friends? If so, you get the idea.

2. Punishment mechanism. If the cartel can restrict output and increase the price above the current competitive level, cartel members have an incentive to cheat by producing more than their allotment. There must be some kind of deterrent to cheating.

3. Entry of new firms. If the cartel members are successful in creating monopoly profits, they are faced with new firms eager to enter. If entry occurs, the cartel loses monopoly power and profit.

› Review Questions

1. For a competitive firm, what is the most important thing to consider in deciding whether to shut down in the short run?
   (A) Compare AVC to MR.
   (B) Compare TR to TC.
   (C) Do not produce if the TFC is not covered by revenue.
   (D) Produce the highest quantity demanded regardless of price.
   (E) Compare P to ATC.

2. Which characteristic is likely a part of a monopoly market but not of monopolistic competition?
   (A) Differentiated products
   (B) Patents and copyrights
   (C) Possibility of profit in the short run
   (D) Deadweight loss exists
   (E) None of the above.

3. If the perfectly competitive price is currently above minimum ATC, we can expect which of the following events in the long run?
   (A) Price rises as firms enter the industry.
   (B) Market equilibrium quantity rises as firms exit the industry.
   (C) Nothing. The industry is currently in long-run equilibrium.
   (D) Profits fall as the market price rises.
   (E) Price falls as firms enter the industry.

4. Which of these situations is not an example of price discrimination?
   (A) Brent works nights, so he chooses to buy bread at 7 a.m. rather than at 7 p.m.
   (B) Bob and Nancy each receive a "$1 off" coupon in the mail, but Bob redeems it while Nancy does not.
   (C) Katie buys 12 Cokes for $3, and Josh buys one Coke at a time for $1.
   (D) Velma likes to go to the movies at the lower afternoon matinee price, and Rosemary would rather pay more for the evening show.
   (E) Jason and Jen go to a popular nightclub. Because it is "Ladies' Night," Jen pays no cover charge, but Jason must pay to enter the club.

Two competing firms are deciding whether to launch a huge costly advertising campaign or maintain the status quo. Use the following matrix showing the profits of this duopoly to respond to question 5.

		FIRM X	
		Advertise	Status Quo
FIRM Y	Advertise	X: $4.5 million Y: $4.5 million	X: $1 million Y: $6 million
	Status Quo	X: $6 million Y: $1 million	X: $5 million Y: $5 million

5. If these firms do not collude, the outcome will be that
   (A) both firms maintain the status quo.
   (B) both firms advertise.
   (C) Firm X advertises and Firm Y maintains the status quo.
   (D) Firm Y advertises and Firm X maintains the status quo.
   (E) Firm X advertises and Firm Y alternates between the status quo and advertising.

6. Deadweight loss occurs in
   (A) monopolistic competition as $P > MC$.
   (B) monopoly markets because $P > MC$.
   (C) oligopoly markets because $P > MC$.
   (D) All of the above.
   (E) None of the above.

› Answers and Explanations

1. **A**—The firm only operates if the total revenue is at least as great as total variable cost. On a per-unit basis, the firm must receive a $P = MR$ that is at least as great as AVC. Since firms pay TFC regardless of production, they are not a factor in whether you should shut down. Choices B, C, and E are wrong because TC and ATC include the fixed costs. Choice D is incorrect because it might not be the profitable strategy, but it is irrelevant to the shutdown decision.

2. **B**—Monopoly has barriers to entry (e.g., patents) and the monopolistic competitive firm does not. Choices A, C, and D are true of monopolistic competition and monopoly.

3. **E**—With $P > ATC$, you should recognize that positive economic profits exist. Firms enter and price falls toward the breakeven point, so any mention of exit or rising prices can be eliminated. Entry also increases the market quantity of the good produced.

4. **A**—If Brent chooses to buy his bread early in the morning rather than in the evening, this is not price discrimination. The other choices describe buying in bulk, redeeming a coupon, or paying a lower price because of the time in which one consumes the good. The nightclub example is price discrimination based upon gender.

5. **B**—For each firm, choosing the costly advertising campaign is the dominant strategy. This is an example of the prisoner's dilemma.

6. **D**—Allocative inefficiency and deadweight loss in *any* market structure is when $P > MC$.

› Rapid Review

Perfect competition: The most competitive market structure is characterized by many small price-taking firms producing a standardized product in an industry in which there are no barriers to entry or exit.

Profit maximizing rule: All firms maximize profit by producing where $MR = MC$.

Breakeven point: The output in perfect competition where ATC is minimized and economic profit is zero.

Shutdown point: The output where AVC is minimized. If the price falls below this point, the firm chooses to shut down or produce zero units in the short run.

Perfectly competitive long-run equilibrium: Occurs when there is no more incentive for firms to enter or exit. $P = MR = MC = ATC$ and $\pi = 0$.

Normal profit: Another way of saying that firms are earning zero economic profits or a fair rate of return on invested resources.

Constant cost industry: Entry (or exit) of firms does not shift the cost curves of firms in the industry.

Increasing cost industry: Entry of new firms shifts the cost curves for all firms upward.

Decreasing cost industry: Entry of new firms shifts the cost curves for all firms downward.

Monopoly: The least competitive market structure; it is characterized by a single producer, with no close substitutes, barriers to entry, and price-making power.

Market power: The ability to set the price above the perfectly competitive level.

Natural monopoly: The case where economies of scale are so extensive that it is less costly for one firm to supply the entire range of demand.

Monopoly long-run equilibrium: $P_m > MR = MC$, which is not allocatively efficient and deadweight loss exists. $P_m > ATC$, which is not productively efficient. $\pi_m > 0$ so consumer surplus is transferred to the monopolist as profit.

Price discrimination: The practice of selling essentially the same good to different groups of consumers at different prices.

Perfect price discrimination: The type of price discrimination in which each consumer pays exactly his or her maximum willingness to pay. Consumer surplus is eliminated, yet the allocatively efficient output is produced.

Monopolistic competition: A market structure characterized by a few small firms producing a differentiated product with easy entry into the market.

Monopolistic competition long-run equilibrium: $P_{mc} > MR = MC$ and $P_{mc} >$ minimum ATC, so the outcome is not efficient, but $\pi_{mc} = 0$.

Excess capacity: The difference between the monopolistic competition output Q_{mc} and the output at minimum ATC. Excess capacity is underused plant and equipment.

Oligopoly: A very diverse market structure characterized by a small number of interdependent large firms, producing a standardized or differentiated product in a market with a barrier to entry.

Four-firm concentration ratio: A measure of industry market power. If the combined market share of the four largest firms is above 40 percent, it is a good indicator of oligopoly.

Noncollusive oligopoly: Models where firms are competitive rivals seeking to gain at the expense of their rivals.

Prisoner's dilemma: A game where the two rivals achieve a less desirable outcome because they are unable to coordinate their strategies.

Dominant strategy: A strategy that is always the best strategy to pursue, regardless of what a rival is doing.

Nash equilibrium: The outcome of a game for which each player's strategy maximizes his or her payoff, given the strategies used by the rival players.

Collusive oligopoly: Models where firms agree to mutually improve their situation.

Cartel: A group of firms that agree not to compete with each other on the basis of price, production, or other competitive dimensions. Cartel members operate as a monopolist to maximize their joint profits.

Factor Markets

IN THIS CHAPTER

Summary: We have invested significant time reviewing the forces of supply and demand in the competitive market for goods and services. In addition, we have investigated the theory behind production and cost, but have not brought market forces to bear on those input, or factor, markets. We begin with the demand for inputs in a perfectly competitive input market, and then move to the supply of inputs and construct a model of wage and employment. We tweak the competitive model by allowing for some monopoly hiring behavior. How is the wage of college professors determined? Can we predict whether employment of steel workers is going to grow or decline? A study of input markets sheds some light on many important microeconomic issues that have critical macroeconomic implications.

Key Ideas
- ✪ Factor Demand
- ✪ Least-Cost Hiring of Inputs
- ✪ Factor Supply
- ✪ Equilibrium in Competitive Factor Markets
- ✪ Noncompetitive Factor Markets

10.1 Factor Demand

Main Topics: *Competitive Factor Markets, Marginal Revenue Product, Profit-Maximizing Resource Employment, MRP$_L$ as Demand for Labor, Derived Demand, Determinants of Resource Demand*

The theory of factor (or resource, or input) demand is applicable to any factor of production, but it is more intuitive if we focus on labor, the production input with which we are all most comfortable. Because we are most familiar with it, most examples below address labor, but later in the chapter we will also look at the market for capital.

Competitive Factor Markets

To best see the theory of factor demand, we assume the simplest market structure. First, we'll assume that the firms are price takers in the product (output) market. Second, we'll assume that they are price takers in the factor (input) market. This means that they cannot impact either the price of their product or the price they must pay to employ more of an input. In a competitive labor market, they can employ as much labor as they wish at the going market-determined wage.

Marginal Revenue Product

Here's a difficult question for any employee to ask: What am I worth to my employer? Sure, I'm a snazzy dresser; I can tell a humorous joke, and my personal hygiene is top-notch. However, the bottom line to my employer is probably more important than these civilities. To build a model of factor demand, economists assert that the demand for a unit of labor is a function of two things important to employers. First, employers are very interested in the marginal productivity of the next unit of labor. If the next worker is going to greatly contribute to the firm's total production, he is likely to be a good hire for the firm. Second, the firm must then receive good value for the production. The value of this production to the firm is the additional, or marginal, revenue that it brings to the firm. Combining the necessary components of marginal productivity of labor and marginal revenue provides **marginal revenue product of labor** (**MRP$_L$**), a measure of what the next unit of a resource, such as labor, brings to the firm. With the assumption of a perfectly competitive output market, the marginal revenue is simply the price of the product. Some textbooks will refer to marginal revenue product as the value of the marginal product (VMP$_L$), while others will reserve VMP$_L$ for the case where price and marginal revenue are not the same. Consult your textbook to see which approach that author prefers.

$$\text{MRP}_L = \frac{\text{Change in total revenue}}{\text{Change in resource quantity}} = \text{MR} \times \text{MP}_L = P \times \text{MP}_L$$

In our examples, we change the resource (labor) by a quantity of one. Table 10.1 revises the hourly production function for Molly's lemonade stand. Recall that in the short run she hires additional units of labor to a fixed level of capital. The competitive price of a cup of lemonade is 50 cents.

Table 10.1

LABOR INPUT (WORKERS PER HOUR)	TOTAL PRODUCT (TP$_L$) (CUPS PER HOUR)	MARGINAL PRODUCT (MP$_L$)	MARGINAL REVENUE (MR = P)	MARGINAL REVENUE PRODUCT (MRP$_L$ = MP$_L$ × MR)
0	0			
1	25	25	$.50	$12.50
2	45	20	$.50	$10.00
3	60	15	$.50	$7.50

Table 10.1—cont'd

LABOR INPUT (WORKERS PER HOUR)	TOTAL PRODUCT (TP$_L$) (CUPS PER HOUR)	MARGINAL PRODUCT (MP$_L$)	MARGINAL REVENUE (MR = P)	MARGINAL REVENUE PRODUCT (MRP$_L$ = MP$_L$ × MR)
4	70	10	$.50	$5.00
5	75	5	$.50	$2.50
6	70	−5	$.50	−$2.50
7	60	−10	$.50	−$5.00

Profit-Maximizing Resource Employment

Yet again, we are faced with a decision that must be based upon marginal benefits and marginal costs. Our decision rule is, and has always been:

- If MB > MC, do more of it.
- If MB < MC, do less of it.
- If MB = MC, stop here.

In the case of resource hiring, the marginal benefit is **MRP$_L$**. The marginal cost of resource hiring is **marginal resource cost (MRC)**, a measure of how much cost the firm incurs from using an additional unit of an input. When the firm is hiring labor in a competitive labor market, MRC is equal to the wage (w).

Some textbooks refer to this as the **marginal factor cost (MFC)** or, when the factor is labor, the **marginal cost of labor (MC$_L$)**. No matter what label your textbook might use, the concept is the same and the labels are often used interchangeably.

$$MRC = \frac{\text{Change in total resource cost}}{\text{Change in resource quantity}} = \text{Wage}$$

With this measure of marginal cost, the profit-maximizing employer of labor would hire to the point where MRP$_L$ = MRC = Wage. Table 10.2 adds a competitive $7.50 hourly wage to Molly's table of lemonade production. At this wage, Molly should employ three hourly workers to her fixed capital.

Table 10.2

TOTAL LABOR INPUT (WORKERS PER HOUR)	PRODUCT (TP$_L$) (CUPS PER HOUR)	MARGINAL PRODUCT (MP$_L$)	MARGINAL REVENUE (MR = P)	MARGINAL REVENUE PRODUCT (MRP$_L$ = MP$_L$ × MR)	MARGINAL RESOURCE COST (MRC = WAGE)
0	0				
1	25	25	$.50	$12.50	$7.50
2	45	20	$.50	$10.00	$7.50
3	*60*	*15*	*$.50*	*$7.50*	*$7.50*
4	70	10	$.50	$5.00	$7.50
5	75	5	$.50	$2.50	$7.50
6	70	−5	$.50	−$2.50	$7.50
7	60	−10	$.50	−$5.00	$7.50

MRP$_L$ as Demand for Labor

If the hourly wage were to rise to $10, Molly would reduce her employment to two workers per hour. If the wage decreases to $5 per hour, she would employ four workers. All else equal, as the price of labor increases, the employment falls and as the price of labor decreases, employment rises. This is the law of demand again! Figure 10.1 illustrates the MRP$_L$ and Molly's hiring at three wages.

Molly's demand for labor is actually represented by the MRP$_L$. It is downward sloping, like any demand curve would be, because of the diminishing marginal productivity of labor in the short run. To move from Molly's demand for labor to the overall market demand for labor, we simply sum up all of the individual firms' MRP$_L$ curves: Market $D_L = \Sigma MRP_L$.

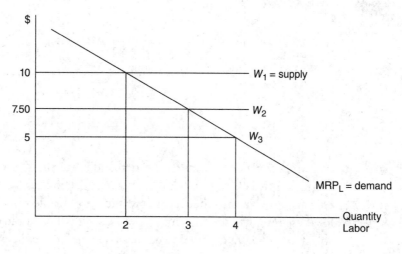

Figure 10.1

Market Wage as Supply of Labor

Under the assumptions of a perfectly competitive labor market, the supply of labor to the individual firm is perfectly elastic and equal to the wage. This means that the firm can employ all of the workers it desires at the going market wage.

- In competitive markets, MRP$_L$ is the firm's downward-sloping labor demand curve.
- In competitive markets, wage is the firm's horizontal labor supply curve.

Derived Demand

Economists say that the demand for an input like labor is derived from the demand for the goods produced by the input. If the weather is hot and demand for lemonade rises, local economists might predict a stronger demand for production resources like lemonade workers, lemons, and sugar. An increase in the demand for a resource means that at any wage, the firm wishes to employ more of that resource. If the demand for lemonade increases and the price rises to $1 per cup, the MRP$_L$ increases at all quantities of labor. This is seen in Figure 10.2.

- You are *very* likely to see the topic of derived demand on the AP exam. To avoid losing points on the free-response question, you *must* make the connection between the price of the product rising and the increased demand for the labor.
- ↑D for product, ↑price of product, ↑MRP$_L$, ↑hiring of labor at the current wage.

Determinants of Resource Demand

The demand for the goods themselves is an important determinant of resource demand, but not the only determinant.

> "Keep answers crisp, graphs labeled, and you are on your way to a 5."
> —Navin, AP Student

Figure 10.2

- *Product demand.* An increase in the demand for textiles—towels, for example—results in an increased price of those goods. The higher price increases the marginal revenue product of resources used in the production of textiles (e.g., textile workers), and this shifts the demand for those resources to the right. Of course, this works in the opposite direction and is probably a more accurate story of what has happened to textile workers in the United States.
- *Productivity (output per resource unit).* If the productivity of the resource increases, the firm has a profit motive to take advantage of that heightened productivity, and the demand for the resource should increase. Productivity of a resource is affected by a few different factors:

  1. *Quantity of other resources.* Give workers more equipment to help production and labor's productivity can be increased. If Molly were to provide her workers with a larger workspace or more manual juicers or pitchers or stirring spoons or measuring cups, they might achieve increased output per worker.
  2. *Technical progress.* Better technology with which to work can increase labor's productivity. Rather than using manual lemon squeezers, Molly invests in electric squeezers that allow for a given number of employees to produce more lemonade every hour.
  3. *Quality of variable resources.* Fertile farmland in the Midwest is a huge productivity advantage over the same acreage of farmland in Nevada. A more educated and trained workforce is an improvement in the quality of the labor and therefore provides more productivity. Maybe Molly employs only those who have completed daylong training at the local community college.

- *Prices of other resources.* Employers hire several different resources, so the demand for one (labor) often depends upon the prices of the others.

  1. *Substitute resources.* If the price of a substitute resource—machinery, for example—falls, it has two competing effects on the demand for labor.

     a. Substitution effect (SE). Because machinery is now relatively less expensive, the firm uses more machinery and decreases demand for labor. For Molly, a lower price of electric lemon squeezers would put pressure on her to decrease the demand for labor.

b. Output effect (OE). Lower machine prices lower production costs (a downward shift in MC), which increases output for the firm and prompts an increased demand for labor. With the lower marginal cost of producing lemonade, Molly sees that she can actually produce more and would therefore need more labor.

c. The net effect of a lower price of capital depends upon the magnitude of each effect. If the SE > OE, demand for labor falls. If the OE > SE, the demand for labor increases.

2. *Complementary resources.* When labor and machine work together, a lower price of the machine makes it more affordable to purchase more machinery but also increases the demand for labor. Interstate trucking companies need trucks, fuel, and drivers. When the price of fuel increases, this can have a negative impact on the demand for drivers. For Molly's firm, if the price of lemons falls, this more affordable complement to labor might increase the demand for labor.

Table 10.3 is a summary of the determinants of labor demand.

Table 10.3

LABOR DEMAND INCREASES IF . . .	LABOR DEMAND DECREASES IF . . .
Demand for the product increases, increasing the price.	Demand for the product decreases, decreasing the price.
The labor becomes more productive, either with more resources available, better technology, or a higher quality workforce.	The labor becomes less productive, either with fewer resources available, lessened technology, or a lower quality workforce.
The price of a substitute resource falls and the OE > SE.	The price of a substitute resource falls and the SE > OE.
The price of a substitute resource rises and the SE > OE.	The price of a substitute resource rises and the OE > SE.
The price of a complementary resource falls.	The price of a complementary resource rises.

10.2 Least-Cost Hiring of Multiple Inputs

Main Topic: *The Least-Cost Hiring Rule*

Finding the best way to cope with scarcity really excites economists. We found that consumers needed to find the best (utility-maximizing) combination of two goods, given the prices and an income constraint. For producers, we would like to find the best (cost-minimizing) combination of two inputs, given the prices and production constraint. To do this, we use the consumer's decision as a model for the producer's decision. The consumer's utility maximizing rule said to find the combination of good X and good Y so that $MU_x/P_x = MU_y/P_y$ while spending exactly his or her income and paying prices P_x and P_y.

Least-Cost Hiring Rule

KEY IDEA

For a producer, we can express the constraint in two equivalent ways. Remember the bridge between production and cost?

1. You must produce Q^* units of output. Now find the least-cost ($TC) way of doing so.

2. You can only spend \$TC. Now find the highest level of output (Q^*).

There is only one combination of two resources (we'll use labor and capital) that satisfies either of these two constraints, and it is found by using this **least-cost rule**. The price of labor is P_L and the price of capital (K) is P_K.

$$MP_L/P_L = MP_K/P_K, \text{ or equivalently, } MP_L/MP_K = P_L/P_K$$

Example:
If each of the inputs is hired at \$1 per unit and at the current amount of labor and capital you have employed, the $MP_L = 100$ and the $MP_K = 10$, clearly, the least-cost rule is not satisfied:

$$100 \text{ units/\$1} > 10 \text{ units/\$1}$$

If you could spend \$1 more on labor, you would see output increase by 100 units. That extra \$1 would come from spending \$1 less on capital, which would decrease output by 10 units. So you spend the same amount of money but get 90 more units of output.

Great deal! In situations like this, where $MP_L/P_L > MP_K/P_K$, the firm is going to find it in its best interest to increase spending on L and decrease spending on K. The law of diminishing marginal returns predicts that as you increase L, MP_L falls. And as you decrease K, MP_K rises. The substitution of labor for capital ceases to be a great deal at the combination of L and K where the ratios of marginal product per dollar are equal again.

SITUATION	FIRM WILL . . .	WHICH CAUSES . . .	AND . . .	UNTIL
$MP_L/P_L > MP_K/P_K$	↑L and ↓K	↓MP_L	↑MP_K	$MP_L/P_L = MP_K/P_K$
$MP_L/P_L < MP_K/P_K$	↑K and ↓L	↓MP_K	↑MP_L	$MP_L/P_L = MP_K/P_K$

Example:
A producer of gadgets pays \$5 for each hour of labor and \$10 for each hour of capital employed. Table 10.4 describes the marginal products of each at various levels of employment. Told that you must produce $Q = 360$ gadgets, find the least-cost combination of labor and capital.

Table 10.4

# OF L EMPLOYED	MPL	# OF K EMPLOYED	MPK
1	50	1	100
2	40	2	90
3	30	3	80
4	20	4	60
5	10	5	45
6	5	6	30

Find all of the combinations of L and K where our rule is satisfied:

$$MP_L/P_L = MP_K/P_K$$
$$\text{or } MP_L/MP_K = \$5/\$10 = .5$$

There are three possibilities where the MP_L is one-half the size of MP_K:

- $L = 1, K = 1$. Total Product = $50 + 100 = 150$
- $L = 2, K = 3$. Total Product = $(50 + 40) + (100 + 90 + 80) = 360$
- $L = 3, K = 4$. Total Product = $(50 + 40 + 30) + (100 + 90 + 80 + 60) = 450$

The best way to produce 360 gadgets is to hire two units of labor and three units of capital at a total cost of TC = $\$5 \times 2 + \$10 \times 3 = \$40$. The same problem could have been modified to use a cost constraint rather than an output constraint.

Told that you can only spend $40, find the combination of labor and capital that maximizes production. Of course, the solution is again $L = 2, K = 3$, and output is 360 gadgets.

10.3 Factor Supply and Market Equilibrium

Main Topics: *Supply of Labor, Wage and Employment Determination, What About Other Resources?*

If you have ever had a job, you have been a small part of the labor supply curve. We quickly investigate labor supply and combine it with labor demand to complete a labor market. It is in this competitive market that wage and employment are determined.

Supply of Labor

Economic theory predicts that as the price of a good increases, suppliers of that good increase the quantity supplied. This is the **law of supply**. If the price of labor (wage) increases, more hours of labor should be supplied. For the most part, this is true, and the market labor supply curve slopes upward. If the hourly wage increased from $5 to $8, most people respond by working more hours, earning more income ($320 per 40-hour workweek), and consuming more goods.

Wage and Employment Determination

Assuming competitive output and input markets, the competitive wage is found at the intersection of labor demand and labor supply. Changing demand and supply influence this wage, and the equilibrium quantity of labor that accompanies it.

Example:

The aging population in the United States is giving a boost to the market for nurses. An increase in the demand for nurses increases both the wage and employment of nurses. This is seen in Figure 10.3.

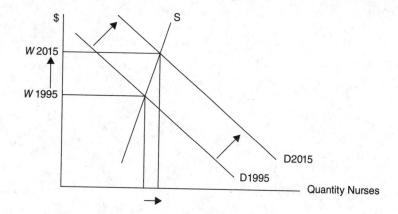

Figure 10.3

What About Other Resources?

Labor is the resource with which most people identify because we have all been, or expect to be, units of labor in a labor market. However, we can use the theory of resource demand to predict how the market for capital (or any other resource) would behave. For example, suppose that the market for capital is also perfectly competitive. If so, then each firm's demand for capital is also derived from the marginal revenue product of capital (MRP_K)

$$MRP_K = P \times MP_K$$

And because the marginal product of capital diminishes, the demand for capital is downward sloping. In a competitive resource market, the firm can hire all of the capital it wants at the marginal factor cost equal to the rental rate of capital (r^*).

Each firm hires the profit-maximizing quantity of capital (K^*) at the point where the MRP_K is equal to the rental rate (r^*). We can see this hiring decision in Figure 10.4.

Figure 10.4

But where does this rental price of capital come from? With many firms hiring capital in this competitive market, the market demand for capital is downward sloping. The market supply curve for capital is upward sloping, and the market determines the competitive price of capital (r^*). This is seen in Figure 10.5.

Market forces, just as in the labor market, would cause the rental rate and quantity of capital to change. For example, if the demand for capital increases, perhaps because of a strong economy and positive corporate expectations, the equilibrium price and quantity of capital in the market would be expected to increase.

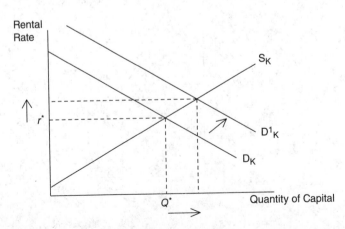

Figure 10.5

10.4 Imperfect Competition in Product and Factor Markets

Main Topics: *Market Power in Product Markets, Market Power in Factor Markets*

We saw in the previous chapter that perfectly competitive markets might not always exist. After all, the conditions for perfect competition are rather strict and not often observed in the "real world." In the sections that follow, we assume that the firm has some market power, first in the product market and then in the factor (labor) market. To no surprise, the outcome of wage and employment differs from the competitive outcome described previously.

Market Power in Product Markets

Perhaps the most important result seen from a firm that has the ability to be a price setter is that the price exceeds marginal revenue. Because $MR < P$ with market power, this has an impact on the marginal revenue product function.

Under perfectly competitive price-taking conditions:
$$MRP_c = MR \times MP_L = P \times MP_L$$

Under conditions of market power:
$$MR < P: MRP_m = MR \times MP_L < MRP_c$$

The result of a lower marginal revenue product function is that the optimal amount of employment falls at all wages. Figure 10.6 illustrates this. In other words, the monopolist hires lesser amounts of all resources, including labor. This should make sense if you recall that monopoly markets produce less output than the competitive market. If the market produces less output, it makes sense that the market would employ fewer resources.

Figure 10.6

- Because $MR < P$, $MRP_m = MR \times MP_L < MRP_c$.
- A monopoly market employs fewer workers than the competitive market.

Market Power in Factor Markets

When a producer has extreme market power in the product market, we label them a price-setting monopolist, and the price of the product is set above marginal revenue. Let's turn this situation around to the factor market. If an employer has extreme market power in the factor market, we label them a wage-setting monopsonist, and we observe the wage set below marginal factor cost.

In a competitive labor market, the firm could employ all it wanted at the market-determined wage. The key difference between **monopsony** and a perfectly competitive labor market is that the employer must increase the wage to increase the quantity of labor that is supplied. In other words, the labor supply to the firm is upward sloping, not horizontal. Marginal factor cost is now greater than the wage. Table 10.5 illustrates how this happens.

Table 10.5

LABOR SUPPLIED TO THE FIRM (L_s)	NECESSARY HOURLY WAGE (W)	TOTAL WAGE BILL = $L_s \times W$	MARGINAL FACTOR COST (MFC)
0		$0	
1	$4	$4	$4
2	$5	$10	$6
3	$6	$18	$8
4	$7	$28	$10
5	$8	$40	$12
6	$9	$54	$14

Example:

Molly's lemonade conglomerate can employ more workers but must increase the wage to do so. However, not only does she have to increase the wage for additional workers but also to her current workers. This creates a situation where $\text{MFC} > W$. See Figure 10.7. Molly still chooses to employ where $\text{MRP}_L = \text{MFC}$, but the wage is determined from the labor supply curve. Graphically the MFC curve lies above the labor supply curve, which means that labor is paid below their MRP_L.

Figure 10.7

- Under monopsony, employers hire $L_m < L_c$.
- Monopsony firms pay $W_m < W_c = \text{MRP}_L$.

Remember that MRP_L measures the value of the last worker to the firm. The outcome that workers receive less than their value to the firm might be alarming. Does this happen?

If you doubt that an employer can get away with such rampant exploitation, I give you a four-letter response: N-C-A-A. A big-time college star athlete might produce, over the course of a four-year career, millions of dollars in revenue to a university. Even if we include the value of four years of tuition, room, and board, the star athlete is compensated well below his or her marginal revenue product. Is it so crazy that many talented college athletes make an early jump to a professional league or in some cases skip college altogether?

› Review Questions

1. Your aunt runs a small firm from her home making apple pies. She hires some friends to help her. Which of the following situations would most likely increase her demand for labor?

   (A) The price of apple peelers/corers rises.
   (B) Your aunt's friends gossip all day, slowing their dough-making process.
   (C) There is a sale on ovens.
   (D) A new study reveals that apples increase your risk of cancer.
   (E) The price of apples increases.

2. The price of labor is $2, and the price of capital is $1. The marginal product of labor is 200, and the marginal product of capital is 50. What should the firm do?

   (A) Increase capital and decrease labor so that the marginal product of capital falls and the marginal product of labor rises.
   (B) Increase capital and decrease labor so that the marginal product of capital rises and the marginal product of labor falls.
   (C) Decrease capital and increase labor so that the marginal product of capital rises and the marginal product of labor falls.
   (D) Decrease capital and increase labor so that the marginal product of capital falls and the marginal product of labor rises.
   (E) Increase both capital and labor until the ratio of marginal products per dollar is equal.

3. A competitive labor market is currently in equilibrium. Which of the following most likely increases the market wage?

   (A) More students graduate with the necessary skills for this labor market.
   (B) Demand for the good produced by this labor is stronger.
   (C) The price of a complementary resource increases.

   (D) The Department of Labor removes the need for workers to pass an exam before they can work in this field.
   (E) Over time, one large employer grows to act as a monopsonist.

Use Table 10.6 to respond to questions 4 and 5.

Table 10.6

WAGE (W)	QUANTITY OF LABOR SUPPLIED	MARGINAL FACTOR COST OF LABOR (MFC)	MARGINAL REVENUE PRODUCT OF LABOR (MRP$_L$)
$3	0		
$4	1	$4	$10
$5	2	$6	$9
$6	3	$8	$8
$7	4	$10	$7

4. If a firm is hiring labor in the perfectly competitive labor market, the wage and employment are

   (A) $3 and 0.
   (B) $4 and 1.
   (C) $5 and 2.
   (D) $6 and 3.
   (E) $7 and 4.

5. If a firm hires labor in a monopsony labor market, the wage and employment are

   (A) $3 and 0.
   (B) $8 and 3.
   (C) $5 and 2.
   (D) $6 and 3.
   (E) $7 and 4.

❯ Answers and Explanations

1. **C**—Since ovens would be a less expensive complementary resource (with more ovens, they can bake more pies), your aunt needs more employees to go along with the extra ovens. Apple corers and peelers are complements, but even if you think they are substitutes, the impact on labor demand is uncertain because of the competing output and substitution effects.

2. **C**—Do a quick ratio of marginal product per dollar. When you see that the $MP_L/P_L > MP_K/P_K$, you notice that the firm is getting more "bang for the buck" with labor. Immediately rule out any choice that says they hire less labor. The only way that MP_L/P_L falls to equal MP_K/P_K is to decrease the capital and increase the labor, causing the MP_K to rise and the MP_L to fall. The firm does this until the marginal products divided by the prices are equal.

3. **B**—The equilibrium wage rises with stronger demand or lessened supply of labor. The stronger demand for the product increases the wage as the demand for labor increases. All other choices either increase the labor supply or decrease the demand, thus decreasing the wage. Emergence of monopsony decreases the wage below competitive levels.

4. **E**—In a competitive labor market, equilibrium is where $W = MRP_L$.

5. **D**—In a monopsony labor market, equilibrium is where $MFC = MRP_L$.

❯ Rapid Review

Marginal revenue product (MRP): Measures the value of what the next unit of a resource (e.g., labor) brings to the firm. $MRP_L = MR \times MP_L$. In a perfectly competitive product market, $MRP_L = P \times MP_L$. In a monopoly product market, $MR < P$ so $MRP_m < MRP_c$.

Marginal resource cost (MRC): Measures the cost the firm incurs from using an additional unit of an input. In a perfectly competitive labor market, MRC = Wage. In a monopsony labor market, the MRC > Wage.

Profit-maximizing resource employment: The firm hires the profit-maximizing amount of a resource at the point where MRP = MRC.

Demand for labor: Labor demand for the firm is the MRP_L curve. The labor demand for the entire market $D_L = \Sigma MRP_L$ of all firms.

Derived demand: Demand for a resource like labor is derived from the demand for the goods produced by the resource.

Determinants of labor demand: One of the external factors that influences labor demand. When these variables change, the entire demand curve shifts to the left or right.

Least-cost rule: The combination of labor and capital that minimizes total costs for a given production rate. Hire L and K so that $MP_L/P_L = MP_K/P_K$ or $MP_L/MP_K = P_L/P_K$.

Monopsonist: A firm that has market power in the factor market, i.e., a wage setter.

CHAPTER 11

Public Goods, Externalities, and the Role of Government

IN THIS CHAPTER

Summary: One of the recurring themes of the first half of this book is that the competitive marketplace provides the most efficient societal outcome where goods are produced at the point where MB = MC, or at the intersection of market supply and market demand. We have not, however, explored the possibility that the demand curve might not capture all of the benefits to society from the consumption of a good. There is also the possibility that the supply curve might not capture all of the costs to society from the production of the good. If these benefits and/or costs are indeed not reflected in the market equilibrium price and quantity, then we conclude that the market has failed to provide the efficient outcome. When this occurs, the government usually needs to step in.

Key Ideas
- ✪ Public and Private Goods
- ✪ Positive and Negative Externalities
- ✪ Income Distribution
- ✪ Tax Structures

11.1 Public Goods and Spillover Benefits

Main Topics: *Private and Public Goods, Spillover Benefits and Positive Externalities*

Private and Public Goods

So far, when discussing goods and services, we have focused on private goods and services. **Private goods** are goods that are both rival and excludable. A bag of potato chips and a cup of herbal tea are both private goods. These are rival in that only one person can consume the good, and so consumption by one consumer necessarily means another cannot. Private goods are excludable in that consumers who do not pay for the good are excluded from consumption.

Public goods, however, are special cases where the goods are both nonrival and nonexcludable. These characteristics mean that one person's consumption does not prevent another from also consuming the good. If a public good is provided to some, it is necessarily provided to all, even if they do not pay for the good. Common examples of public goods are national defense, local fire and police services, space exploration, and environmental protection.

Who Pays?

In the case of private goods, each individual decides whether he or she is going to pay the going price. If the marginal benefit to me is at least as high as the price, I might decide to purchase and consume the good. For private goods, those who want the good badly enough are the ones who pay.

Maybe you have confronted the difficulty in paying for a public good if you have been assigned a group project in school. If each group member receives the same grade, regardless of his or her level of effort, some members of the group might slack off and benefit from the hard work of the others. If this sounds familiar, you have experienced the **free-rider problem.** The free-rider problem pops up whenever some members of the community understand that they can consume the public good while others provide for it.

A small town has a community meeting to decide how to pay for local police protection. The mayor passes a collection plate around the room, and we each make a voluntary donation toward this public good. There are some difficulties with paying for a public good in this way. How much do I use or value the next unit of police services in my protection? Is this more than, less than, or the same as my neighbor's use and value of police protection? It is impossible to answer this question, and even if it were possible to determine how much my neighbor values police service, maybe he won't pay his fair share. After all, if police protection is going to be provided to the entire community, and this protection cannot be denied to anyone, some members of the community might become **free riders**. The free-rider problem and the nonexcludable nature of public goods require that the government collect taxes to pay for their provision.

Spillover Benefits and Positive Externalities

In graduate school I rented a small house on a dead-end street. On the other side of the street, two older ladies had an immaculately landscaped yard with gorgeous rosebushes. Riding my mountain bike home from campus, I was happy to see, and smell, the results of their hard yard work. I'm sure that I was not the only neighbor who felt that way. When one person's consumption of a good provides utility to a third party who has not directly purchased the good, there exist **spillover benefits** that are not reflected in the market price of that good. In my case, my neighbors went to the trouble, expense, and effort to beautify their yard. In the process, they beautified the neighborhood and provided benefits to those of us who received utility from the landscaping and the roses. This situation is described as a **positive externality** and is illustrated in Figure 11.1.

Figure 11.1

The market demand curve $D_{private}$ for roses (labeled MPB for marginal private benefits) captures the private benefits received by consumers of roses but does not capture the additional benefits received by neighbors of those who consumed roses. Figure 11.1 incorporates the spillover benefits to the market for roses. The private demand curve, which does not include the spillover benefits, lies below the societal demand curve (labeled MSB for marginal social benefits) by an amount equal to the per-unit spillover benefits. The market produces only Q_{mkt} roses, but the optimal amount is greater at Q_{social}. Because the market produces less than the socially optimal amount, it is said that there is an underallocation of resources to rose production and deadweight loss is the result. In other words, society wants more than the market provides.

- The existence of spillover benefits in a market results in an underallocation of resources in that market. In other words, there is not enough of a good thing.
- In the presence of a positive externality, at Q_{mkt}, the MSB is greater than MPB due to spillover benefits. At the market quantity, MSB > MSC.
- Because the market ignores the spillover benefits, deadweight loss exists and is seen as the shaded area between MSB and MPB and between Q_{social} and Q_{mkt}. There is no deadweight loss at the socially optimal output where MSC = MSB.

The ladies who lived across the street from my house were essentially providing a public good that we might call "community beautification," and the rest of us were free riding on their activity. How could we have contributed to the provision of the public good? Maybe we could have brought these ladies cash donations, or we could have volunteered our labor. Each of these gestures would have lessened their burden and freed up their private resources to provide even more landscaping for the neighborhood.

Subsidies

On a larger scale, this type of market failure can be remedied through government intervention. Our goal as economic policy makers is to move the equilibrium quantity from Q_{mkt} to Q_{social}. One solution might be to provide a subsidy to gardeners equal to the amount of the spillover benefit that their activity provides to the community. By sending a check (or voucher) to the ladies, they would have increased their demand for roses and other landscaping and shifted the private demand out to equal the social demand. This is seen in Figure 11.2. The price received by the firm has risen to P_{firm}, but when the consumer applies the voucher, the actual price to the consumer is lower at P_{cons}.

Another possibility is to provide a subsidy to producers of roses. This type of subsidy would result in an outward shift in the supply curve so that the equilibrium quantity of roses would be at Q_{social}. This policy is seen in Figure 11.3. The price to consumers, P_{cons}, is also lower in this case, while producers receive, with the subsidy, P_{firm}.

Figure 11.2

Figure 11.3

11.2 Pollution and Spillover Costs

Main Topics: *Spillover Costs and Negative Externalities*

Another kind of market failure occurs when there are additional costs associated with production of a good that are not reflected in the market price. Pollution of all kinds is a classic example.

Spillover Costs and Negative Externalities

Almost anyone who has walked down a busy street has experienced secondhand smoke. Even a nonsmoker, having spent just a minute walking next to a smoker, can smell smoke on his or her clothes. While the smoker has chosen to pay the market price of tobacco, the nonsmoker also pays a price for that choice, either in minor disutility or worsened health. When one person's consumption of a good imposes disutility on a third party who has not directly purchased the good, there exist **spillover costs** that are not reflected in the market price of that good. A situation in which polluters impose costs upon third parties is called a **negative externality**.

The existence of spillover costs from a negative externality means that not all of the costs of production are captured by the market supply curve $S_{private}$. In the Midwest, the burning of coal produces most electricity. The private cost of electricity production includes the coal, the labor, and capital at the plant. But the burning of coal imposes environmental costs in the form of air, water, and land pollution. These costs actually make people, not to mention the planet, sick! These societal costs are not found in the market price (P_{mkt}) of charging your cellphone or running the dishwasher. The difference between the private cost and the societal cost of producing electricity is seen in Figure 11.4. The private supply curve (labeled MPC for marginal private cost), which does not include the spillover costs, lies below the societal supply curve (labeled MSC for marginal social cost). The market produces Q_{mkt} units of electricity, but the optimal amount is less at Q_{social}. Because the market produces more than the socially optimal amount, it is said that there is an overallocation of resources to electricity production, so a deadweight loss exists. In other words, society wants less than the market provides.

- The existence of spillover costs in a market results in an overallocation of resources in that market. In other words, there is too much of a bad thing.
- In the presence of a negative externality, at Q_{mkt}, the MSC is greater than MPC due to spillover costs. At the market quantity, MSC > MSB.
- Because the market ignores the spillover costs, deadweight loss exists and is seen as the shaded area between MSC and MPC and between Q_{social} and Q_{mkt}. At the socially efficient quantity, MSC = MSB, and there is no deadweight loss.

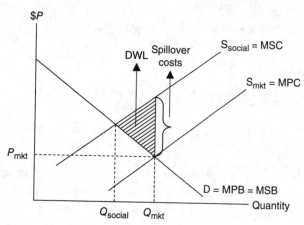

Figure 11.4

So how could cigarette smokers alleviate the discomfort that they impose upon their nonsmoking citizens? The aim of any such policy is to try to move the spillover costs away from the third-party victims and back upon those who produce the externality.

Pollution Taxes

Rather than allow the spillover costs to fall externally on members of society, the goal of pollution taxes is to internalize these costs by imposing a tax on the production or consumption of goods that create negative externalities. Our goal is to move the market equilibrium quantity closer to the socially optimal quantity of electricity. Suppose government imposes a tax, equal to the spillover cost, on every unit of coal that our power plant uses to produce electricity. This pollution tax results in an inward, or upward, shift of the private supply curve so that it equals the social supply curve. See Figure 11.5. The price of running the dishwasher has increased, but now that price incorporates all of the costs of electricity, including the effects of pollution on the environment and human health.

In some cases, a tax may be imposed on consumers, if they are responsible for the negative externality. For example, in major metropolitan areas, traffic is a serious problem and millions of commuters create significant amounts of pollution. We might increase the

Figure 11.5

automobile registration tax or create a system of toll highways so that the users of automobiles and the commuters themselves must pay an additional price for that behavior. We have seen that any time the price increases, quantity demanded (driving) must fall.

Be careful when designing a tax to remedy a negative externality. We must tax those who are imposing the spillover costs on society. Would you tax the nonsmoker to fix the problem of secondhand smoke? Hardly.

KEY IDEA

11.3 Income Distribution and Tax Structures

Main Topics: *Equity as a Goal; Marginal and Average Tax Rates; Progressive, Regressive, and Proportional Taxes*

In the case of pollution and other negative externalities, the marketplace fails to protect the victims of spillover costs. In the case of public goods or other positive externalities, the market fails to provide an adequate quantity to satisfy the needs of society. As we saw previously, the government is called to action to move the market outcome closer to the societal efficient outcome. The government is also called to action to remedy issues of equity, or fairness. This section discusses equity, distribution of income, and tax structures to move closer to a more equitable outcome.

Equity as a Goal

While we tout the efficiency of competitive markets with a fervor that approaches deification, the one thing even the most efficient market does not do is provide equity, or fairness. Some consumers can afford a new Mercedes; some cannot. Yet I doubt that this is a good example of the unfairness of markets. But some consumers cannot afford pediatric services for their infant children. Even if these services are exchanged at the efficient quantity where the marginal social benefit is equal to the marginal social cost, even the most die-hard advocates of the free market can see that it is an outcome that should be remedied through some form of income redistribution.

An Equal Share?

There are some who propose that the economic resources should be equally divided amongst all members of society. This egalitarian, or equal-share, view seems fair but has at least one serious criticism. **Egalitarianism** suffers from an issue of compensation that fails to match productivity. In other words, the incentives to work hard, take risks, and seek a competitive advantage are greatly reduced. If you were guaranteed an equal share of the resources, how hard would you work?

Example:

All students in your class are assured of being compensated with a B, regardless of the effort and productivity that might merit a B. C-level students lack the motivation to become more productive because they are guaranteed compensation above their productivity. A-level students lack the motivation to produce A-level work because they know compensation falls below that. The high-productivity students get disenchanted and disgruntled, and work even less.

Productivity Share?

If egalitarianism suffers from a lack of productivity incentives, maybe everyone's share of economic resources should be based upon individual productivity. In other words, this **marginal productivity theory** says your wage is a function of your marginal revenue product. If markets are competitive, this can be quite efficient. In theory, this could even be fair. The flaw in this method of income distribution is that not all citizens are given a fair shake at demonstrating to the labor market their true marginal revenue product. Think of all of the advantages, large or small, that you were lucky enough to be born with. Now imagine all of them being removed from your past and present. Productive individuals who have few advantages can overcome obstacles with hard work, but some societal barriers (e.g., discrimination, a disability) prevent them from ever receiving a compensation equal to their productivity.

How Do We Measure the Income Distribution?

There are a couple of common ways to see a nation's income distribution. Whether or not we think this is "fair" is another question entirely.

1. *Quintiles.*

Economists sort households from the lowest incomes to the highest incomes and then divide that range into fifths, or **quintiles**. In each quintile lies 20 percent of all households. Table 11.1 illustrates the income distribution in 2000 and 2010 as published by the Census Bureau. If income were perfectly distributed, each 20 percent of the families in the United States would have 20 percent of the total income.

Table 11.1

QUINTILE	% OF TOTAL INCOME (2000)	% OF TOTAL INCOME (2010)
Lowest 20%	3.6%	3.3%
Second 20%	8.9%	8.5%
Third 20%	14.8%	14.6%
Fourth 20%	23.0%	23.4%
Highest 20%	49.8%	50.2%
Total	100.0%	100.0%

2. *Lorenz Curve and Gini Ratio.*

The above quintile distribution can be graphically illustrated with a **Lorenz curve** (see Figure 11.6). The farther the Lorenz curve lies below the hypothetical line of perfect equality, the more unequal the distribution of income. This distance of the actual distribution of income from the line of perfect equality is calculated by constructing a **Gini ratio**, the area of the gap between the perfect equality line and the Lorenz curve (A) as a ratio of the entire area (A + B). The closer the Gini ratio is to zero, the more equal the distribution. The closer to one, the more unequal the income distribution.

$$\text{Gini ratio} = \text{Area A} / (\text{Area A} + \text{Area B})$$

- The closer the Gini ratio gets to zero, the more equal the distribution of income.
- The closer the Gini ratio gets to one, the more unequal the distribution of income.

What Are the Sources of Inequality?

The market is not always a good mechanism for distributing income equally. There are some commonly accepted factors for income inequality:

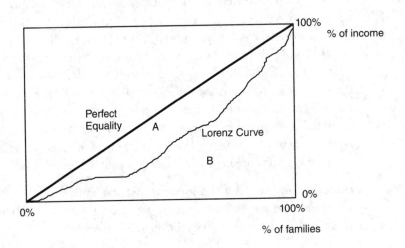

Figure 11.6

- *Ability.* Because natural ability is not distributed equally, income is not distributed equally. This factor would explain why some quarterbacks or artists are more highly paid than other quarterbacks or artists.
- *Human capital.* Individuals augment their ability with education and training, resulting in higher income. Not everyone attains the same level of human capital, so income is not equally distributed.
- *Discrimination.* Despite social progress, discrimination is a hurdle that might not be surmountable even with high levels of ability and human capital.
- *Preferences.* Some individuals, even with high ability and human capital, prefer to maximize utility with more leisure and less labor.
- *Market power.* We learned that monopoly and monopsony markets are detrimental to consumers and workers. The more market power held in the hands of the few, the more unequal the distribution of income.
- *Luck and connections.* Some are born into prosperity, and some are lucky enough to stumble upon the right connections.

Can Income Be Redistributed?

The economic system in the United States emphasizes a productivity-based distribution of resources, but we know that this system does not overcome all of the equity issues that are theoretically solved by egalitarianism. We have decided that the government should have a role in income distribution. The idea behind redistribution of income is that the government collects taxes from one segment of society and transfers it to another. These transfers come in the form of social programs like government housing, Medicare, or public education. And while most agree that these programs are essentially good, how government decides to tax is a hotly debated issue along philosophical and political grounds. We summarize the nature of progressive, regressive, and proportional taxes, and use the marginal and average concepts again in this new context.

Marginal and Average Tax Rates

Marginal tax rate is the rate paid on the last dollar earned. This is found by taking the ratio of the change in taxes divided by the change in income:

$$\text{Marginal tax rate} = (\Delta \text{ taxes due})/(\Delta \text{ taxable income})$$

Example:

If my income rises by $100 and the taxes that I owe the government rise by $25, the marginal tax rate is 25 percent on those additional $100.

Average tax rate is the proportion of total income paid to taxes. It is calculated by dividing the total taxes owed by the total taxable income:

$$\text{Average tax rate} = (\text{Total taxes due})/(\text{Total taxable income})$$

Example:

If my monthly taxable income is $1,000 and $200 is deducted for taxes, my average tax rate is 20 percent.

Progressive, Regressive, and Proportional Taxes

The way in which a redistributive tax works depends upon how the average tax rate changes as income changes.

A Progressive Tax

A **progressive tax** exists if as income increases, the average tax rates increase. The federal income tax works this way. If your household income is above a certain minimum level but below a certain maximum level (a tax bracket), you might pay an average of 20 percent of your income in taxes. If your household income rises above that upper limit and falls into a higher tax bracket, your average tax rate might increase to 24 percent. A **tax bracket** is a range of income on which is applied a given marginal tax rate. This structure is designed so that the lowest incomes pay taxes at a much lower rate than the highest incomes.

A Regressive Tax

A tax is **regressive** if the average tax rate falls as income rises. A sales tax on consumption is a good example of a regressive tax.

Example:

Two unmarried consumers with no children both shop at the grocery store in a state with a 5 percent sales tax. One consumer, Bill, earns a modest $20,000 and spends $10,000 annually on food at the store. He pays $500 in sales tax. A second consumer, Mary, earns $200,000, or 10 times as much as Bill. Can we expect her to spend 10 times as much on food? Doubtful. Let's be generous and say that Mary spends $20,000 annually on food at the grocery store and pays $1,000 in sales tax. Everyone in the state pays 5 percent sales tax on his or her consumption spending, but as a percentage of income, Bill pays a much higher average tax rate.

$$\text{Bill's average tax rate} = \$500/\$20,000 = 2.5\%$$

$$\text{Mary's average tax rate} = \$1,000/\$200,000 = .5\%$$

A Proportional Tax

A proportional tax exists if a constant tax rate is applied regardless of income. Many politicians, on the grounds of a more streamlined way of taxing the population, have proposed this kind of "flat tax." Corporate taxes are taxed at a flat rate of approximately 21 percent and are one of few examples of a proportional tax in the United States. Some U.S. states have adopted a proportional income tax rather than the more traditional progressive tax on income.

Example:
Melanie and Max earn $30,000 and $60,000, respectively. A proportional tax of 10% would require that Melanie pays $300 and Max pays $600 in taxes.

> Review Questions

1. In the figure below, X represents

   (A) spillover benefits.
   (B) a potential producer subsidy to eliminate an externality.
   (C) a potential consumer subsidy to eliminate an externality.
   (D) both A and C.
   (E) A, B, and C.

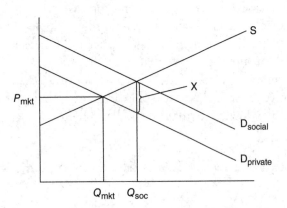

2. Which of the following scenarios best describes a negative externality?

   (A) A roommate has an extensive music library, and you share the same taste in music.
   (B) Your neighbor has a swimming pool, and you have an open invitation to come on over for a pool party.
   (C) Your neighbor has a swimming pool, and her six-year-old child has his first-grade friends over every day for a pool party.
   (D) Your roommate's mom has decided that your apartment needs cable and pays for it.
   (E) Your dad has purchased a new sports coupe and has agreed that you can drive it to the prom.

3. Which of the following is the best example of a public good?

   (A) A lighthouse on a rocky coastline
   (B) Tickets to the Super Bowl
   (C) A granola bar
   (D) A cup of coffee
   (E) A magazine subscription

4. Production of energy (i.e., electricity, natural gas, heating oil) creates a negative externality in the form of air pollution blown to communities downwind from the source of the pollution. Of the choices below, which is the most appropriate policy to remedy this negative externality?

   (A) a per-unit tax on consumers of subway tickets and city bus passes
   (B) a per-unit tax on producers of energy
   (C) a per-unit subsidy for energy consumers
   (D) a per-unit tax on consumers of energy-efficient lightbulbs
   (E) a per-unit subsidy for energy producers

5. Jason earns $1,000 a week and pays a total of $200 in taxes. Jennifer earns $2,000 a week and pays a total of $300 in taxes. We can conclude from this information that their income is taxed with a(n)

(A) progressive tax.
(B) proportional tax.
(C) regressive tax.
(D) tax bracket.
(E) egalitarian tax.

6. You learn that one nation has a Gini ratio of .25 and another nation has a Gini ratio of .85. Based on this you might conclude

(A) the nation with the higher Gini ratio has a more equal distribution of wealth and income.
(B) the nation with the higher Gini ratio has a more unequal distribution of citizens with college degrees.
(C) the nation with the lower Gini ratio has more societal barriers like discrimination.
(D) the nation with the higher Gini ratio has fewer societal barriers like discrimination.
(E) the nation with the lower Gini ratio has more oligopolistic industries.

› Answers and Explanations

1. **E**—This vertical distance between society's demand curve and the market demand curve represents spillover benefits, or additional benefits to society not captured by market demand. However, it could also be the amount of a producer or consumer subsidy if the government chose to eliminate the externality.

2. **C**—A negative externality is a situation where a third party is harmed by the actions of consumers and/or producers. The first-grade pool party is the best candidate for such a situation, as all of the other choices are likely to benefit you, rather than impose cost upon you.

3. **A**—A public good is a good that is nonrival and nonexcludable. In other words, if one person consumes it, all others can still consume it.

4. **B**—The presence of the negative externality should rule out any choice that refers to a subsidy of either producers or consumers of energy. To reduce consumption and production, we must

reduce the market quantity, not encourage more of it. Subsidies could be used to encourage more energy-efficient behavior, but choices A and D would actually inhibit this kind of action. The per-unit tax on producers of the negative externality is the most appropriate choice, as the tax shifts the market supply inward, making it closer to the socially optimal supply of energy.

5. **C**—Jennifer's weekly income is twice Jason's, yet she pays less than double his taxes. This is a regressive tax. A proportional tax would require Jennifer to pay $400, and a progressive tax would require that she pay more than $400 in weekly taxes.

6. **B**—The distribution of human capital is a factor in determining the distribution of income and wealth. A nation that has a more unequal distribution of educational attainment would therefore likely have a more unequal distribution of income.

› Rapid Review

Private goods: Goods that are both rival and excludable. Only one person can consume the good at a time, and consumers who do not pay for the good are excluded from consumption. Examples include a tube of toothpaste or an airline ticket.

Public goods: Goods that are both nonrival and nonexcludable. One person's consumption does not prevent another from also consuming the good, and if it is provided to some, it is necessarily provided to all, even if they do not pay for the good. Examples are local police services and national defense.

Free-rider problem: In the case of a public good, some members of the community know that they can consume the public good while others provide for it. This results in a lack of private funding for the good and requires that the government provide it.

Spillover benefits: Additional benefits to society, not captured by the market demand curve from the production of a good, result in a price that is too high and a market quantity that is too low. Resources are underallocated to the production of this good.

Positive externality: Exists when the production of a good creates utility (the spillover benefits) for third parties not directly involved in the consumption or production of the good.

Marginal private benefit curve (MPB): The MPB reflects the additional benefit received by actual consumers of a good; the market demand curve.

Marginal social benefit curve (MSB): The MSB reflects the additional benefit received by all members of society, including both those who actually consume the good and those who receive spillover benefits from that consumption; the socially optimal demand curve.

Spillover costs: Additional costs to society, not captured by the market supply curve from the production of a good, result in a price that is too low and market quantity that is too high. Resources are overallocated to the production of this good.

Negative externality: Exists when the production of a good imposes disutility (the spillover costs) upon third parties not directly involved in the consumption or production of the good.

Marginal private cost curve (MPC): The MPC reflects the additional cost incurred by actual producers of a good; the market supply curve.

Marginal social cost curve (MSC): The MSC reflects the additional cost incurred by all members of society, including those who actually produce the good and those who incur spillover costs from that production; the socially optimal supply curve.

Egalitarianism: The philosophy that all citizens should receive an equal share of the economic resources.

Marginal productivity theory: The philosophy that a citizen should receive a share of economic resources proportional to the marginal revenue product of his or her productivity.

Marginal tax rate: The rate paid on the last dollar earned. This is found by taking the ratio of the change in taxes divided by the change in income.

Average tax rate: The proportion of total income paid to taxes. It is calculated by dividing the total taxes owed by the total taxable income.

Progressive tax: The proportion of income paid in taxes rises as income rises. An example is the personal income tax.

Tax bracket: A range of income on which a given marginal tax rate is applied.

Regressive tax: The proportion of income paid in taxes decreases as income rises. An example is a sales tax.

Proportional tax: A constant proportion of income is paid in taxes no matter the level of income. An example is a "flat tax" or the corporate income tax.

Lorenz curve: A graphical representation of a nation's income distribution.

Gini ratio: A measure of a nation's income inequality. This measure uses a scale between zero and one. The closer it lies to zero, the more equal the distribution of income.

STEP 5

Build Your Test-Taking Confidence

AP Microeconomics Practice Exam 1
AP Microeconomics Practice Exam 2

AP Microeconomics Practice Exam 1

SECTION I: Multiple-Choice Questions
ANSWER SHEET

1 (A) (B) (C) (D) (E)	21 (A) (B) (C) (D) (E)	41 (A) (B) (C) (D) (E)
2 (A) (B) (C) (D) (E)	22 (A) (B) (C) (D) (E)	42 (A) (B) (C) (D) (E)
3 (A) (B) (C) (D) (E)	23 (A) (B) (C) (D) (E)	43 (A) (B) (C) (D) (E)
4 (A) (B) (C) (D) (E)	24 (A) (B) (C) (D) (E)	44 (A) (B) (C) (D) (E)
5 (A) (B) (C) (D) (E)	25 (A) (B) (C) (D) (E)	45 (A) (B) (C) (D) (E)
6 (A) (B) (C) (D) (E)	26 (A) (B) (C) (D) (E)	46 (A) (B) (C) (D) (E)
7 (A) (B) (C) (D) (E)	27 (A) (B) (C) (D) (E)	47 (A) (B) (C) (D) (E)
8 (A) (B) (C) (D) (E)	28 (A) (B) (C) (D) (E)	48 (A) (B) (C) (D) (E)
9 (A) (B) (C) (D) (E)	29 (A) (B) (C) (D) (E)	49 (A) (B) (C) (D) (E)
10 (A) (B) (C) (D) (E)	30 (A) (B) (C) (D) (E)	50 (A) (B) (C) (D) (E)
11 (A) (B) (C) (D) (E)	31 (A) (B) (C) (D) (E)	51 (A) (B) (C) (D) (E)
12 (A) (B) (C) (D) (E)	32 (A) (B) (C) (D) (E)	52 (A) (B) (C) (D) (E)
13 (A) (B) (C) (D) (E)	33 (A) (B) (C) (D) (E)	53 (A) (B) (C) (D) (E)
14 (A) (B) (C) (D) (E)	34 (A) (B) (C) (D) (E)	54 (A) (B) (C) (D) (E)
15 (A) (B) (C) (D) (E)	35 (A) (B) (C) (D) (E)	55 (A) (B) (C) (D) (E)
16 (A) (B) (C) (D) (E)	36 (A) (B) (C) (D) (E)	56 (A) (B) (C) (D) (E)
17 (A) (B) (C) (D) (E)	37 (A) (B) (C) (D) (E)	57 (A) (B) (C) (D) (E)
18 (A) (B) (C) (D) (E)	38 (A) (B) (C) (D) (E)	58 (A) (B) (C) (D) (E)
19 (A) (B) (C) (D) (E)	39 (A) (B) (C) (D) (E)	59 (A) (B) (C) (D) (E)
20 (A) (B) (C) (D) (E)	40 (A) (B) (C) (D) (E)	60 (A) (B) (C) (D) (E)

AP Microeconomics Practice Exam 1

SECTION I

Multiple-Choice Questions
Time—1 hour and 10 minutes
60 questions

For the multiple-choice questions that follow, select the best answer and fill in the appropriate letter on the answer sheet.

1. At the birthday party of your best friend, you see Skylar help himself to a second piece of cake. For this individual, it must be the case that

   (A) the marginal benefit of the second piece of cake is less than the marginal cost.
   (B) the total benefit received from eating cake is falling.
   (C) the ratio of marginal benefit over marginal cost is less than one.
   (D) the marginal benefit of the second piece of cake is greater than the marginal cost.
   (E) Skylar is irrationally consuming too much cake.

2. Nancy has the choice to spend one hour studying for an exam, mowing the lawn for one hour at a wage of $6, or babysitting her niece for one hour at a wage of $8. If we know that Nancy has chosen to study for the exam, which of the following is true?

   (A) The benefit received from studying is greater than the opportunity cost of $8.
   (B) The opportunity cost of studying is $14, which is less than the benefit received from studying.
   (C) Nancy is indifferent to both studying and mowing the lawn.
   (D) Nancy's behavior is irrational, since babysitting was clearly superior to all other options.
   (E) Nancy is indifferent to both babysitting and mowing the lawn.

3. Suppose the market for roses is currently in equilibrium. If the supply of roses falls, while at the same time the demand for roses rises, what can you say about the price and quantity of roses in the market?

   (A) Price and quantity both rise.
   (B) Price rises, but the change in quantity is ambiguous.
   (C) Price and quantity both fall.
   (D) Quantity rises, but the change in price is ambiguous.
   (E) Neither price nor quantity change, as these shifts offset one another.

4. The United States is trading salmon to Peru in exchange for anchovies. If these nations are trading based upon relative opportunity costs, what must be the case?

   (A) The United States has comparative advantage in anchovy production, and Peru has comparative advantage in salmon production.
   (B) The United States has comparative advantage in salmon production, and Peru has comparative advantage in anchovy production.
   (C) The United States has absolute advantage in anchovy production, and Peru has absolute advantage in salmon production.
   (D) The United States has absolute advantage in salmon production, and Peru has absolute advantage in anchovy production.
   (E) The United States has comparative advantage in salmon production, and Peru has absolute advantage in anchovy production.

5. Which of the following is the best example of a public good?

   (A) Private violin lessons
   (B) The volunteer fire department in your community
   (C) A $1 ticket for admission to a museum
   (D) A bag of potato chips
   (E) A history textbook

6. A typical characteristic of capitalist market economies is

   (A) government ownership of land and capital.
   (B) extensive price controls.
   (C) centralized government decision making to determine production limits.
   (D) an absence of scarcity.
   (E) private ownership of economic resources.

Questions 7 to 9 refer to the graph below.

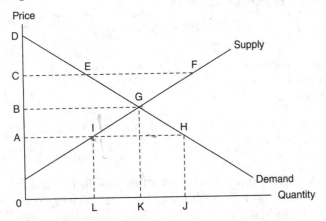

7. Assuming no government involvement in this market, if the current price were at the level of 0A, we would expect

   (A) a surplus in the market to be eliminated by rising prices.
   (B) a shortage in the market to be eliminated by falling prices.
   (C) a surplus in the market to be eliminated by falling prices.
   (D) a shortage in the market to be eliminated by rising prices.
   (E) a decrease in quantity supplied and an increase in quantity demanded as the price rises.

8. If the market is initially in equilibrium, which of the following would create a new equilibrium at point H?

   (A) A decrease in consumer income if this good is normal.
   (B) An increase in the price of a substitute for this good.
   (C) A decrease in the cost of a production input for this good.
   (D) An increase in the number of consumers of this good.
   (E) An increase in consumer income if this good is normal.

9. If the price were to rise from 0B to 0C,

   (A) dollars spent on this good would increase if demand for the good were price elastic.
   (B) dollars spent on this good would decrease if demand for the good were price inelastic.
   (C) dollars spent on this good would increase if demand for the good were price inelastic.
   (D) dollars spent on this good would increase if demand for the good were unitary price elastic.
   (E) dollars spent on this good would decrease if demand for the good were unitary price elastic.

10. Every day Melanie spends her lunch money consuming apples, at $1 each, and oranges, at $2 each. At her current level of consumption, Melanie's marginal utility of apples is 12 and her marginal utility of oranges is 18. If she has already spent all of her lunch money, how should Melanie change her consumption decision to maximize utility?

    (A) She should make no changes; she is consuming the utility maximizing combination of apples and oranges.
    (B) She should increase her apple consumption and decrease her orange consumption until the marginal utility per dollar is equal for both.
    (C) She should decrease her apple consumption and increase her orange consumption until the marginal utility per dollar is equal for both.
    (D) She should increase her apple consumption and decrease her orange consumption until the marginal utility is equal for both.
    (E) She should decrease her apple consumption and increase her orange consumption until the marginal utility is equal for both.

11. When the production or consumption of a good creates a positive externality, it is deemed a market failure because at the market quantity

    (A) the marginal social benefit exceeds the marginal social cost.
    (B) the marginal social cost exceeds the marginal social benefit.
    (C) society produces too much of the good.
    (D) the private benefits from consuming the good exceed the social benefits.
    (E) a surplus of the good always exists without government intervention.

12. Which of the following would best complete a short definition of economics? "Economics is the study of . . ."

   (A) how unlimited resources are allocated between scarce wants.
   (B) how money is circulated through the economy.
   (C) how corporations maximize the share price of their stock.
   (D) how nations trade goods and services in a global marketplace.
   (E) how scarce resources are allocated to satisfy unlimited wants.

13. Suppose the price elasticity of demand for cigarettes is less than one. When an excise tax is imposed on cigarette production, it changes the price, quantity, and consumer spending in which of the following ways?

	PRICE	QUANTITY	SPENDING
(A)	Decrease	Increase	Increase
(B)	Decrease	Decrease	Decrease
(C)	Increase	Decrease	Decrease
(D)	Increase	Decrease	Increase
(E)	Increase	Increase	Increase

14. Which of the following is true of a price floor?

   (A) The price floor shifts the demand curve to the left.
   (B) An effective floor creates a shortage of the good.
   (C) The price floor shifts the supply curve of the good to the right.
   (D) To be an effective floor, it must be set above the equilibrium price.
   (E) The government sets the price floor to assist consumers who are exploited at the equilibrium price.

15. You are told that the income elasticity for skateboards is +1.5. This means that

   (A) a 10-percent increase in income produces a 15-percent increase in consumption of skateboards. Skateboards are a normal luxury good.
   (B) a 10-percent increase in income produces a 15-percent increase in consumption of skateboards. Skateboards are an inferior good.
   (C) a 10-percent increase in income produces a 15-percent decrease in consumption of skateboards. Skateboards are an inferior good.
   (D) a 10-percent increase in the price of skateboards produces a 15-percent decrease in consumption of skateboards. Skateboards are a price elastic good.
   (E) a 10-percent increase in the price of skateboards produces a 15-percent decrease in consumption of skateboards. Skateboards are a price inelastic good.

16. Which of the following causes the supply curve of paper to shift to the left?

   (A) Paper producers expect lower paper prices in the months ahead.
   (B) The price of pencils, a complement to paper, increases.
   (C) Improvements are made in the technology used to produce paper.
   (D) Household income falls.
   (E) Environmental concerns reduce the yearly amount of timber that can be harvested.

Computers

Corn

17. Using the diagram above, which of the following might have caused the outward movement of the production possibility frontier?

   (A) A decrease in the availability of fertile farmland
   (B) A plague of destructive grasshoppers
   (C) An increase in the productivity of the labor force
   (D) A severe and long-lasting drought
   (E) A decline in the rate of technological improvements

18. Suppose the county government sends each parent a coupon that can be used to subsidize the cost of sending each child to daycare. What would you expect to occur in the market for daycare services?

    (A) The demand for daycare falls, lowering the market price.
    (B) The demand for daycare rises, increasing the market price.
    (C) The supply of daycare rises, lowering the market price.
    (D) The supply of daycare falls, increasing the market price.
    (E) A permanent shortage of daycare services exists.

19. Monopoly deadweight loss is the result of

    (A) setting the price above marginal cost.
    (B) setting the price above average total cost.
    (C) monopoly output being greater than the competitive output.
    (D) long-run normal profits.
    (E) marginal revenue equaling marginal cost.

20. The market for Cincinnati Reds baseball tickets is currently in equilibrium. Which of the following events would most likely increase the consumer surplus received by Reds fans?

    (A) The Reds offer discounted parking for all home games.
    (B) The Reds increase hot dog prices to reflect a higher cost of buns.
    (C) The city of Cincinnati is undertaking a huge highway construction project that strands fans in pregame traffic jams for hours.
    (D) The Reds must increase ticket prices to afford the most talented players.
    (E) Fans must pay a steep service charge in order to purchase tickets online or over the phone.

21. If Matt's total utility from consuming bratwurst increased at a constant rate, no matter how many bratwurst Matt consumed, what would Matt's demand curve for bratwurst look like?

    (A) Vertical
    (B) Horizontal
    (C) Downward sloping
    (D) Upward sloping
    (E) First upward, but eventually downward sloping

22. When a firm is earning a normal profit from the production of a good, it is true that

    (A) total revenues from production are equal to explicit costs.
    (B) explicit costs are equal to implicit costs.
    (C) total revenues from production are equal to implicit costs.
    (D) total revenues from production are equal to the sum of explicit and implicit costs.
    (E) implicit costs are greater than explicit costs.

23. You are told that the cross-price elasticity between goods X and Y is +2.0. This means that

    (A) goods X and Y are normal goods.
    (B) goods X and Y are inferior goods.
    (C) goods X and Y are complementary goods.
    (D) goods X and Y are substitute goods.
    (E) demand for good X is twice as elastic as demand for good Y.

24. Which of the following is an example of a long-run adjustment for the owners of a small café?

    (A) The owners switch from whole wheat to sourdough bread.
    (B) The owners hire several part-time workers to cover the dinner shifts.
    (C) The owners work overtime on a busy weekend.
    (D) The owners install more energy-efficient lightbulbs in all of the light fixtures.
    (E) The owners buy the office next door, and this doubles the customer seating.

25. If total product of labor is rising at an increasing rate,

    (A) marginal product of labor is rising.
    (B) marginal product of labor is at its minimum.
    (C) marginal product of labor is at its maximum.
    (D) marginal cost is rising.
    (E) average product of labor is at its minimum.

26. The demand curve for a perfectly competitive firm's product is

    (A) downward sloping and equal to the market demand curve.
    (B) perfectly elastic.
    (C) perfectly inelastic.
    (D) "kinked" at the going market price.
    (E) the same as the firm's marginal cost curve.

27. Which of the following is true in the long run in perfect competition?

(A) $P = MR = MC = ATC$
(B) $P = MR = MC > ATC$
(C) $P > MR = MC = ATC$
(D) $P = MR > MC = ATC$
(E) $P > MR = MC > ATC$

28. If the market price is above the perfectly competitive firm's average total cost curve, we expect that in the long run,

(A) the industry contracts as firms exit the market.
(B) the industry expands as firms exit the market.
(C) the industry contracts as firms enter the market.
(D) the industry expands as firms enter the market.
(E) the government seeks to regulate the market to ensure efficient outcomes.

29. If a market is organized by a cartel, we can expect

(A) normal profits for all cartel firms.
(B) an incentive for cartel firms to cheat on the cartel agreement.
(C) profit maximization by individual firms in the cartel.
(D) allocative efficiency.
(E) perfectly competitive prices.

30. Jason cleans swimming pools in a perfectly competitive local market. A profit maximizer, he can charge $10 per pool to clean 9 pools per day, incurring total variable costs of $80 and total fixed costs of $20. Which of the following is true?

(A) Jason should shut down in the short run, with economic losses of $20.
(B) Jason should shut down in the short run, with economic losses of $10.
(C) Jason should clean 9 pools per day, with economic losses of $20.
(D) Jason should clean 9 pools per day, with economic losses of $10.
(E) Jason should clean 9 pools per day, with economic profits of $10.

31. Which of the following might explain how a price decrease might cause a decrease in quantity demanded and an upward-sloping demand curve?

(A) The good is inferior and the income effect is stronger than the substitution effect.
(B) The good is normal and the income effect is stronger than the substitution effect.
(C) The good is normal and the income effect is weaker than the substitution effect.
(D) The good is inferior and a luxury.
(E) The good is highly subsidized, creating a large increase in marginal utility per dollar.

32. For the perfectly competitive firm, the profit-maximizing decision to shut down is made when the price

(A) falls below minimum average total cost.
(B) is greater than minimum average variable cost, but lower than minimum average total cost.
(C) falls below minimum average variable cost.
(D) is equal to minimum average total cost.
(E) is equal to average fixed cost.

33. Declining populations of tuna in the Atlantic Ocean have likely had which of the following impacts on the wages of tuna fishermen, the employment of tuna fishermen, and real estate prices in New England fishing towns?

	FISHERMAN WAGES	EMPLOYMENT OF FISHERMEN	REAL ESTATE PRICES
(A)	Decrease	Increase	Increase
(B)	Decrease	Decrease	Decrease
(C)	Decrease	Decrease	Increase
(D)	Increase	Decrease	Decrease
(E)	Increase	Increase	Increase

34. Which of the following is true of monopoly markets?

(A) Deadweight loss exists in the short run, but not in the long run.
(B) A homogenous product allows for long-run entry of competing firms.
(C) Collusion between close rivals creates pricing above marginal cost.
(D) Barriers to entry allow for the power to set prices above marginal cost.
(E) Allocative efficiency is guaranteed because marginal revenue equals marginal cost.

Questions 35 and 36 refer to the graph below.

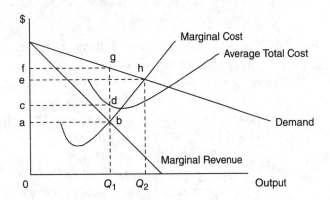

35. If this firm were a profit-maximizing monopolist, the price and output would be which of the following?

(A) 0a and Q1
(B) 0c and Q1
(C) 0e and Q1
(D) 0e and Q2
(E) 0f and Q1

36. Deadweight loss is equal to which of the following areas?

(A) abcd
(B) cdfg
(C) 0abQ1
(D) Q1Q2gh
(E) bdgh

Two competing firms are deciding whether to enter a new market or maintain the status quo. Use the following profit matrix to respond to question 37.

		FIRM X	
		Enter Market	**Status Quo**
FIRM Y	**Enter Market**	X: $3 million Y: $3 million	X: $1 million Y: $6 million
	Status Quo	X: $6 million Y: $1 million	X: $5 million Y: $5 million

37. If these firms do not collude, the outcome will be

(A) both firms maintain the status quo.
(B) both firms enter the market.
(C) Firm X enters the market and Firm Y maintains the status quo.
(D) Firm Y enters the market and Firm X maintains the status quo.
(E) both firms alternate between entering the market and maintaining the status quo.

38. When the marginal product of labor is equal to the average product of labor,

(A) marginal product of labor is at its maximum.
(B) marginal cost of production is at its minimum.
(C) marginal cost is equal to minimum average variable cost.
(D) average total cost is at its minimum.
(E) total product of labor is at its maximum.

Questions 39 to 41 refer to the graph below.

39. The area 0abQ is equal to

(A) total cost.
(B) total variable cost.
(C) total fixed cost.
(D) marginal cost.
(E) average product of labor.

40. The curve labeled 1 represents which of the following?

(A) Marginal cost
(B) Marginal product of labor
(C) Average total cost
(D) Average variable cost
(E) Average fixed cost

41. If this firm was operating in a perfectly competitive market, and the price was equal to 0g, economic profit would be equal to which of the following areas?

    (A) abcd
    (B) cdgh
    (C) cdef
    (D) eghf
    (E) abgh

42. Which is true of monopolistic competition?

    (A) Firms earn long-run economic profits.
    (B) $P = MR = MC = ATC$.
    (C) Firms spend money to differentiate and advertise their products.
    (D) In the long run the market is allocatively efficient.
    (E) Excess capacity is eliminated in the long run.

43. If firms are entering an industry that is monopolistically competitive, we would expect

    (A) the demand for existing firms to shift rightward.
    (B) the market price of the product to increase.
    (C) the demand for existing firms to become more inelastic.
    (D) economic profits to rise for all firms.
    (E) the demand for existing firms to shift leftward.

44. Monopolistic competition is said to be productively inefficient because

    (A) the long-run price is above minimum average total cost.
    (B) long-run profits are positive.
    (C) firms engage in collusive behavior.
    (D) there exist no barriers to entry.
    (E) there exist diseconomies of scale.

45. One of the reasons that the government discourages and regulates monopolies is that

    (A) producer surplus is lost and consumer surplus is gained.
    (B) monopoly prices ensure productive efficiency but cost society allocative efficiency.
    (C) monopoly firms do not engage in significant research and development.
    (D) consumer surplus is lost with higher prices and lower levels of output.
    (E) lower prices and higher levels of output create deadweight loss.

46. What is one reason why the government discourages collusion between large firms in the same industry?

    (A) Collusive output levels tend to increase, driving the price above competitive levels.
    (B) Consumer surplus falls as the price is driven downward.
    (C) Collusive output levels tend to decrease, driving the price down to competitive levels.
    (D) Joint profit maximization drives profits downward, forcing colluding firms to exit the industry.
    (E) Joint profit maximization costs society consumer surplus as the price rises above competitive levels.

47. In a competitive labor market for housepainters, which of the following would increase the demand for housepainters?

    (A) An effective minimum wage imposed on this labor market.
    (B) An increase in the price of gallons of paint.
    (C) An increase in the construction of new houses.
    (D) An increase in the price of mechanical painters so long as the output effect exceeds the substitution effect.
    (E) An increase in home mortgage interest rates.

48. If a monopsony labor market suddenly were transformed into a perfectly competitive labor market, how would the wage and employment change?

    (A) Both would increase.
    (B) Both would decrease.
    (C) The wage would remain constant, but employment would increase.
    (D) The wage would fall, but employment would increase.
    (E) The wage would rise, but employment would decrease.

49. Which of the following is most likely to be true in the long run for a monopoly firm?

    (A) $P = MR = MC = ATC$
    (B) $P = MR = MC > ATC$
    (C) $P > MR = MC = ATC$
    (D) $P = MR > MC = ATC$
    (E) $P > ATC > MR = MC$

Questions 50 and 51 refer to the table below, which describes employment and production of a firm.

UNITS OF LABOR	TOTAL PRODUCT	PRICE OF OUTPUT
0	0	$2
1	8	$2
2	20	$2
3	30	$2
4	38	$2
5	44	$2

50. The marginal revenue product of the fourth unit of labor is equal to

(A) $19.
(B) $16.
(C) $8.
(D) $20.
(E) $2.

51. If the wage paid to all units of labor is $20, how many units of labor are employed?

(A) 1
(B) 2
(C) 3
(D) 4
(E) 5

52. An industry described as an oligopoly would most likely have

(A) normal profits in the long run.
(B) no opportunities for collusive behavior.
(C) significant barriers to entry.
(D) price-taking behavior.
(E) one firm with no close rivals.

53. An effective minimum wage in the market for fast-food workers is likely to produce

(A) an increase in the demand for fast-food workers.
(B) a decrease in the supply of fast-food workers.
(C) a shortage of fast-food workers.
(D) a lower price of fast-food products.
(E) a surplus of fast-food workers.

54. In order to hire the least-cost combination of labor and capital, the firm must do which of the following?

(A) Find the combination of labor and capital where the marginal product of labor is equal to the marginal product of capital.
(B) Find the combination of labor and capital where the ratio of the marginal product of labor to the marginal product of capital is equal to one.
(C) Find the combination of labor and capital where the marginal product of labor divided by the price of labor is equal to the marginal product of capital divided by the price of capital.
(D) Find the combination of labor and capital where the price of labor is equal to the price of capital.
(E) Find the combination of labor and capital where the marginal revenue product of labor is equal to the marginal revenue product of capital.

55. More college students are graduating with BA degrees in economics. Given this trend, we would expect the wage of economists, the employment of economists, and the demand for economics textbooks to change in which of the following ways?

	ECONOMIST WAGES	EMPLOYMENT OF ECONOMISTS	DEMAND FOR ECONOMICS TEXTBOOKS
(A)	Decrease	Increase	Increase
(B)	Decrease	Decrease	Decrease
(C)	Increase	Decrease	Decrease
(D)	Increase	Decrease	Increase
(E)	Increase	Increase	Increase

56. Which of the following is the best example of a negative externality and the appropriate plan for eliminating it?

(A) Air pollution from a factory blows downwind and harms children in a small community. Tax the citizens of the community.
(B) Your neighbor plants a fragrant blooming cherry tree in her front yard. Give a tree subsidy to your neighbor.
(C) The waste from a hog farm pollutes a neighbor's drinking water. Give a subsidy to the hog farmer.
(D) Diesel-burning cars, trucks, and buses are creating smog in your city. Eliminate a subsidy for people who purchase electric vehicles.
(E) Air pollution from a power plant is blowing downwind and harming the trees in your community. Tax the production of electricity.

57. A perfectly competitive employer hires labor up to the point where

(A) wage = marginal factor cost.
(B) wage = marginal product of labor.
(C) wage = marginal revenue.
(D) wage = marginal revenue product of labor.
(E) wage = price of the good produced by the labor.

58. The sales tax that you pay at the grocery store is commonly labeled a

(A) progressive tax.
(B) regressive tax.
(C) proportional tax.
(D) excise tax.
(E) tax bracket.

59. Which of the following is the best example of the free-rider effect?

(A) You and a friend take a road trip to Florida in your friend's car. You pay for the gas.
(B) In exchange for tutoring your friend in economics, she helps you with your geometry assignment.
(C) You have ordered a big college football game on pay-per-view, and several of your buddies show up unannounced to watch it at your place.
(D) You buy your date dinner, but your date insists on leaving a tip for the server.
(E) A local Girl Scout troop is giving a "free" carwash. You give them a $5 donation.

Question 60 refers to the graph below.

60. If the market for this good was in equilibrium at $Q2$ but the socially optimal output was $Q1$, the government could best remedy this ____ of resources by legislating a ____ on ____ of the good.

(A) underallocation, per-unit tax, consumers
(B) overallocation, per-unit subsidy, consumers
(C) underallocation, per-unit tax, producers
(D) overallocation, per-unit subsidy, producers
(E) overallocation, per-unit tax, producers

› Answers and Explanations

1. **D**—You have to assume that Skylar evaluated the marginal benefits and marginal costs of the second piece of cake and decided that he should consume it.

2. **A**—The opportunity cost is the value of the most attractive alternative (in this case, the babysitting wage).

3. **B**—If demand increases and supply decreases, the price definitely rises. The quantity is ambiguous and depends upon which effect is stronger. Draw these shifting curves in the margin of your exam book.

4. **B**—Trading nations specialize in the good in which they have lower opportunity costs. A nation trades this good to the other in exchange for the good for which it does not have comparative advantage.

5. **B**—Public goods like police and fire protection are received by all citizens, even if they do not pay.

6. **E**—The citizens privately own resources in capitalist systems.

7. **D**—Prices below equilibrium create shortages, but they do not last.

8. **C**—A rightward shift in supply would move the market to point H and lower input prices would do just that.

9. **C**—If $E_d < 1$, a given percent increase in the price outweighs the percent decrease in quantity demanded, thus increasing total dollars spent on the good.

10. **B**—The utility maximizing rule requires that MU/P is equal for both goods. Now the MU/P is greater for apples than for oranges. Melanie consumes more apples and fewer oranges, which lowers MU of apples and increases the MU of oranges.

11. **A**—Market equilibrium occurs where marginal private benefit equals marginal cost to society. With a positive externality, the MSB > MPB at the market quantity.

12. **E**—This is the definition of economics!

13. **D**—Excise taxes shift a supply curve leftward, increase price, and decrease quantity. If $E_d < 1$, cigarette consumers spend more on cigarettes.

14. **D**—Price floors are legal minimum prices so they are set above equilibrium. A surplus results.

15. **A**—When $E_I > 0$, it is a normal good. When $E_I > 1$, it is a luxury good.

16. **E**—Restricting the supply of a raw material to paper would increase the price of the production input and decrease the supply of paper.

17. **C**—Economic growth is the result of better, or more economic, resources or more technological progress. A more productive labor force increases the PPF for both goods.

18. **B**—A subsidy given to consumers acts as an increase in income. Demand for daycare rises, raising the price of daycare.

19. **A**—If $P = MC$, the market is allocatively efficient and there is no deadweight loss. If the monopoly $P > MC$, DWL emerges.

20. **A**—Anything that effectively lowers the price of attending the Reds game increases CS.

21. **B**—Downward-sloping demand is the result of diminishing marginal utility. This consumer's MU is constant, so the demand curve for bratwurst is horizontal.

22. **D**—Normal profits are also thought of as break-even economic profits.

23. **D**—If $E_{xy} > 0$, goods are substitutes.

24. **E**—Long-run adjustments change the production capacity of a firm.

25. **A**—MP_L tells you how TP_L is changing when more labor is hired. If more labor is increasing TP_L at a faster and faster rate, MP_L is rising.

26. **B**—Perfectly competitive firms are price takers, so demand for each firm's product is horizontal: $E_d = \infty$.

27. **A**—A defining outcome of long-run equilibrium in perfect competition.

28. **D**—If $P > ATC$, positive short-run economic profits exist. Long-run entry expands the market.

29. **B**—Cartels are illegal collusive agreements to lower output, raise the price, and maximize joint profits. Each member has an incentive to cheat by producing a little more.

30. **D**—TR > TVC, so Jason does not shut down. Subtracting all costs from TR, he is losing $10 per day.

31. **A**—Income and substitution effects work in opposite directions for inferior goods. A lower price prompts a substitution effect, increasing quantity demanded of the good. A lower price increases purchasing power, and for an inferior good, it decreases consumption. If the income effect outweighs the substitution effect, we can see an upward-sloping demand curve.

32. **C**—This is the shutdown point.

33. **B**—Decreased labor demand lowers wage and employment. Lower incomes and higher unemployment decrease real estate prices.

34. **D**—Barriers to entry are the key to monopoly pricing power.

35. **E**—Find the output where MR = MC and the price is found vertically at the demand curve.

36. **E**—DWL is the area above MC and below the demand curve, between the monopoly output and the perfectly competitive output.

37. **B**—Entering is a dominant strategy for both firms.

38. **C**—MC and AVC are inverses of MP_L and AP_L. Because $MP_L = AP_L$ at the maximum of AP_L, MC = AVC at the minimum of AVC.

39. **C**—Familiarity with cost curves identifies curve 4 as AFC. The area of this rectangle is $Q \times$ AFC = TFC.

40. **A**—Quickly recognize this as MC.

41. **D**—The profit rectangle is the quantity multiplied by the vertical distance between price and ATC.

42. **C**—With product differentiation, monopolistically competitive firms spend money to promote their product as different from the others.

43. **E**—Entry of new firms takes market share from existing firms, so demand curves begin to shift to the left.

44. **A**—Profits are normal and $P =$ ATC, but unlike perfect competition, $P >$ minimum ATC, so the industry is not productively efficient.

45. **D**—Lost CS is a big reason why government keeps an eye on the monopoly power of firms.

46. **E**—Colluding members of an oligopoly act as a monopolist, restraining competition, restricting output, and increasing the price.

47. **C**—This is the idea of derived demand.

48. **A**—Monopsony lowers both wage and employment when compared to the competitive labor market.

49. **E**—Like the competitive firm, the monopolist produces where MR = MC, but $P >$ ATC, which is most likely even further above MR = MC.

50. **B**—MRP = MP $\times$ P. Calculate MP by looking at the difference in TP as one more unit of labor is hired.

51. **C**—Labor is hired to the point where $W =$ MRP, so quickly find the point in the table where MP = 10, which when multiplied by P = $2 gives you MRP = $20.

52. **C**—This is a main identifier of oligopoly.

53. **E**—Minimum wages are price floors in a labor market. A surplus results.

54. **C**—This choice describes the least-cost rule for hiring inputs.

55. **A**—Increased labor supply lowers the wage, increases employment, and increases demand for goods that are "tools of the trade."

56. **E**—The appropriate fix to a negative externality is to tax either the producers or the consumers of electricity.

57. **D**—This describes the choice that is made by employers in competitive labor markets.

58. **B**—Sales taxes are typical examples of regressive taxes.

59. **C**—Free riders receive the benefit of a public good without contributing to its production.

60. **E**—If equilibrium output exceeds the socially desirable output, resources are overallocated to production of this good. This negative externality can be fixed with a tax on producers or sometimes on consumers.

AP Microeconomics Practice Exam 1

SECTION II

Free-Response Questions
Planning time—10 minutes
Writing time—50 minutes

At the conclusion of the planning time, you have 50 minutes to respond to the following three questions. Approximately half of your time should be given to the first question, and the second half should be divided evenly between the remaining two questions. Be careful to clearly explain your reasoning and to provide clear labels to all graph axes and curves.

1. The soybean market is a constant cost industry and Bob's Beans is a perfectly competitive soybean producer. The market price of soybeans is currently below average total cost, but above Bob's shutdown point.

   (A) Using two correctly labeled graphs, show the soybean market side by side with Bob's Beans. Clearly indicate which graph represents the market and which represents Bob's Beans. In your graphs, identify

      i. the equilibrium price and quantity in the soybean market, labeled P_{mkt} and Q_{mkt}, respectively.
      ii. the profit-maximizing quantity produced by Bob's Beans, labeled Q_b.
      iii. the area of economic profit or loss for Bob's Beans.

   (B) Will the number of firms in the soybean market increase, decrease, or stay the same in the long run? Explain.

   (C) Suppose now that Bob's Beans is a monopoly producer of soybeans currently setting a price that exceeds average total cost. In a correctly labeled graph, show a profit-maximizing monopolist and indicate each of the following:

      i. The profit-maximizing monopoly output, labeled Q_m
      ii. The monopoly price, labeled P_m
      iii. The area of economic profit or loss for Bob's Beans

2. Eli's lemonade stand employs only labor and lemons to produce lemonade. The table below shows how total production changes at different combinations of labor and lemons. Lemonade sells in a competitive market at $1 per cup.

HOURS OF LABOR	TOTAL PRODUCTION	POUNDS OF LEMONS	TOTAL PRODUCTION
0	0	0	0
1	12	1	9
2	22	2	17
3	30	3	23
4	36	4	27
5	39	5	29
6	40	6	30

   (A) In competitive input markets, each hour of labor costs $6 to employ and each pound of lemons costs $2 to employ. If Eli has a $14 budget for hiring inputs, identify the least-cost combination of labor and lemons.

   (B) At the least-cost combination of labor and lemons, calculate each of the following:

      i. The output produced. Show your work.
      ii. The economic profit earned. Show your work.

   (C) Now suppose that the market demand for lemonade shifts to the right.

      i. All else equal, how does this change in lemonade demand affect Eli's demand for labor? Explain.
      ii. Will Eli's employment of labor increase, decrease, or stay the same?

3. Assume that the market for pork is perfectly competitive, but the production of pork on hog farms generates pollution that seeps into the ground and can pollute the local well-water supply.

(A) In a correctly labeled graph, illustrate the market for pork and identify:

　i. The market equilibrium price and quantity of pork, labeled P_{mkt} and Q_{mkt}, respectively.

　ii. The socially optimal price and quantity of pork, labeled P_e and Q_e, respectively.

(B) Assuming that local residents do not enjoy having polluted drinking water, in your graph in part (A), show each of the following.

　i. The marginal social cost curve, labeled MSC

　ii. The marginal social benefit curve, labeled MSB

　iii. The deadweight loss, if any, shaded completely

(C) Suppose the government grants a subsidy to pork consumers equal to the marginal external cost of the polluted water. Will this increase, decrease, or have no effect on the deadweight loss? Explain.

› Free-Response Grading Rubric

Note: Based on my experience, these point allocations roughly approximate the weighting on similar questions on the AP examinations. I have also tried to provide you with notations on where points would likely be deducted for responses that were not acceptable enough for full credit. However, be aware that every year the point allocations change and partial credit is awarded differently.

Question 1 (10 points)

Part (A): 4 points
These points are graphing points.

- One point is earned for drawing a correctly labeled graph of the soybean market with P_{mkt} and Q_{mkt}. The market demand curve must be downward sloping and the market supply curve must be upward sloping.
- One point is earned for showing a horizontal demand curve on the firm's graph extended from the market equilibrium price, P_{mkt}.
- One point is earned for identifying the firm's profit-maximizing quantity, Q_b, at marginal cost equal to marginal revenue.
- One point is earned for showing the firm's average total cost (ATC) curve and marginal cost (MC) passing through the minimum point of ATC, and P < ATC and P > AVC, at Q_b.

You cannot have a downward-sloping MR curve here.

 TIP 1: On graphing problems, you can lose a point for not indicating which variables lie on each graphical axis. In this case, it would be as simple as a $ and a Q.

TIP 2: When asked to identify equilibrium price and quantity, make it clear to the reader that you know where these are found. The preferred way to do this is to use dashed lines from the intersection to the axes. You should also use the labeling given to you in the prompt. If you are told to label the market output Q_m and the firm's output Q_f, you are wise to play along.

TIP 3: Draw your graphs large enough for you to clearly identify the area of profit/loss. If your graph is the size of a postage stamp, it becomes more difficult for you to identify all relevant parts. It is also very tough for the reader to find all of the points.

When completing graphs, label everything and indicate direction of change and you will lose fewer points.

Part (B): 2 points
i. One point is earned for stating that the number of firms will decrease.
    One point is earned for explaining that because of short-run losses, firms will begin to exit the soybean market.

Part (C): 4 points
• One point is earned for drawing a correctly labeled graph of the monopoly showing downward-sloping demand (D) and marginal revenue (MR) curves with the MR curve below the demand curve.
• One point is earned for showing the profit-maximizing quantity, labeled Q_M, where $MR = MC$.
• One point is earned for both showing the profit-maximizing price, labeled P_M, from the demand curve at Q_M, and above the average total cost (ATC) curve.
• One point is earned for shading the correct area of economic profit.

Note: I've also shaded the areas of consumer surplus and deadweight loss, which were not required in this practice problem. Because a more thorough analysis of monopoly has been asked on recent exams, be sure that you can identify monopoly profit, deadweight loss, and consumer surplus.

Question: So I've messed up the monopoly quantity; have I lost all points in part (C)?

Answer: Again, maybe not, but the rest of your response must be consistent with the incorrectly labeled output. In the figure below I have tried to replicate one possible incorrectly identified output, but consistent price and profit.

An Alternative Scoring for Part (C).

This graph shows output where demand intersects MC, not where MR = MC. This response cannot be given the point for a correct level of output. However, you would likely get a point for a correctly drawn monopoly figure, a price P_m that is consistent with the Q_m in this figure, and a profit area that is also consistent with Q_m and P_m.

Question 2 (5 points)

Part (A): 1 point
One point is earned for stating that Labor = 1, Lemons = 4

TIP: Quickly write down the marginal products and highlight the options that satisfy the least-cost condition that states that the ratio of the (MPL/MPK) must be equal to the ratio of the input prices (w/r). With the price of labor being $6 and the price of lemons $2, find those ratios that are 3:1 and ignore all other possibilities.

Part (B): 2 points
i. One point is earned for calculating Output = 39 (12 from 1 labor and 27 from 4 lemons)
ii. One point is earned for calculating Total revenue = $1 × 39 = $39
    − Total cost = $6 × 1 + $2 × 4 = $14
    Economic profit = $25

If you do not show your work, you will *not* earn these points.

Note: If you happened to pick an incorrect combination of labor and lemons in part (A), it may be possible to receive both points in part (B) if you find the consistent level of output and profit.

Part (C): 2 points
- One point is earned for stating that Eli's demand for labor will increase and for the explanation that the increase in the price of lemonade increases the marginal revenue product of labor ($MRP_L = P \times MP_L$)
- One point is earned for stating that Eli's employment of labor will increase.

Question 3 (5 points)

Part (A): 1 point
One point is earned for drawing a correctly labeled supply and demand graph with P_{Mkt} and Q_{mkt} labeled.

Part (B): 3 points
- One point is earned for drawing the MSC curve above the MPC, or supply curve.
- One point is earned for labeling the demand curve MSB.
- One point is earned for shading the correct area of the deadweight loss.

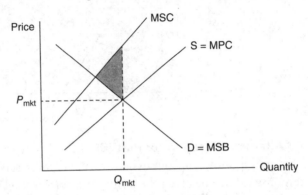

Part (C): 1 point
One point is earned for stating that the subsidy would increase the deadweight loss and for the explanation that a subsidy will increase the quantity of pork exchanged in the market. Since the market already produces more than the socially optimal quantity of pork, a subsidy will only worsen this over-allocation of resources.

Scoring and Interpretation

AP Microeconomics Practice Exam 1

Multiple-Choice Questions:

Number of correct answers: _____
Number of incorrect answers: _____
Number of blank answers: _____
Did you complete this part of the test in the allotted time? <u>Yes/No</u>

Free-Response Questions:

1. _____/10
2. _____/5
3. _____/5

Did you complete this part of the test in the allotted time? <u>Yes/No</u>

Calculate Your Score:

Multiple-Choice Questions:

$$\frac{\rule{3cm}{0.4pt}}{\text{(\# right)}} = \frac{\rule{3cm}{0.4pt}}{\text{MC raw score}}$$

Free-Response Questions:

Free-Response Raw Score $= (1.50 \times \text{Score 1}) + (1.50 \times \text{Score 2}) + (1.50 \times \text{Score 3}) = \rule{2cm}{0.4pt}$

Add the raw scores from the multiple-choice and free-response sections to obtain your total raw score for the practice exam. Use the table below to determine your grade, remembering these are rough estimates using questions that are not actually from AP exams, so do not read too much into this conversion from raw score to AP score.

MICROECONOMICS #1	
RAW SCORE	APPROXIMATE AP GRADE
73–90	5
58–72	4
45–57	3
33–44	2
0–32	1

AP Microeconomics Practice Exam 2

SECTION I: Multiple-Choice Questions
ANSWER SHEET

1 Ⓐ Ⓑ Ⓒ Ⓓ Ⓔ
2 Ⓐ Ⓑ Ⓒ Ⓓ Ⓔ
3 Ⓐ Ⓑ Ⓒ Ⓓ Ⓔ
4 Ⓐ Ⓑ Ⓒ Ⓓ Ⓔ
5 Ⓐ Ⓑ Ⓒ Ⓓ Ⓔ
6 Ⓐ Ⓑ Ⓒ Ⓓ Ⓔ
7 Ⓐ Ⓑ Ⓒ Ⓓ Ⓔ
8 Ⓐ Ⓑ Ⓒ Ⓓ Ⓔ
9 Ⓐ Ⓑ Ⓒ Ⓓ Ⓔ
10 Ⓐ Ⓑ Ⓒ Ⓓ Ⓔ
11 Ⓐ Ⓑ Ⓒ Ⓓ Ⓔ
12 Ⓐ Ⓑ Ⓒ Ⓓ Ⓔ
13 Ⓐ Ⓑ Ⓒ Ⓓ Ⓔ
14 Ⓐ Ⓑ Ⓒ Ⓓ Ⓔ
15 Ⓐ Ⓑ Ⓒ Ⓓ Ⓔ
16 Ⓐ Ⓑ Ⓒ Ⓓ Ⓔ
17 Ⓐ Ⓑ Ⓒ Ⓓ Ⓔ
18 Ⓐ Ⓑ Ⓒ Ⓓ Ⓔ
19 Ⓐ Ⓑ Ⓒ Ⓓ Ⓔ
20 Ⓐ Ⓑ Ⓒ Ⓓ Ⓔ

21 Ⓐ Ⓑ Ⓒ Ⓓ Ⓔ
22 Ⓐ Ⓑ Ⓒ Ⓓ Ⓔ
23 Ⓐ Ⓑ Ⓒ Ⓓ Ⓔ
24 Ⓐ Ⓑ Ⓒ Ⓓ Ⓔ
25 Ⓐ Ⓑ Ⓒ Ⓓ Ⓔ
26 Ⓐ Ⓑ Ⓒ Ⓓ Ⓔ
27 Ⓐ Ⓑ Ⓒ Ⓓ Ⓔ
28 Ⓐ Ⓑ Ⓒ Ⓓ Ⓔ
29 Ⓐ Ⓑ Ⓒ Ⓓ Ⓔ
30 Ⓐ Ⓑ Ⓒ Ⓓ Ⓔ
31 Ⓐ Ⓑ Ⓒ Ⓓ Ⓔ
32 Ⓐ Ⓑ Ⓒ Ⓓ Ⓔ
33 Ⓐ Ⓑ Ⓒ Ⓓ Ⓔ
34 Ⓐ Ⓑ Ⓒ Ⓓ Ⓔ
35 Ⓐ Ⓑ Ⓒ Ⓓ Ⓔ
36 Ⓐ Ⓑ Ⓒ Ⓓ Ⓔ
37 Ⓐ Ⓑ Ⓒ Ⓓ Ⓔ
38 Ⓐ Ⓑ Ⓒ Ⓓ Ⓔ
39 Ⓐ Ⓑ Ⓒ Ⓓ Ⓔ
40 Ⓐ Ⓑ Ⓒ Ⓓ Ⓔ

41 Ⓐ Ⓑ Ⓒ Ⓓ Ⓔ
42 Ⓐ Ⓑ Ⓒ Ⓓ Ⓔ
43 Ⓐ Ⓑ Ⓒ Ⓓ Ⓔ
44 Ⓐ Ⓑ Ⓒ Ⓓ Ⓔ
45 Ⓐ Ⓑ Ⓒ Ⓓ Ⓔ
46 Ⓐ Ⓑ Ⓒ Ⓓ Ⓔ
47 Ⓐ Ⓑ Ⓒ Ⓓ Ⓔ
48 Ⓐ Ⓑ Ⓒ Ⓓ Ⓔ
49 Ⓐ Ⓑ Ⓒ Ⓓ Ⓔ
50 Ⓐ Ⓑ Ⓒ Ⓓ Ⓔ
51 Ⓐ Ⓑ Ⓒ Ⓓ Ⓔ
52 Ⓐ Ⓑ Ⓒ Ⓓ Ⓔ
53 Ⓐ Ⓑ Ⓒ Ⓓ Ⓔ
54 Ⓐ Ⓑ Ⓒ Ⓓ Ⓔ
55 Ⓐ Ⓑ Ⓒ Ⓓ Ⓔ
56 Ⓐ Ⓑ Ⓒ Ⓓ Ⓔ
57 Ⓐ Ⓑ Ⓒ Ⓓ Ⓔ
58 Ⓐ Ⓑ Ⓒ Ⓓ Ⓔ
59 Ⓐ Ⓑ Ⓒ Ⓓ Ⓔ
60 Ⓐ Ⓑ Ⓒ Ⓓ Ⓔ

AP Microeconomics Practice Exam 2

SECTION I

Multiple-Choice Questions
Time—1 hour and 10 minutes
60 questions

For the multiple-choice questions that follow, select the best answer and fill in the appropriate letter on the answer sheet.

1. Land, labor, capital, and entrepreneurial talent are often referred to as

   (A) production possibilities.
   (B) goods and services.
   (C) unlimited human wants.
   (D) opportunity costs.
   (E) scarce economic resources.

2. The law of increasing costs is useful in describing

   (A) a demand curve.
   (B) a marginal benefit curve.
   (C) a linear production possibility frontier.
   (D) a concave production possibility frontier.
   (E) a total fixed costs curve.

3. Which of the following is likely to have a demand curve that is the least elastic?

   (A) Demand for the perfectly competitive firm's output
   (B) Demand for the oligopoly firm's output with a homogenous product
   (C) Demand for the oligopoly firm's output with a differentiated product
   (D) Demand for the monopolistically competitive firm's output
   (E) Demand for the monopoly firm's output

4. The figure above shows the production possibility frontiers (PPFs) for two nations that produce crabs and cakes. If these nations specialize and trade based on the principle of comparative advantage, which of the following trade agreements benefit both nations?

   (A) Nation A trades three crabs to Nation B in exchange for two cakes.
   (B) Nation A trades three cakes to Nation B in exchange for three crabs.
   (C) Nation A trades one cake to Nation B in exchange for two crabs.
   (D) Nation A trades one crab to Nation B in exchange for two cakes.
   (E) Nation A trades four crabs to Nation B in exchange for six cakes.

5. Which of the following scenarios would increase a nation's production possibility frontier (PPF)?

   (A) The nation's system of higher education slowly declines in quality.
   (B) The nation invests in research and development of new technology.
   (C) The nation's infant mortality rate increases.
   (D) Environmental pollution severely damages the health of the population.
   (E) Mineral reserves are exhausted.

6. A rational consumer who is eating Girl Scout cookies stops eating when

(A) the total benefit equals the total cost of eating cookies.
(B) the marginal benefit equals the marginal cost of the next cookie.
(C) the marginal cost of eating cookies is maximized.
(D) the marginal benefit of eating cookies is minimized.
(E) the price of the cookie equals the total benefit of the next cookie.

7. A competitive market for coffee, a normal good, is currently in equilibrium. Which of the following would most likely result in an increase in the demand for coffee?

(A) Consumer income falls.
(B) The price of tea rises.
(C) The wage of coffee plantation workers falls.
(D) Technology in the harvesting of coffee beans improves.
(E) The price of coffee brewing machines rises.

8. Which of the following certainly lowers the equilibrium price of a good exchanged in a competitive market?

(A) The demand curve shifts to the right.
(B) The supply curve shifts to the left.
(C) The demand curve shifts to the left, and the supply curve shifts to the right.
(D) The demand curve shifts to the right, and the supply curve shifts to the left.
(E) Both the demand and supply curves shift to the left.

9. An effective price ceiling in the market for good X likely results in

(A) a persistent surplus of good X.
(B) a persistent shortage of good X.
(C) an increase in the demand for good Y, a substitute for good X.
(D) a decrease in the demand for good Z, a complement with good X.
(E) a rightward shift in the supply curve of good X.

10. Which of the following goods is likely to have the most elastic demand curve?

(A) Demand for white Ford minivans
(B) Demand for automobiles
(C) Demand for Ford automobiles
(D) Demand for American-made automobiles
(E) Demand for a Ford minivan

11. Which of the following is a fundamental aspect of the free market system?

(A) A high degree of government involvement.
(B) Public ownership of resources.
(C) Private property.
(D) Central planners set wages and prices.
(E) Employers consult government agencies for guidance in hiring workers with appropriate job skills.

12. The elasticity of supply is typically greater when

(A) producers have fewer alternative goods to produce.
(B) producers have less time to respond to price changes.
(C) producers are operating near the limits of their production.
(D) producers have less access to raw materials necessary for production.
(E) producers have more time to respond to price changes.

13. Good X is exchanged in a competitive market. Which of the following is true if an excise tax is now imposed on the production of good X?

(A) If the demand curve is perfectly elastic, the price rises by the amount of the tax.
(B) The consumer's burden of the tax rises as the demand curve is more elastic.
(C) Consumer surplus rises as a result of the tax.
(D) The consumer's burden of the tax rises as the demand curve is less elastic.
(E) If the demand curve is perfectly inelastic, the price does not rise as a result of the tax.

14. Which of the following is an implicit cost for the owner of a small store in your hometown?

(A) The wage that is paid to the assistant manager
(B) The cost of purchasing canned goods from a wholesale food distributor
(C) The value placed on the owner's skills in an alternative career
(D) The cost of cooling the refrigerated meat display
(E) The price of placing an advertisement in the local newspaper

15. Suppose a price floor is installed in the market for coffee. One result of this policy would be

(A) a decrease in the demand for coffee-brewing machines.
(B) a persistent shortage of coffee in the market.
(C) an increase in consumer surplus due to lower coffee prices.
(D) an increase in the demand for coffee.
(E) a decrease in the profits for the owners of coffee plantations.

Questions 16 and 17 refer to the table below, which describes employment and production of a firm that hires labor and produces output in competitive markets. The competitive price of the product is $.50.

UNITS OF LABOR	TOTAL PRODUCT
0	0
1	11
2	20
3	27
4	32
5	35

16. Which unit of labor has marginal revenue product equal to $1.50?

(A) 1st
(B) 2nd
(C) 3rd
(D) 4th
(E) 5th

17. If the wage paid to all units of labor is $4.50, how many units of labor are hired?

(A) 1
(B) 2
(C) 3
(D) 4
(E) 5

18. Which of the following is true of the perfectly competitive firm in the short run?

(A) The firm earns a normal profit.
(B) The firm shuts down if the price falls below average total cost.
(C) The firm earns positive economic profit.
(D) The firm maximizes profit by producing where the price equals marginal revenue.
(E) The firm may earn positive, negative, or normal profits.

Questions 19 to 21 refer to the figure below.

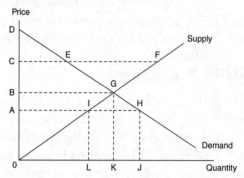

19. If the current price is 0B, we would expect

(A) a surplus in the market to be eliminated by rising prices.
(B) a shortage in the market to be eliminated by falling prices.
(C) a surplus in the market to be eliminated by falling prices.
(D) quantity demanded to be equal to quantity supplied as the market is in equilibrium.
(E) a shortage in the market to be eliminated by rising prices.

20. If the price were to fall from 0C to 0A, which of the following would be true?

(A) Dollars spent on this good would increase if demand for the good were price inelastic.
(B) Dollars spent on this good would decrease if demand for the good were price elastic.
(C) Dollars spent on this good would increase if demand for the good were price elastic.
(D) Dollars spent on this good would increase if demand for the good were unitary price elastic.
(E) Dollars spent on this good would decrease if demand for the good were unitary price elastic.

21. If the market is in equilibrium, which of the following areas corresponds to producer surplus?

    (A) BGD
    (B) 0AHJ
    (C) 0DGK
    (D) 0BG
    (E) 0BGK

22. The downward-sloping demand curve is partially explained by which of the following?

    (A) Substitution effects and income effects
    (B) The law of increasing marginal costs
    (C) The principle of comparative advantage
    (D) The law of diminishing marginal returns to production
    (E) The least-cost principle

23. Dorothy has daily income of $20, each cup of coffee costs $P_c = \$1$, and each scone costs $P_s = \$4$. The table below provides us with Dorothy's marginal utility (MU) received in the consumption of each good. As a utility-maximizing consumer, which combination of coffee and scones should Dorothy consume each day?

CUPS OF COFFEE	MU OF COFFEE	# OF SCONES	MU OF SCONES
1	10	1	30
2	8	2	24
3	6	3	20
4	4	4	16
5	2	5	14
6	1	6	8

    (A) 2 coffee and 2 scones
    (B) 5 coffee and 6 scones
    (C) 3 coffee and 2 scones
    (D) 4 coffee and 4 scones
    (E) 4 coffee and 16 scones

24. You are told that the Gini coefficient of income inequality has risen from .35 to .85. Which of the following is a likely cause of this change?

    (A) Market power in the factor and output markets has increased.
    (B) Labor market discrimination has been eliminated.
    (C) The distribution of wealth and property has become more equitable.
    (D) The vast majority of adults have achieved at least a college degree.
    (E) The tax system has become even more progressive.

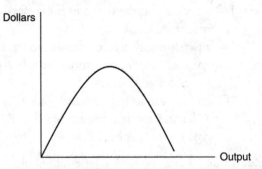

25. The figure above best represents which of the following functions?

    (A) Total product of labor
    (B) Total revenue
    (C) Total cost
    (D) Total utility
    (E) Total short-run economic profits

26. If it is true that bacon and eggs are complementary goods, then

    (A) the income elasticity of bacon is positive and the income elasticity for eggs is negative.
    (B) the price elasticity for eggs is greater than the price elasticity for bacon.
    (C) the cross-price elasticity between bacon and eggs is negative.
    (D) the income elasticity of bacon is negative and the income elasticity for eggs is positive.
    (E) the cross-price elasticity between bacon and eggs is positive.

27. A firm employs variable amounts of labor to a fixed amount of capital to produce output. If the daily wage paid to labor increases, how does this affect the firm's costs?

	TOTAL VARIABLE COST	TOTAL FIXED COST	TOTAL COST
(A)	Decrease	No change	Decrease
(B)	Decrease	Decrease	Decrease
(C)	Increase	Decrease	No change
(D)	Increase	No change	Increase
(E)	Increase	Increase	Increase

28. Diminishing marginal returns to short-run production begin when

(A) the average product of labor begins to fall.
(B) the total product of labor begins to fall.
(C) marginal product of labor becomes negative.
(D) average variable cost begins to rise.
(E) marginal product of labor begins to fall.

29. Which of the following is a characteristic of perfect competition?

(A) Firms produce a homogeneous product.
(B) Barriers to entry exist.
(C) Firms are price-setting profit maximizers.
(D) The government regulates the price so that deadweight loss is eliminated.
(E) Long-run positive profits are available.

UNITS OF LABOR	TOTAL PRODUCT (TP$_L$)
0	0 cups
1	5
2	15
3	30
4	40
5	45
6	40
7	30

30. The table above shows how hiring increasing amounts of labor to a fixed amount of capital affects the hourly output of Eli's lemonade stand. Based on this table of production data, which of the following can be said?

(A) Diminishing marginal returns begins with the first worker hired.
(B) Marginal cost begins to rise at the sixth worker hired.
(C) Total product is maximized at the third worker hired.
(D) Average product begins to decline with the first worker hired.
(E) Diminishing marginal returns begins with the fourth worker hired.

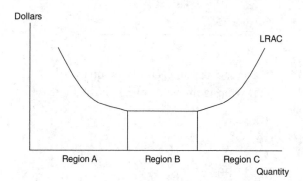

31. The figure above shows the long-run average cost curve of a competitive firm. Which of the following choices best describes Region B in the diagram?

(A) Economies of scale
(B) Diseconomies of scale
(C) Constant returns to scale
(D) Diminishing returns to scale
(E) Increasing returns to scale

32. The market for good X is currently in equilibrium. Which of the following choices would *not* cause both a decrease in the equilibrium price of good X and a decrease in the equilibrium quantity of good X?

(A) A decrease in consumer income and good X is a normal good.
(B) An increase in consumer income and good X is an inferior good.
(C) An increase in the price of good Y, a complement for good X.
(D) A decrease in the price of good Y, a substitute for good X.
(E) An increase in the number of consumers in the market for good X.

Questions 33 and 34 refer to the figure below, which shows cost curves for a competitive firm.

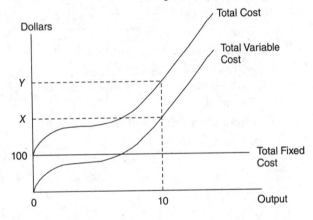

33. If average variable cost at a quantity of 10 is $25, what is the value of $Y in the figure above?

(A) $250
(B) $25
(C) $35
(D) $1,000
(E) $350

34. At a quantity of 10, what is the value of $(Y − X)?

(A) $100
(B) $25
(C) $10
(D) $35
(E) $350

35. The demand for labor falls if

(A) labor productivity falls.
(B) the price of the good produced by labor rises.
(C) the price of a complementary input falls.
(D) demand for the good produced by labor rises.
(E) a minimum wage is removed from the labor market.

Questions 36 and 37 refer to the graph below.

36. The curve labeled 4 represents which of the following?

(A) Marginal cost
(B) Marginal product of labor
(C) Average total cost
(D) Average fixed cost
(E) Average variable cost

37. Where is the shutdown point for this perfectly competitive firm?

(A) Any price below curve 4
(B) Any price below 0c
(C) Any price below curve 3
(D) Any price below curve 2
(E) Any quantity less than Q

38. If a market for a good is producing a negative externality,

(A) at the market output the marginal costs to society exceed the private marginal costs of production.
(B) at the market output the marginal benefits to society exceed the private marginal costs of production.
(C) at the market output the marginal costs to society exceed the total benefits to society.
(D) at the market output the private marginal costs of production exceed the marginal costs to society.
(E) at the market output the marginal benefits to society exceed the marginal costs to society.

39. Which of the following is a characteristic of a monopoly market?

(A) Firms produce a homogeneous product.
(B) Barriers to entry exist.
(C) Firms are price-taking profit maximizers.
(D) Deadweight loss is eliminated through entry of competing firms in the long run.
(E) In the long run the firm earns normal profits.

40. A monopolist may be able to maintain long-run positive profit due to

(A) deadweight loss.
(B) economies of scale in production.
(C) a price that is set equal to average total cost.
(D) perfectly elastic demand for the product.
(E) entry of new firms that keep the price high.

Questions 41 and 42 refer to the graph below.

41. If this firm were a profit-maximizing monopolist, the price, output, and profit would be

	PRICE	OUTPUT	PROFIT
(A)	$P5$	$Q1$	$Q1 \times (c-b)$
(B)	$P5$	$Q1$	$Q1 \times P1$
(C)	$P4$	$Q2$	$Q2 \times (P4-P1)$
(D)	$P1$	$Q1$	$Q1 \times (P5-P1)$
(E)	$P3$	$Q3$	$Q3 \times P3$

42. Consumer surplus in the monopolist market is equal to the area

(A) abce.
(B) abcf.
(C) $P5$cd.
(D) $0Q1aP1$.
(E) $P1P5$ca.

43. The top six firms in an oligopolistic industry have market shares of 25%, 25%, 15%, 10%, 6%, and 3%. Many smaller firms split the rest of the market. What is the value of the four-firm concentration ratio?

(A) 65%
(B) 54%
(C) 75%
(D) 34%
(E) 50%

44. Which of the following statements is true of a consumer's utility-maximizing behavior?

    (A) As consumption of good X increases, total utility increases at an increasing rate.
    (B) The consumer should stop consuming good X when marginal utility is maximized.
    (C) The consumer has maximized utility between two goods X and Y when the quantities of the two goods are equalized.
    (D) Utility maximization occurs when the marginal utilities per dollar for goods X and Y are equalized.
    (E) As consumption of good X increases, the marginal utility per dollar spent on good X also increases.

45. Oligopoly has at times been the subject of government antitrust regulation. Which of the following is a reason for this government regulation?

    (A) Price is approximately equal to marginal cost.
    (B) Price is approximately equal to average total cost.
    (C) Deadweight loss lessens over time.
    (D) Consumer surplus is lost as market power increases.
    (E) Market efficiency is maximized.

46. The production of chicken often results in offending odors that are picked up by the wind and blown over rural communities. This is an example of a _____ externality, the result of which are spillover _____ and an _____ of resources to chicken production.

    (A) negative, costs, underallocation
    (B) negative, benefits, overallocation
    (C) negative, benefits, underallocation
    (D) positive, costs, overallocation
    (E) negative, costs, overallocation

47. Which of the following choices is true of both perfectly competitive firms and monopolistically competitive firms?

    (A) Barriers to entry
    (B) Homogenous products
    (C) Normal profits in the long run
    (D) Excess capacity
    (E) Price-setting behavior

48. The monopolistically competitive price is above marginal revenue because

    (A) firms have differentiated products.
    (B) firms are price takers.
    (C) firms produce a homogenous product.
    (D) the market is allocatively efficient.
    (E) profits are normal in the long run.

49. Deadweight loss in industries with market power is a result of

    (A) profit-maximizing output occurs where price equals marginal revenue.
    (B) profit-maximizing output occurs where price exceeds marginal cost.
    (C) profit-maximizing output occurs where price equals marginal cost.
    (D) profit-maximizing output occurs where price exceeds average total cost.
    (E) profit-maximizing output occurs where price equals average total cost.

50. If the government wishes to regulate a natural monopoly so that it earns a normal profit, it sets

    (A) Price = Marginal cost.
    (B) Marginal revenue = Marginal cost.
    (C) Price = Average total cost.
    (D) Price = Marginal revenue.
    (E) Marginal revenue = Average total cost.

51. Which of the following would improve the efficiency of a monopoly market?

(A) The government regulates the monopolist to produce the output where marginal revenue equals marginal cost.
(B) The government provides additional legal barriers to entry.
(C) The government subsidizes the monopolist so that they achieve even greater economies of scale.
(D) The government eliminates trade barriers on potential foreign producers.
(E) The government regulates the monopolist to produce the output where monopoly profits are maximized.

52. Which of the following increases the demand for interstate truck drivers?

(A) An increase in the wage of truck drivers
(B) An increase in the supply of truck drivers
(C) An increase in the price of diesel fuel, which is used to power semitrucks
(D) A decrease in the demand for interstate shipping
(E) A decrease in the price of semitrucks

53. A monopsony employer hires labor up to the point where

(A) wage = marginal factor cost.
(B) marginal factor cost = marginal product of labor.
(C) marginal factor cost = marginal revenue product of labor.
(D) wage = marginal revenue product of labor.
(E) wage = price of the good produced by the labor.

54. The price of labor is $5 and the price of capital is $10 per unit. Using the table below, what is the least-cost combination of labor and capital that should be hired to produce 18 units of output?

UNITS OF LABOR	MARGINAL PRODUCT OF LABOR	UNITS OF CAPITAL	MARGINAL PRODUCT OF CAPITAL
1	6	1	8
2	4	2	6
3	3	3	5
4	2	4	4
5	1	5	2

(A) 1 Labor and 2 Capital
(B) 4 Labor and 8 Capital
(C) 2 Labor and 1 Capital
(D) 5 Labor and 5 Capital
(E) 3 Labor and 2 Capital

55. A cartel is often the result of

(A) perfectly competitive firms that agree to produce a homogenous product.
(B) oligopoly competitors that agree to restrict output to maximize joint profits.
(C) a monopoly that has been regulated by the government.
(D) a natural monopoly that has evolved into a perfectly competitive industry.
(E) monopolistically competitive firms that have agreed to earn normal profits in the long run.

56. Suppose the state requires hairdressers and manicurists to pass a series of exams to be certified cosmetologists. How does this policy change the supply of cosmetologists, the equilibrium wage, and the price of a manicure?

	SUPPLY OF COSMETOLOGISTS	WAGE	PRICE OF MANICURES
(A)	Decrease	Increase	Increase
(B)	Decrease	Decrease	Decrease
(C)	Increase	Decrease	Decrease
(D)	Increase	Decrease	Increase
(E)	Increase	Increase	Increase

57. The local market for bankers is currently in equilibrium. Which of the following increases the local wage paid to bankers?

    (A) Internet banking at home is becoming more popular.
    (B) More college students are majoring in finance and economics, majors that make them attractive as bank employees.
    (C) The price of banking software, a complementary resource to bankers, rises.
    (D) Several banks in the local market merge and consolidate many operations.
    (E) The price of automatic teller machines, a substitute for bankers, decreases and the output effect is greater than the substitution effect.

58. The U.S. government collects tax revenue, buys military equipment from many private firms, and uses this equipment to provide national defense to all Americans. This is a good example of

    (A) a natural monopoly.
    (B) an excise tax on military equipment.
    (C) a regressive tax.
    (D) a public good.
    (E) deadweight loss.

59. Which of the following scenarios is the best example of a positive externality?

    (A) Your neighbor has a swimming pool and throws loud late-night parties.
    (B) Your neighbor has a swimming pool and allows you free access.
    (C) Your neighbor has a swimming pool and the powerful chlorine odor blows into your open dining room window.
    (D) Your neighbor has a swimming pool and allows you to use it in exchange for letting his kids use your swing.
    (E) Your neighbor has a swimming pool that is conducive for the breeding of mosquitoes.

60. Because of the free-rider effect, the private marketplace tends to

    (A) provide the allocatively efficient amount of a public good.
    (B) produce too much of a public good, requiring the government to intervene and tax the production of it.
    (C) produce a public good in the amount where the marginal benefit to society equals the marginal cost to society.
    (D) produce too little of the public good, requiring the government to intervene and provide it for all.
    (E) produce too little of the public good, requiring the government to intervene and ban it.

› Answers and Explanations

1. **E**—Know the four scarce economic resources.

2. **D**—A concave PPF exhibits the law of increasing costs. As more of a good is produced, opportunity costs rise. This is because resources are not perfectly substitutable between the production of different goods.

3. **E**—Demand is more elastic if there are more substitute goods. A monopolist has no close substitutes so is likely the least elastic demand.

4. **A**—Nation A has comparative advantage in crab production, and Nation B has comparative advantage in cake production. Nation A specializes in crabs and Nation B specializes in cakes, so avoid any option suggesting the opposite. Choice A is the only one that allows both to consume beyond the PPF.

5. **B**—Nations that invest in research and technology expect the PPF to expand, the key to economic growth.

6. **B**—Rational decision makers consume right up to the point where the MB of the next cookie is exactly equal to the MC of the next cookie.

7. **B**—Tea is a coffee substitute. Higher tea prices increase coffee demand.

8. **C**—Leftward demand shifts coupled with rightward supply shifts put downward pressure on prices.

9. **B**—Price ceilings are legal maximum prices set below the equilibrium price. A shortage results.

10. **A**—The more narrowly a good is defined, the more elastic demand.

11. **C**—Private property is fundamental to the free market economy.

12. **E**—The supply curve is more elastic as more time elapses.

13. **D**—If the demand curve is more inelastic (more vertical), a greater burden of an excise tax falls upon consumers and less upon producers.

14. **C**—The opportunity cost of starting a small store is the salary given up in the next best alternative for the entrepreneur's skills.

15. **A**—A price floor is a legal minimum price set above the equilibrium price. Higher coffee prices decrease the demand for complementary goods like coffee machines.

16. **E**—$P \times MP_L = MRP_L$.

17. **B**—At the second worker, wage = MRP_L.

18. **E**—In perfect competition, short-run profits may be positive or negative, or normal, but long-run profits are always normal.

19. **D**—This is the equilibrium price.

20. **C**—When the price falls and quantity demanded rises, consumer spending on the good ($P \times Q$) can change in two directions. If $E_d > 0$, a percent decrease in price increases quantity demanded by a greater percent, increasing spending on the good.

21. **D**—PS is the area under the price and above supply.

22. **A**—Substitution and income effects explain the law of demand.

23. **D**—Using the utility maximizing rule, set $MU_c/\$1 = MU_s/\$4$. There are three options where the MU_c is four times the MU_s, and only one of those options uses exactly $20 of daily income.

24. **A**—The Gini coefficient measures income inequality. The closer it gets to one, the more unequal the income distribution. One explanation for inequality is more market power in product and input markets. This redistributes CS to monopoly producers and/or employers.

25. **B**—Quickly look at the graph to eliminate some possibilities. With dollars on the y-axis, this curve cannot represent TP_L (output on the y-axis) or total utility (utility on the y-axis). The other key is that this curve has a value of zero dollars at an output of zero. TC = TFC at zero output and short-run economic losses equal TFC at zero output.

26. **C**—If the price of eggs rises, demand for bacon falls if they are complementary; $E_{xy} < 0$.

27. **D**—Labor is a variable cost so there is no change in TFC, but an increase in TVC and TC.

28. **E**—This defines diminishing marginal returns and is often missed by students, who make the mistake of identifying falling TP_L, rather than falling MP_L, with diminishing returns.

29. **A**—Know the characteristics of all market structures.

30. **E**—The fourth worker is the first to have lower MP_L than the worker before.

31. **C**—Constant returns exist when a larger firm has constant LRAC.

32. **E**—All other choices *would* produce a decrease in the demand for good X and would therefore decrease both the price and quantity. You are looking for the only choice that would *not*. More consumers for good X would increase demand and increase both the price and quantity.

33. **E**—Since you know that AVC is $25 at $Q = 10$, TVC is $250. Adding this to the given $100 of TFC produces $350 of total cost at $Q = 10$.

34. **A**—The vertical distance between TC and TVC is TFC.

35. **A**—Demand for labor is the MRP_L curve. Higher labor productivity increases labor demand.

36. **D**—AFC declines as output rises.

37. **C**—The shutdown point is at $P <$ AVC.

38. **A**—With no externality, MSB = MSC. With a negative externality, MSC > MPC = MSB for the good.

39. **B**—Barriers to entry are a defining characteristic of monopoly.

40. **B**—Economies of scale are a common barrier to entry; a key to maintaining long-run positive profits.

41. **A**—Find the output level where MR = MC and locate the price from the demand curve. Profit is equal to $Q \times (P -$ ATC) at that output.

42. **C**—CS is the area above price and under demand.

43. **C**—A four-firm concentration ratio is the sum of the market share of the four largest firms in an industry.

44. **D**—Utility-maximizing consumers do not equate the units of two goods, they equate MU/P for each good.

45. **D**—As industries approach monopoly, prices rise, lowering CS.

46. **E**—Negative externalities, like "fowl" odors, impose spillover costs upon third parties. These costs, ignored by the market, reflect an over-allocation of resources to chicken production.

47. **C**—Know the characteristics of all market structures.

48. **A**—Product differentiation results in a small degree of price-setting ability and downward-sloping demand curves for the firms. $P =$ ATC and profits are normal in the long run, and this output level does not occur where ATC is minimized. This defines excess capacity.

49. **B**—DWL emerges when output is moved away from where $P =$ MC.

50. **C**—If $P =$ ATC, economic profit is zero, or normal.

51. **D**—Allowing more foreign competition lessens market power of a monopolist and improves efficiency as the price falls closer to MC.

52. **E**—Semitrucks are a complementary resource to the truck drivers. If the price falls, demand for the labor rises.

53. **C**—The monopsony hiring decision.

54. **C**—Use the least-cost rule of $MP_L/\$5 = MP_K/\$10$ to find the optimal combination of labor and capital. There are three combinations of labor and capital where the MP_K is twice the MP_L, but only one choice produces 18 units of output. Remember that adding the marginal products provides the total product.

55. **B**—This describes a cartel.

56. **A**—Certification exams decrease labor supply and raise the wage in the market. A higher wage increases the MC of producing the good, which raises the price of the good.

57. **E**—If the price of a substitute resource falls, labor demand can increase if the output effect is greater than the substitution effect.

58. **D**—Know your public goods.

59. **B**—You are the recipient of a spillover benefit from your neighbor's purchase of a pool.

60. **D**—The private marketplace underprovides for a public good because free riders benefit from the good without paying for it. Government must provide the public good.

AP Microeconomics Practice Exam 2

SECTION II

Free-Response Questions
Planning time—10 minutes
Writing time—50 minutes

At the conclusion of the planning time, you have 50 minutes to respond to the following three questions. Approximately half of your time should be given to the first question, and the second half should be divided evenly between the remaining two questions. Be careful to clearly explain your reasoning and to provide clear labels to all graph axes and curves.

1. The graph below shows a firm that has monopolized the market for gadgets.

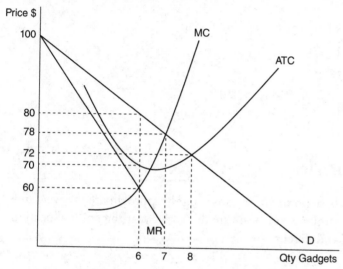

(A) Using the values in the graph, identify the following:

   i. The profit-maximizing quantity
   ii. The price of a gadget when the monopolist has maximized profit
   iii. The allocatively efficient output

(B) Using the values in the graph, calculate the following and show your work:

   i. Monopoly profit
   ii. Consumer surplus

(C) Suppose the government levies a lump-sum tax on the monopolist.

   i. Will output increase, decrease, or stay the same? Explain.
   ii. Will deadweight loss increase, decrease, or stay the same? Explain.
   iii. Will profit increase, decrease, or stay the same?

2. Assume the following about the market for gizmos:

- Gizmos are sold in a competitive market.
- Gizmos have no close substitute.
- The demand for gizmos is price inelastic but not perfectly inelastic.

Suppose now that the government imposes a per-unit excise tax on producers of gizmos.

(A) Using a correctly labeled graph, show the impact of the excise tax on each of the following in the gizmos market:

   i. The change to price and quantity, after the tax
   ii. The area of tax revenue collected by the government
   iii. Deadweight loss from the tax

(B) Given that demand for gizmos is price inelastic, will consumer spending on gizmos increase, decrease, or remain constant after the tax is imposed? Explain.

3. Two rival firms operate in an oligopoly and, once a year, choose an advertising strategy. The firms can choose between an expensive television and radio advertising campaign (costly ads) or an inexpensive direct-mail advertising campaign (cheap ads). Television and radio cost more but reach more potential customers. Each firm decides their advertising strategy independently on January 1, 2019, and, once chosen, cannot alter the decision until January 1, 2020. The table below summarizes the profits each firm would earn given their own, and their rival's, strategy. Use this matrix to answer the following questions.

FIRM 1		FIRM 2	
		Costly Ads	Cheap Ads
	Costly Ads	Firm 1: $100 Firm 2: $100	Firm 1: $250 Firm 2: $75
	Cheap Ads	Firm 1: $75 Firm 2: $250	Firm 1: $200 Firm 2: $200

(A) Suppose Firm 1 chooses *Costly Ads* and Firm 2 chooses *Cheap Ads*.

Identify the profit for Firm 1.

(B) It is now January 1, 2019, and each firm must independently make the advertising strategy decision. Is there a dominant strategy for Firm 2 in this game? Explain.

(C) If each firm chooses the advertising strategy independently without collusion, what is the outcome of this game?

(D) Is the outcome of this game an example of a "prisoner's dilemma"? Explain your answer.

› Free-Response Grading Rubric

Note: Based on my experience, these point allocations roughly approximate the weighting on similar questions on the AP examinations. Be aware that every year the point allocations differ and partial credit is awarded differently.

Question 1 (10 points)

Part (A): 3 points

i. One point is earned for identifying 6 as the profit maximizing output.
ii. One point is earned for identifying $80 as the price.
iii. One point is earned for identifying that 7 units would be allocatively efficient (where $P = MC$).

Part (B): 2 points

i. One point is earned for calculating, with work shown, that $\pi = 6 \times (\$80 - \$70) = \$60$.
ii. One point is earned for calculating, with work shown, that $CS = .5 \times 6 \times \$20 = \$60$.

Part (C): 5 points

i. One point is earned for stating that output will not change.
One point is earned for explaining that the lump-sum tax does not affect marginal revenue or marginal cost.
ii. One point is earned for stating that deadweight loss doesn't change.
One point is earned for explaining that because output doesn't change, and the demand curve still intersects MC at 7 units, the difference between profit maximizing and allocatively efficient output levels is the same.
iii. One point is earned for stating that profit decreases.

Question 2 (5 points)

Part (A): 4 points

These are all graphing points, so to get all points, you must perfectly identify all curves, axes, and directional shifts.

One point is earned for drawing a correctly labeled graph showing the supply curve shifting upward by the amount of a tax.

When you are given the flexibility to use your own labeling, use arrows to clearly demonstrate that you know that price is rising and quantity is falling.

i.   One point is earned for showing that the price increases and quantity decreases after the tax.
ii. One point is earned for identifying tax revenue as the area of the rectangle yP_2DW.
iii. One point is earned for showing deadweight loss as the area of the triangle DWL shown above.

TIP: In a question like this, there are very few partial credit possibilities. You either get the graphing points or you do not.

Part (B): 1 point

One point is earned for stating that consumer spending increases because the percent increase in the price is greater than the percent decrease in quantity. It is also accurate to refer to proportional changes.

TIP: This explanation point is the more difficult of the two necessary parts of the correct answer and serves to differentiate students. In the past you might have also received credit for saying "a *large* increase in the price outweighs a *small* decrease in quantity." It is much more accurate to refer to proportional or percentage changes, and in recent years, the rubric has been more stringent on this point.

Question 3 (5 points)

Part (A): 1 point

This is a point for just being able to read the payoff matrix in this game. Since we know that Firm 1 is choosing *Costly Ads*, then you must focus on the top half of the matrix. If Firm 2 is choosing *Cheap Ads*, then the game ends in the top right square.

One point is earned for stating $250.

Part (B): 1 point

The key here is obviously to know what it means to have a dominant strategy. A dominant strategy is one that is always superior to the other option, no matter what the rival firm is doing. For example, if Firm 2 plays *Costly Ads*, Firm 1 should do the same because $100 (*Costly Ads*) beats $75 (*Cheap Ads*). If Firm 2 were to play *Cheap Ads*, Firm 1 would play *Costly Ads* because $250 (*Costly Ads*) beats $200 (*Cheap Ads*). So Firm 1 would always play *Costly Ads*. The same is true of Firm 2.

One point is earned for stating yes, playing *Costly Ads* is a dominant strategy for Firm 2. Because, no matter what Firm 1 is doing, this strategy always beats *Cheap Ads*.

Part (C): 1 point

One point is earned for stating that the outcome is that both firms earn $100 because, without collusion, both will play the dominant strategy, *Costly Ads*.

Part (D): 2 points

A prisoner's dilemma is a situation where playing the dominant strategy produces an outcome that, in hindsight, could have been better for both if the firms could have colluded and coordinated their strategies.

One point for stating that yes, it is an example of a prisoner's dilemma.

One point for explaining that both firms could have improved profits ($200 each versus $100 each) by colluding with a selection of *Cheap Ads*.

Scoring and Interpretation

AP Microeconomics Practice Exam 2

Multiple-Choice Questions:

Number of correct answers: _____

Number of incorrect answers: _____

Number of blank answers: _____

Did you complete this part of the test in the allotted time? <u>Yes/No</u>

Free-Response Questions:

1. _____/10
2. _____/5
3. _____/5

Did you complete this part of the test in the allotted time? <u>Yes/No</u>

Calculate Your Score:

Multiple-Choice Questions:

$$\frac{}{\text{(\# right)}} = \frac{}{\text{MC raw score}}$$

Free-Response Questions:

$$\text{Free-Response Raw Score} = (1.50 \times \text{Score 1}) + (1.50 \times \text{Score 2}) +$$
$$(1.50 \times \text{Score 3}) = \underline{\hspace{2cm}}$$

Add the raw scores from the multiple-choice and free-response sections to obtain your total raw score for the practice exam. Use the table below to determine your grade, remembering these are rough estimates using questions that are not actually from AP exams, so do not read too much into this conversion from raw score to AP score.

MICROECONOMICS #2	
RAW SCORE	APPROXIMATE AP GRADE
73–90	5
58–72	4
45–57	3
33–44	2
0–32	1

Appendixes

Further Reading
Websites
Glossary
Important Formulas and Conditions

FURTHER READING

Dodge, Eric, and Melanie Fox. *Economics Demystified.* New York: McGraw-Hill, 2012.

Krugman, Paul, and Robin Wells. *Economics,* 5th ed. New York: Worth Publishers, 2019.

Mankiw, N. Gregory. *Principles of Economics,* 8th ed. Mason, OH: Thomson South-Western, 2017.

McConnell, Campbell L., Stanley L. Brue, and Sean Flynn. *Economics,* 21st ed. New York: McGraw-Hill/Irwin, 2019.

Here is a list of websites that you might find useful in your preparation for the AP Microeconomics exam.

https://apstudent.collegeboard.org/home

www.economy.com/dismal

www.economist.com/research/Economics

www.councilforeconed.org

absolute advantage The ability to produce more of a good with the same quantity of resources, or the same quantity of goods with fewer resources than all other producers.

absolute (or money) prices The price of a good measured in units of currency.

accounting profit The difference between total revenue and total explicit cost.

all else equal The assumption that all other variables are held constant so that we can predict how a change in one variable affects a second. Also known as the "ceteris paribus" assumption.

allocative efficiency Production of the combination of goods and services that provides the most net benefit to society. This is achieved when the MSB = MSC of the next unit.

average fixed cost (AFC) Total fixed cost divided by output.

average product of labor (AP$_L$) Total product divided by the labor employed.

average tax rate The proportion of total income paid to taxes.

average total cost (ATC) Total cost divided by output.

average variable cost (AVC) Total variable cost divided by output.

capitalist market system (capitalism) An economic system based upon the fundamentals of private property, freedom, self-interest, and prices.

cartel Firms that agree to maximize their joint profits rather than compete.

circular flow of economic activity (or circular of goods and services) A model that shows how households and firms circulate resources, goods, and incomes through the economy. This basic model is expanded to include the government and the foreign sector.

collusive oligopoly Models where firms agree to work together to mutually improve their situation.

comparative advantage The ability to produce a good at lower opportunity cost than all other producers.

complementary goods Two goods that provide more utility when consumed together than when consumed separately.

constant returns to scale The horizontal range of long-run average total cost where LRAC is constant over a variety of plant sizes.

constant returns to scale in production The long-run outcome when output exactly doubles from a doubling of all inputs.

constrained utility maximization Given prices and income, a consumer stops consuming a good when the price paid for the next unit is equal to the marginal utility received.

consumer surplus The difference between a buyer's willingness to pay and the price actually paid.

cross-price elasticity of demand A measure of how sensitive the consumption of good X is to a change in the price of good Y.

deadweight loss The lost net benefit to society caused by a movement from the competitive market equilibrium.

decreasing returns to scale in production The long-run outcome when output less than doubles from a doubling of all inputs.

demand curve Shows the quantity of a good demanded at all prices.

demand for labor Shows the quantity of labor demanded at all wages. Labor demand for a firm hiring in a competitive labor market is MRP$_L$.

demand schedule A table showing quantity demanded for a good at all prices.

derived demand Demand for a resource arising from the demand for the goods produced by the resource.

determinants of demand The external factors that shift demand to the left or right.

determinants of supply The external factors that influence supply. When these variables change, the entire supply curve shifts to the left or right.

diseconomies of scale The upward part of the long-run average total cost curve where LRAC rises as plant size rises.

disequilibrium Any price where the quantity demanded does not equal the quantity supplied.

domestic price The equilibrium price of a good in a nation without trade.

dominant strategy A strategy that is always the best strategy to pursue, regardless of what a rival is doing.

economic costs The sum of explicit and implicit costs of production.

economic growth The increase in an economy's PPF over time.

economic profit The difference between total revenue and total economic cost.

economics The study of how society allocates scarce resources.

economies of scale The downward part of the long-run average total cost curve where LRAC falls as plant size rises.

egalitarianism The philosophy that all citizens should receive an equal share of the economic resources.

elasticity Measures the sensitivity, or responsiveness, of a choice to a change in an external factor.

elasticity along the demand curve At the midpoint of a linear demand curve, $E_d = 1$. Above the midpoint demand is elastic, and below the midpoint demand is inelastic.

excess capacity The difference between the long-run output in monopolistic competition and the output at minimum average total cost.

excess demand The difference between quantity demanded and quantity supplied. A shortage.

excess supply The difference between quantity supplied and quantity demanded. A surplus.

excise tax A per-unit tax on a specific good or service.

explicit costs Direct, purchased, out-of-pocket costs, paid to resource suppliers outside the firm. Also referred to as accounting costs.

exports Goods and services produced domestically but sold abroad.

factors of production Inputs or resources that go into the production function to produce goods and services.

firm An organization that employs factors of production to produce a good or service that it hopes to profitably sell.

fixed inputs Production inputs that cannot be changed in the short run.

four-firm concentration ratio The sum of the market share of the four largest firms in an industry.

free rider An individual who receives the benefit of a good without incurring any cost for the good.

free-rider problem The lack of private funding for, or production of, a public good due to the presence of free riders.

game theory An approach for modeling the strategic interactions of firms in oligopoly markets.

Gini ratio A measure of income inequality. As the Gini ratio gets closer to zero, the more equally the income is distributed. As the Gini ratio gets closer to one, the more unequally the income is distributed.

human capital The amount of knowledge and skills that labor can apply to the work that they do.

implicit costs Indirect, nonpurchased, or opportunity costs of resources provided by the entrepreneur.

imports Goods produced abroad but consumed domestically.

incidence of tax The division of a tax between consumers and producers.

income effect Due to a higher price, the change in quantity demanded that results from a change in the consumer's purchasing power (or real income).

income elasticity A measure of how sensitive consumption of a good is to a change in consumers' income.

increasing returns to scale in production The long-run outcome when output more than doubles from a doubling of all inputs.

inferior goods A good for which demand decreases with an increase in consumer income.

law of demand All else equal, when the price of a good rises, the quantity demanded of that good falls.

law of diminishing marginal returns As successive units of a variable input are added to a fixed input, beyond some point the marginal product declines.

law of diminishing marginal utility In a given time period, as consumption of an item increases, the marginal (additional) utility from that item falls.

law of increasing costs As more of a good is produced, the greater is its opportunity (or marginal) cost.

law of increasing marginal cost As a producer produces more of a good, the marginal cost rises. This is very similar to the idea of increasing opportunity costs.

law of supply All else equal, when the price of a good rises, the quantity supplied of that good rises.

least-cost rule The combination of labor and capital that minimizes total costs for a given production rate is where $MP_L/P_L = MP_K/P_K$.

long run A period of time long enough for the firm to alter all production inputs, including capital and the plant size.

Lorenz curve A graphical device that shows how a nation's income is distributed across the nation's households.

luxury A good for which the proportional increase in consumption exceeds the proportional increase in income.

marginal The next unit, or increment of, an action.

marginal analysis Making decisions based upon weighing the marginal benefits and costs of that action. The rational decision maker chooses an action if $MB \geq MC$.

marginal benefit (MB) The additional benefit received from the consumption of the next unit of a good or service.

marginal cost (MC) The additional cost of producing one more unit of output.

marginal productivity theory The theory that a citizen's share of economic resources is proportional to the marginal revenue product of his or her labor.

marginal product of labor (MP_L) The change in total product resulting from a change in the labor input.

marginal resource cost (MRC) The change in a firm's total cost from the hiring of an additional unit of an input. Some authors refer to this as marginal factor cost (MFC) or the marginal cost of labor MC_L.

marginal revenue product of labor (MRP) The change in a firm's total revenue from the hiring of an additional unit of labor. If the output market is competitive, some authors call this the value of the marginal product (VMP) of labor.

marginal social benefit The additional benefit that society receives from the consumption of the next unit of a good or service.

marginal social cost The additional cost that society incurs from the production of the next unit of a good or service.

marginal tax rate The rate paid on the last dollar earned, calculated by taking the ratio of the change in taxes divided by the change in income.

marginal utility The change in an individual's total utility from the consumption of an additional unit of a good or service.

market A group of buyers and sellers involved in the exchange of a good or service.

market economy An economic system in which resources are allocated through the decentralized decisions of firms and consumers.

market equilibrium Exists at the only price where the quantity supplied equals the quantity demanded. Or, it is the only quantity where the price consumers are willing to pay is exactly the price producers are willing to accept.

market failure A market outcome for which the quantity produced is not allocatively efficient ($MSB \neq MSC$) and either too many or too few units are produced.

market power The ability to set a price above the perfectly competitive level.

monopolistic competition A market structure characterized by a few small firms producing a differentiated product with easy entry into the market.

monopoly A market structure in which one firm is the sole producer of a good with no close substitutes in a market with entry barriers.

monopsony A factor market in which there is a sole firm that has market power, i.e., a wage setter.

Nash equilibrium The outcome of a game for which each player's strategy maximizes his or her payoff, given the strategies used by the rival players.

natural monopoly The case where economies of scale are so extensive that it is less costly for one firm to supply the entire range of demand than for multiple firms to share the market.

necessity A good for which the proportional increase in consumption is less than the proportional increase in income.

negative externality The existence of spillover costs upon third parties from the production or consumption of a good.

noncollusive oligopoly Models of industries in which firms are competitive rivals seeking to gain at the expense of their rivals.

nonrenewable resources Natural resources that cannot replenish themselves.

normal goods A good for which demand increases with an increase in consumer income.

normal profit The opportunity cost of the entrepreneur's talents. Another way of saying the firm is earning zero economic profit.

oligopoly A very diverse market structure characterized by a small number of interdependent large firms, producing either a standardized or differentiated product in a market with a barrier to entry.

opportunity cost The value of the sacrifice made to pursue a course of action.

perfect price discrimination The type of price discrimination in which each consumer pays exactly his or her maximum willingness to pay.

perfectly elastic $E_d = \infty$. In this special case, the demand curve is horizontal, meaning consumers have an instantaneous and infinite response to a change in price.

perfectly inelastic $E_d = 0$. In this special case, the demand curve is vertical and there is absolutely no response to a change in price.

positive externality The existence of spillover benefits upon third parties from the production or consumption of a good.

price ceiling A legal maximum price above which the product cannot be sold.

price discrimination The sale of the same product to different groups of consumers at different prices.

price elasticity of demand (E_d) Measures the sensitivity of consumers' quantity demanded for good X when the price of good X changes.

price elasticity of supply (E_s) Measures the sensitivity of producers' quantity supplied for good X when the price of good X changes.

price floor A legal minimum price below which the product cannot be sold.

prisoner's dilemma A game where the two rivals achieve a less desirable outcome because they are unable to coordinate their strategies.

private goods Goods that are both rival and excludable.

producer surplus The difference between the price received and the marginal cost of producing the good.

production function The mechanism for combining production resources, with existing technology, into finished goods and services.

production possibilities The different quantities of goods that an economy can produce with a given amount of scarce resources.

production possibility curve (or frontier) A graphical device that shows the combination of two goods that a nation can efficiently produce with available resources and technology.

productive efficiency Production of maximum output for a given level of technology and resources. On the cost side, a given quantity of output is being produced at the lowest possible cost.

productivity The quantity of output that can be produced per worker in a given amount of time.

profit maximizing resource employment The firm hires a resource up to the point where MRP = MRC.

progressive tax A tax where the proportion of income paid in taxes rises as income rises.

proportional tax A tax where the proportion of income paid in taxes is constant no matter the level of income.

protective tariff An excise tax levied on an imported good that is produced in the domestic market so that it may be protected from foreign competition.

public goods Goods that are both nonrival and nonexcludable.

quintiles When you rank household income from lowest to highest, each quintile represents 20 percent of all households.

quota A maximum amount of a good that can be imported into the domestic market.

regressive tax A tax where the proportion of income paid in taxes decreases as income rises.

relative prices The price of one unit of good X measured not in currency, but in the number of units of good Y that must be sacrificed to acquire good X.

renewable resources Natural resources that can replenish themselves if they are not overharvested.

resources Also called factors of production, these are commonly grouped into the four categories of labor, physical capital, land or natural resources, and entrepreneurial ability.

revenue tariff An excise tax levied on goods that are not produced in the domestic market.

scarcity The imbalance between limited productive resources and unlimited human wants.

shortage A situation in which, at the going market price, the quantity demanded exceeds the quantity supplied.

short run A period of time too short to change the size of the plant, but many other, more variable resources can be adjusted to meet demand.

specialization Production of goods, or performance of tasks, based upon comparative advantage.

spillover benefits Additional benefits to society, not captured by the market demand curve from the production of a good.

spillover costs Additional costs to society, not captured by the market supply curve from the production of a good.

subsidy A government transfer, either to consumers or producers, on the consumption or production of a good.

substitute goods Two goods are consumer substitutes if they provide essentially the same utility to the consumer.

substitution effect The change in quantity demanded resulting from a change in the price of one good relative to the price of other goods.

supply curve Shows the quantity of a good supplied at all prices.

supply schedule A table showing quantity supplied for a good at various prices.

surplus A situation in which, at the going market price, the quantity supplied exceeds the quantity demanded.

tax bracket A range of income on which a given marginal tax rate is applied.

technology A nation's knowledge of how to produce goods in the best possible way.

total cost (TC) The sum of total fixed and total variable costs at any level of output.

total fixed costs (TFC) Production costs that do not vary with the level of output.

total product of labor (TP$_L$) The total quantity of output produced for a given quantity of labor employed.

total revenue The price of a good multiplied by the quantity of that good sold.

total revenue test Total revenue rises with a price increase if demand is price inelastic and falls with a price increase if demand is price elastic.

total utility The total happiness received from consumption of a number of units of a good.

total variable costs (TVC) Production costs that change with the level of output.

total welfare The sum of consumer surplus and producer surplus. Some authors label this as total surplus.

trade-offs The reality of scarce resources implies that individuals, firms, and governments are constantly faced with difficult choices that involve benefits and costs.

unit elastic demand $E_d = 1$. The percentage change in price is equal to percentage change in quantity demanded.

utility Happiness, or benefit, or satisfaction, or enjoyment gained from consumption of goods and services.

utility maximizing rule The consumer chooses amounts of goods X and Y, with their limited income, so that the marginal utility per dollar spent is equal for both goods.

utils A hypothetical unit of measurement often used to quantify utility; aka "happy points."

variable inputs Production inputs that the firm can adjust in the short run to meet changes in demand for the firm's output.

world price The global equilibrium price of a good when nations engage in trade.

IMPORTANT FORMULAS AND CONDITIONS

Chapter 5

1. Optimal Decision Making: $MB = MC$

2. Opportunity Cost from a Production Possibility Curve (PPC):

   Good X: The slope of the PPC

   Good Y: The inverse of the slope of the PPC

Chapter 6

1. Market Equilibrium:

   $Q_d = Q_s$

2. Shortage:

   $Q_d - Q_s$

3. Surplus:

   $Q_s - Q_d$

4. Total Welfare:

   $=$ Consumer surplus $+$ Producer surplus

Chapter 7

1. Price Elasticity of Demand:

   $E_d = $ (%Δ in quantity demanded of good X)/ (%Δ in the price of good X)

2. Percentage Change:

   %$\Delta = 100 \times$ (New value – Old value)/ Old value

3. Total Revenue:

   $=$ Price $\times$ Quantity demanded

4. Income Elasticity:

   $E_I = $ (%Δ Q_d good X)/(%Δ income)

5. Cross-Price Elasticity:

   $E_{x,y} = $ (%Δ Q_d good X)/(%Δ price good Y)

6. Price Elasticity of Supply:

   $E_s = $ (%Δ in quantity supplied of good X)/ (%Δ in the price of good X)

7. Marginal Utility:

   $MU = \Delta TU/\Delta Q$

8. Utility Maximizing Rule:

   $MU_x/P_x = MU_y/P_y$ or $MU_x/MU_y = P_x/P_y$

9. Revenue from a Tariff:

   $=$ Per-Unit Tariff $\times$ Units Imported

Chapter 8

1. Accounting Profit:

   TR – Explicit costs

2. Economic Profit:

   TR – Explicit costs – Implicit costs

3. Marginal Product of Labor:

   $MP_L = \Delta$ in TP_L/Δ in L

4. Average Product of Labor:

   $AP_L = TP_L/L$

5. Total Costs:

   $TC = TVC + TFC$

6. Marginal Costs:

   $MC = \Delta TVC/\Delta Q$

7. Average Fixed Cost:

   $AFC = TFC/Q$

8. Average Variable Cost:

   $AVC = TVC/Q$

9. Average Total Cost:

   $ATC = TC/Q = AFC + AVC$

10. Marginal Cost and Marginal Product of Labor:

    $MC = w/MP_L$

11. Average Variable Cost and Average Product of Labor:

$$AVC = w/AP_L$$

Chapter 9

1. Profit Maximization Point:

$$MR = MC$$

2. Demand for Firm's Product (Perfectly Competitive Market):

$$P = MR = AR$$

3. Profit:

$$\pi = TR - TC = P \times q_e - TC = q_e \times (P - ATC)$$

4. Breakeven Point:

$$P = ATC$$

5. Shutdown Point:

$$P < AVC \text{ or } TR < TVC$$

6. Allocative Efficiency:

Produce output q where $P_c = MR = MC$

7. Excess Capacity in Monopolistic Competition:

$$Q_{atc} - Q_{mc}$$

8. Perfectly Competitive Long-Run Equilibrium:

$$P = MR = AR = MC = ATC$$

9. Monopoly Long-Run Equilibrium:

$$P_m > MR = MC$$

Chapter 10

1. Marginal Revenue Product:

$$= \frac{\text{Change in total revenue}}{\text{Change in resource quantity}}$$

$$= MR \times MP_L$$

a. Under perfectly competitive price-taking conditions:

$$MRP_c = MR \times MP_L = P \times MP_L$$

b. Under conditions of market power, $MR < P$:

$$MRP_m = MR \times MP_L < MRP_c$$

2. Marginal Resource Cost:

$$= \frac{\text{Change in total resource cost}}{\text{Change in resource quantity}}$$

$$= \text{Wage (in a competitive resource market)}$$

3. Least-Cost Hiring Rule:

$$MP_L/P_L = MP_K/P_K \text{ or equivalently,}$$

$$MP_L/MP_K = P_L/P_K$$

4. Profit Maximizing Resource Employment:

$$MRP = MRC$$

5. Monopsony Hiring Decision:

$$MFC = MRP > W$$

Chapter 11

1. Socially Optimal Output:

$$MSB = MSC$$

2. Marginal Tax Rate:

$$= (\Delta \text{ taxes due})/(\Delta \text{ taxable income})$$

3. Average Tax Rate:

$$= (\text{Total taxes due})/(\text{Total taxable income})$$

The Cross-Platform Prep Course

McGraw Hill's multi-platform course gives you a variety of tools to help you raise your test scores. Whether you're studying at home, in the library, or on-the-go, you can find practice content in the format you need—print, online, or mobile.

Print Book

This print book gives you the tools you need to ace the test. In its pages you'll find smart test-taking strategies, in-depth reviews of key topics, and ample practice questions and tests. See the Welcome section of your book for a step-by-step guide to its features.

Online Platform

The Cross-Platform Prep Course gives you additional study and practice content that you can access *anytime, anywhere*. You can create a personalized study plan based on your test date that sets daily goals to keep you on track. Integrated lessons provide important review of key topics. Practice questions, exams, and flashcards give you the practice you need to build test-taking confidence. The game center is filled with challenging games that allow you to practice your new skills in a fun and engaging way. And, you can even interact with other test-takers in the discussion section and gain valuable peer support.

Getting Started

To get started, open your account on the online platform:

Go to the URL shown on the inside front cover

↓

Enter your access code

↓

Provide your name and e-mail address to open your account and create a password

↓

Click "Start Studying" to enter the platform

It's as simple as that. You're ready to start studying online.

Your Personalized Study Plan

First, select your test date on the calendar, and you'll be on your way to creating your personalized study plan. Your study plan will help you stay organized and on track and will guide you through the course in the most efficient way. It is tailored to *your* schedule and features daily tasks that are broken down into manageable goals. You can adjust your test date at any time and your daily tasks will be reorganized into an updated plan.

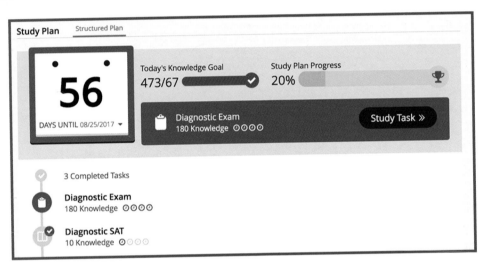

You can track your progress in real time on the Study Plan Dashboard. The "Today's Knowledge Goal" progress bar gives you up-to-the minute feedback on your daily goal. Fulfilling this every time you log on is the most efficient way to work through the entire course. You always get an instant view of where you stand in the entire course with the Study Plan Progress bar.

If you need to exit the program before completing a task, you can return to the Study Plan Dashboard at any time. Just click the Study Task icon and you can automatically pick up where you left off.

Practice Tests

One of the first tasks in your personalized study plan is to take the Diagnostic Test. At the end of the test, a detailed evaluation of your strengths and weaknesses shows the areas where you need the most focus. You can review your practice test results either by the question category to see broad trends or question-by-question for a more in-depth look.

The full-length tests are designed to simulate the real thing. Try to simulate actual testing conditions and be sure you set aside enough time to complete the full-length test. You'll learn to pace yourself so that you can work toward the best possible score on test day.

Lessons

The lessons in the online platform are divided into manageable pieces that let you build knowledge and confidence in a progressive way. They cover the full range of topics that you're likely to see on your test.

After you complete a lesson, mark your confidence level. (You must indicate a confidence level in order to count your progress and move on to the next task.) You can also filter the lessons by confidence levels to see the areas you have mastered and those that you might need to revisit.

> *Use the bookmark feature to easily refer back to a concept or leave a note to remember your thoughts or questions about a particular topic.*

Practice Questions

All of the practice questions are reflective of actual exams and simulate the test-taking experience. The "Review Answer" button gives you immediate feedback on your answer. Each question includes a rationale that explains why the correct answer is right and the others are wrong. To explore any topic further, you can find detailed explanations by clicking the "Help me learn about this topic" link.

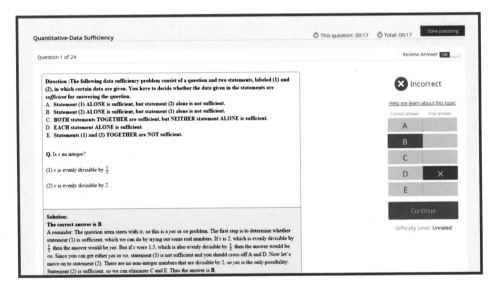

You can go to the Practice Dashboard to find an overview of your performance in the different categories and sub-categories.

Dashboard

The dashboard is constantly updating to reflect your progress and performance. The Percentile Rank icon shows your position relative to all the other students enrolled in the course. You can also find information on your average scores in practice questions and exams.

A detailed overview of your strengths and weaknesses shows your proficiency in a category based on your answers and difficulty of the questions. By viewing your strengths and weaknesses, you can focus your study on areas where you need the most help.

Flashcards

The hundreds of flashcards are perfect for learning key terms quickly, and the interactive format gives you immediate feedback. You can filter the cards by category and confidence level for a more organized approach. Or, you can shuffle them up for a more general challenge.

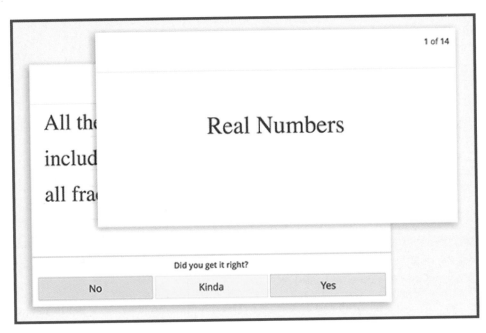

Another way to customize the flashcards is to create your own sets. You can either keep these private or share or them with the public. Subscribe to Community Sets to access sets from other students preparing for the same exam.

Game Center

Play a game in the Game Center to test your knowledge of key concepts in a challenging but fun environment. Increase the difficulty level and complete the games quickly to build your highest score. Be sure to check the leaderboard to see who's on top!

Social Community

Interact with other students who are preparing for the same test. Start a discussion, reply to a post, or even upload files to share. You can search the archives for common topics or start your own private discussion with friends.

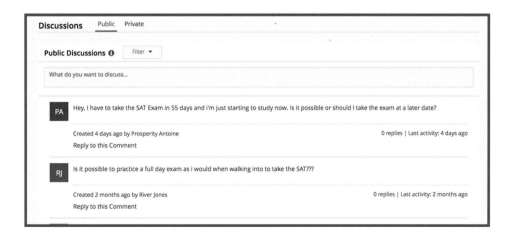

Mobile App

The companion mobile app lets you toggle between the online platform and your mobile device without missing a beat. Whether you access the course online or from your smartphone or tablet, you'll pick up exactly where you left off.

Go to the iTunes or Google Play stores and search "McGraw-Hill Education Cross-Platform App" to download the companion iOS or Android app. Enter your e-mail address and the same password you created for the online platform to open your account.

Now, let's get started!